DATE DUE

WOMEN AND NEW REPRODUCTIVE TECHNOLOGIES:
Medical, Psychosocial, Legal, and Ethical Dilemmas

Edited by
Judith Rodin
Yale University

Aila Collins
Karolinska Institute

LEA LAWRENCE ERLBAUM ASSOCIATES, PUBLISHERS
1991 Hillsdale, New Jersey   Hove and London

Lawrence Erlbaum Associates, Inc., Publishers
365 Broadway
Hillsdale, New Jersey 07642

Library of Congress Cataloging-in-Publication Data

Women and new reproductive technologies : medical, psychosocial,
   legal, and ethical dilemmas / edited by Judith Rodin, Aila Collins.
        p.   cm.
   Based on a conference sponsored by the John D. and Catherine T.
MacArthur Foundation Network on the Determinants and Consequences of
Health Promoting and Health Damaging Behavior, held June 16–18, 1987
in Key Biscayne, Flordia.
   Includes bibliographical references and index.
   ISBN 0-8058-0919-8
   1. Human reproductive technology — Congresses.   2. Human
reproductive technology — Social aspects — Congresses.
   3. Reproductive technology — Law and legislation — Congresses.
   4. Women — Congresses.   I. Rodin, Judith.   II. Collins, Aila.
III. John D. and Catherine T. MacArthur Foundation Network on the
Determinants and Consequences of Health Promoting and Health
Damaging Behaviors.
   [DNLM: 1. Ethics, Medical — congresses.   2. Reproduction Technics —
congresses.   3. Reproduction Technics — legislation — congresses.
   4. Reproduction Technics — psychology.   5. Social Environment —
congresses.   6. Women — congresses.   WQ 205 W872 1987]
   RG133.5.W65   1991
   DNLM/DLC
   for Library of Congress   90-14148
                                                                        CIP

Printed in the United States of America
10   9   8   7   6   5   4   3   2   1

Contents

Preface

The theme of this book is reproduction and how it is viewed on the threshold of the 21st century. The perspectives of many disciplines are brought to bear on the staggering new opportunities, challenges, and problems that now face those who wish to have a child. The book is based on a conference sponsored by the John D. and Catherine T. MacArthur Foundation Network on the Determinants and Consequences of Health-Promoting and Health-Damaging Behaviors, whose mission is to bring together investigators from multiple disciplines for collaborative discussions and research that promote our understanding of successful adaptation and good health, as well as of illness and disease.

At the conference we explored numerous domains where women's health and women's lives have been changed profoundly by the explosion of new technologies emerging in the last decades of the 20th century. In addition to reproduction, we reviewed new technologies and their impact in the areas of contraception, menopause, and breast cancer treatment. We want to thank all the participants at the conference whose ideas and comments enriched the meeting and are reflected especially in our two chapters of the present book. Those participating included: Nancy Adler, PhD; Nancy Cantor, PhD; Ellen Wright Clayton, MD; Aila Collins, PhD; Donald Coustan, MD; Alan De Cherney, MD; Lorraine Dennerstein, PhD; David Dodd; Nancy Dye, PhD; Ruth Faden, PhD; Marianne Frankenhaeuser, PhD; M. R. C. Greenwood, PhD; Florence Haseltine, MD, PhD; Britt-Marie Landgren, MD; Sandra Levy, PhD; Richard Love, MD; Virginia Olesen, PhD; Anne Peterson, PhD; Rayna Rapp, PhD; Anthony Reading, PhD;

Judith Rodin, PhD; Sheryl Ruzek, PhD; Philip Sarrel, MD; John Steege, MD; Caroline Whitbeck, PhD; Deborah Wingard, PhD.

We chose to highlight reproduction in this volume because in bringing medical technology to bear on creating life, the profound ethical, legal, social, and psychological issues surrounding the use of technology come perhaps most sharply into focus. Many disciplines and many perspectives speak to this question and we have tried to represent a broad spectrum of them in the present volume.

In addition to the conference participants, many other people were crucial to the completion of this book. We thank Debbie Whitney-Saltiel for her key role in organizing the meeting, Grace Castellazzo for orchestrating the work needed to move a set of conference papers to an integrated book, and Barbara Faulkner for her excellent administrative and secretarial assistance. We are especially appreciative of the support provided by the John D. and Catherine T. MacArthur Foundation for the exciting meeting that led to this project.

ACKNOWLEDGMENTS

Many people contributed time and effort to this volume, and their contributions are gratefully acknowledged. Debbie Whitney-Saltiel helped to organize the meeting on which this book is based. Grace Castellazzo organized and reorganized the chapters, and dealt with all matters of conceptual framing with both the authors and the publishers. Gloria Fontana orchestrated all the indexing and cheerfully took on some last-minute editing as well. Barbara Faulkner retyped much of the material.

The John D. and Catherine T. MacArthur Foundation supports the Health and Behavior Research Network, which sponsored the conference and preparation of chapters. Their commitment to this particular activity, and to fostering multidisciplinary discussions, has been quite important in helping new ideas to develop and see the light of day.

We are also grateful to Robin Weisberg and the staff at LEA for working so quickly and efficiently.

Finally, we thank our coauthors and contributors for their distinguished efforts and ideas.

Judith Rodin
Aila Collins

1

The New Reproductive Technologies: Overview of the Challenges and Issues

Judith Rodin
Yale University

Aila Collins
Karolinska Institute

Major breakthroughs in medical technology affect everyone. The life span has been dramatically extended. The role of medical science is to compress morbidity—to push illness further and further to the end of the life span so that people will enjoy many more years in good health than ever before (Fries, 1980). Although the impact of technology is widely felt across the life span, those technologies that have changed the nature and process of reproduction may be of greatest consequence to women. To take only a few examples, infertile couples now have many more ways to have natural children, genetic testing provides opportunities for families to make decisions about what type of child they will have, and new ways of monitoring fetal development bring more precision to childbearing than ever before.

Despite these dramatic opportunities, however, the new reproductive technologies are not without problems. The authors of the following chapters explore the complex array of benefits and problems presented by the new reproductive technologies. The issues are complex, and the debate often acrimonious. More significant than the question of whether the technologies are good or bad, however, are the questions related to for whom they are good, in what instances, and for whom they should be made accessible. These thorny issues can be debated at multiple levels, from the ethical implications, to the social and psychological consequences for society and for the individual, to the legal and the medical outcomes. All viewpoints are represented in this book and each chapter highlights a different array of problems and opportunities.

UNIFYING THEMES AND ISSUES

Fundamental to all the chapters are four major themes. They are emphasized differentially in each chapter, but they represent the major threads
that integrate and distinguish the various perspectives held by the authors of
this book.

The Impact of Technology on Women's Lives

All the chapters suggest that the new technological interventions have had
a significant impact — both positive and negative — on the quality of women's lives. As Dye points out, "Technology development cannot always be
viewed as a straightforward narrative of progress." Although technology is
not all good or all bad, often its effects are dramatic. Pervasive in the use
of the new technologies is the view that it can solve all our problems, and
many of the current authors believe this view is dangerous — that we are a
society looking for a high technology "fix." Several question whether "doing
everything possible" is always the right answer.

The new technologies create tensions within individuals, between members of families, and among members of society. This has a profound
impact on the quality of women's lives. Health and safety risks are not the
only considerations one must make with regard to the applications of these
new technologies. We must take account of the effects of these technologies
on human relationships, including those between patient and health-care
provider, between members of families, and among members of communities.

Many of the authors believe that women are struggling to strike a
balance — wishing to take advantage of the new advances in medical
technologies and pharmacology, but not wanting a natural process like
reproduction to become entirely medicalized. They argue that many women
are resisting the emerging view that pregnancy and procreation are medical
problems comparable to other states of disease. This tension is enmeshed in
the use of technology and the increased intervention of medical practice into
reproduction.

Many of the authors emphasize that whether or not women and their
families value high technology depends on class and culture. Women of
lower socioeconomic status and in some traditional cultures may be less
likely to use or to value the high technologies. Social factors must be
recognized as important determinants of acceptance and resistance to
technological innovations, of how these innovations emerge and are
disseminated, and of whom they affect.

The new technologies may alter the quality of women's lives because, with their use, efficiency has become an important medical motive. The public health-care system had at its roots the goal of effectiveness. Effective health care was assumed to ensure that the least capable individual would be able to receive high quality medical care. What has happened in recent years, however, is that medicine may have switched from effectiveness to efficiency as a primary motive. According to some of the authors, many aspects of medical decision making now revolve around the goal of efficient health care. For example, with the development of fetal monitors, the nurse now can "handle" four or five women in the labor room at once. Undoubtedly, this is a more efficient process; but the costs of this efficiency in terms of human relationships, are explored by several authors in this book.

The Role of Women

The second major theme emphasizes the fact that the opportunities to use technologies have political and social meanings and consequences regarding the role of women, and how women and children are viewed in society. There are numerous and complex sets of issues surrounding this general principle. Certainly the roles of women have changed; they have entered the work force in increasing numbers, have delayed childbearing, and are having fewer children. All of these demographic shifts affect the nature and meaning of decisions about reproduction and the technologies that are used to facilitate it.

These new technologies define women in certain ways. For example, as we describe later, some believe that they may relegate women to the role of "fetal containers," whereas others feel that the status of women is enhanced by increased options associated with reproduction. Reciprocally, our perception of the role of women in society in part determines which technologies we seek to create and how we adopt them. For example, the meaning of fertility for a woman and for a society influences how they perceive technology and their aspirations for the use of technology. There is a strong ideology surrounding motherhood in our culture, and the new technologies bring confusion to this previously clearer role. Surrogacy is perhaps the most complicated of these, adding the dimension of genetic motherhood to already complex distinctions between biological and social parenthood.

Indeed, the roles of all individuals in society are defined by how these new technologies are used, what they mean regarding our definitions of when life begins, and how the very beginning of life is managed and engineered. Creation, for so long viewed as natural and mysterious, now can be technologically engineered. Our roles as individuals and as members of society are altered profoundly by that fact.

Who will benefit from these procedures is another essential part of the debate. Access to these is dependent on economic factors, culture, race, and social class. The development of reproductive technologies poses many questions about the ranking of priorities and the allocation of scarce resources. Thus, high technology tends to create further schisms in society between rich and poor and between one subculture and another. If there is not equal access, there is the risk that in the future only the poor will have children with disabilities and we will become more callous as a society to the needs of the disabled. The question of which babies we will allow to be born is crucial — an issue raised only with the emergence of the new technologies. The very meaning of disability is changed as a consequence of the new technologies. Some of the authors are concerned that stigmatization toward disability will increase and women will be pushed to get rid of "bad" babies.

Many of the authors believe that society and women are engaged in a power struggle that is highlighted in the application and expansion of reproductive technology. Some would argue that women do and should "own" reproduction to a great degree and, as they contend with both the opportunities and problems provided by the new technologies, they are representing perhaps metaphorically how they are working out their role in the power structure of society.

The Individual Versus Society

A third fundamental common theme is the question of individual choice as a right versus society's needs and responsibilities. Certainly most people would agree that there are moral, ethical, and legal obligations that limit fundamental choice. But an individual rights model pervades our current health-care system, with the emergence of informed consent being the most notable and tangible marker. Faden, Ruzek, Whitbeck, and Clayton all focus on issues and concerns about individual liberties and social equality, made all the more dramatic by increasingly technological, powerful, and impersonal medical care.

The individual rights model raises significant moral, ethical, and legal issues. How far should individual decision making go? For example, new types of genetic testing currently being developed will allow for determination of whether the woman is carrying a fetus with risk factors for later diseases, not only for major disability at birth. Should an individual be allowed to terminate such a pregnancy, or should a society concerned with rising health costs demand the termination of this fetus? These are questions we will be facing in only a few years.

Currently, we are witnessing a movement away from the principle of informed consent to the principle of shared decision making as the primary medical ethos. Many of the authors grapple with not only who should decide, but how the negotiation around the decision should occur, including what types of communication skills are necessary and how the decisions will take account of risks to the psyche and moral integrity, as well as to life and property. Faden and Whitbeck in particular emphasize these issues. Rapp, in her chapter on the discourse of this negotiation, focuses attention on what is communicated in the decision-making discussion and how it is communicated implicitly and explicitly, verbally and nonverbally.

Fetus as Patient

The fourth major theme is the role of the fetus as patient. Before the 1880s, the mother was viewed as the primary actor in the drama of giving birth. From that point on, with the development of the modern medical science of obstetrics and gynecology, both the mother and the fetus were viewed as patients. And now many would argue that the fetus is viewed as the focal point and the mother as secondary. These changes are based on an increasing knowledge of prenatal development and the new reproductive technology, which make the fetus seem more accessible. Through prenatal diagnosis, the fetus has become a new type of patient, for whom therapies are being developed.

For the first time, discussions center on issues such as the relationship between women's rights for bodily integrity and the rights of the fetus for protection. Certainly, as Faden points out, most women will choose what is good for their fetus; but the law has come to feel that this is not always true and has stepped in to protect the rights of the fetus over the rights of mothers in many recent decisions. Several of the authors grapple with the stunning implications of this subtle social and legal shift in viewpoint. By defining pregnancy as a conflict between woman and her fetus, judges and physicians see themselves as advocates of the fetus (Hubbard, 1990). Clayton cites recent cases in the United States where legal personhood has been attributed to the fetus in order to assert control over pregnant women's lifestyles and birth choices. The most dramatic cases have involved forced cesarean sections. As Clayton emphasizes, these cases are of great symbolic significance because they convey powerful messages about women's moral and legal status. Robertson (1989) predicted that suits by children against their mothers for prenatal injuries will be recognized by courts in the future. He further assumes that a woman's obligation to a fetus whom she has decided to carry to term may require her to avoid work, leisure-time activities, and medication that could be harmful to the fetus.

Women's capacity to procreate raises other issues where the law has become deeply involved, for example, abortion, choices to opt out of the health-care system to deliver one's baby, artificial insemination, surrogate motherhood, and embryo transfer. Many of these have the potential to relegate women to the role of "fetal containers" (Annas, 1986), or to reduce women to the status of "motherships" or "carriers of precious cargo" (Gallagher, 1989).

The emergence of fetal rights as a movement, according to analyses by Clayton, Ruzek, and Whitbeck, adds confusion and an aura of adversity to the relationship between mother and fetus. Acts of law regarding this dyad now often replace moral decisions and have power over choices that some would argue are best for the family as a whole to make. Advances in medical technologies brought the interests of the unborn clearly into focus, and they are forcing society and the law to determine when and whether we should intervene and care more deeply for the benefit of the unborn than either for the mother or for the children already among us.

When a woman is carrying a fetus that she will care for as a baby and a child, these issues are complex enough. But with the advent of surrogacy, ever more complicated questions arise. For example, how do we or should we compel a woman to do things for a baby that will not be hers to rear? What are the rights and responsibilities of the woman carrying the fetus in contrast to the woman who ultimately will mother and raise the child? Who could have imagined, even 20 years ago, that such issues would be presently confronting society?

PERSPECTIVES OF EACH CHAPTER

Each chapter highlights one or more of these prevailing themes. Through this discussion of the benefits and potential disadvantages in the use of the new reproductive technologies, we attempt to highlight the sets of issues they create for society at large, for women in general, and for those individuals who are exposed to them in particular.

The first chapter, by Nancy Dye, reviews historical considerations of women's reproductive health and argues that the relationship between women's health and technology has rarely if ever been clear-cut, in part because the development of new technologies and decisions about their use always have been embedded in social and cultural contexts, and in part because not all technological interventions have carried benefits for women. Her analysis shows that technology, cultural attitudes toward women, and social choices about health care are all interconnected.

Dye uses two historical examples, the first dealing with fertility decline and contraceptive technology, the second dealing with 19th-century gynecological practice, to help illustrate the ways in which technology, cultural attitudes toward women, and social choices about health have intersected.

Building on this historical analysis, we move in the next chapter to a prime example of a dramatic, currently available reproductive technology. According to Thatcher and DeCherney, a vast, clinically oriented science has grown around in vitro technologies and human reproduction, which have become the final common path for the treatment of infertility. Thatcher and DeCherney are physicians and scientists, and they present a clinical view of the scientific and medical value of in vitro fertilization. They suggest that from their perspective, in vitro manipulation of reproduction is a great advantage provided to families by today's medical science. They emphasize the potential value of this and future technological break-throughs to aid and advance the reproductive process.

Implicit in the discussion of current reproductive technologies is the assumption that women freely choose to use them. Informed consent, a relatively recent development, presumes the role of individual responsibility with regard to the use of the technologies we review. It derives from the individual rights model, and is based on the assumption that when an individual is informed adequately, she will make a reasonable choice and then be responsible for the consequences of that choice. In the next chapter, Faden addresses the issue of informed consent.

Faden describes the history of informed consent and examines the informed consent issues raised by new genetic and other diagnostic tech-nologies in the reproductive area. In her chapter, which focuses on a variety of these issues from a social policy prospective, she raises four areas for discussion: the meaning of autonomous decision making in the face of these new technologies, the question of whether any parental choice ought to be permissible in the use of these technologies, the dilemma of whether testing should ever be compulsory, and the issues surrounding maternal consent to fetal testing where fetal therapy is possible.

Faden argues that patients need to understand their role in medical decision making, not just the specific treatment alternatives available to them. Informed consent emerged in response to the extreme imbalance in the way decisions were made by the health-care system. Informed consent intended to empower patients and recognize their rights in decision making. However, the need for consent is sometimes seen as conflicting with the principle of medical beneficence, the view that doctor knows best and that there is a treatment of great benefit. Faden argues that women patients are often seen as less capable of making decisions than men. And informed consent has not always been used for their benefit.

In the next chapter, Whitbeck argues against the individualistic informed consent model from a moral/philosophical point of view. She views technology as embedded in the modern tendency to think of everything as a potential resource. She argues that to regard everything, even ourselves, as a potential resource is to inclusively regard all possible goals or ends as on a par. As a result, the efficient use of resources in pursuit of goals is taken implicitly as a primary social value.

Whitbeck argues that the concept of moral right has predominated the medical ethics literature. It leads to questions regarding the relevant rights and obligations of persons occupying various roles and the correct ordering of these rights and obligations vis-à-vis other values. She asserts that the concept of the moral right and concepts of cost and benefit are the moral concepts that are reconciled most readily with the individualistic model of the person assumed in economic ideology. Although these are used increasingly in medical decision making, she argues that the economic ideology is likely to blind us to the sorts of ethical issues raised by the application of new medical technologies. Whitbeck emphasizes the fact that technology always exchanges one set of problems and vulnerabilities for another. Thus, we cannot assume either that technology per se is bad or that technology can solve perennial human problems.

In the next chapter, Ruzek continues this argument from a social/ethical perspective. Ruzek argues that we must explore moral frameworks beyond the individual rights model to guide our decisions about the application of childbirth technologies. Does society benefit, she asks, by laws that restrain physicians or coerce women? She addresses some of the problematic issues surrounding birth that derive from the individual rights model. In her discussion, she directs attention to the fact that some birth technologies have become accepted as standards of care without regard to rigorous scientific evidence of safety or efficacy, or of their social and psychological consequences. She speculates on why and how some technologies and not others come to be regarded as standards of care. From her perspective, low technology strategies may often be of greater benefit to the woman and society. She, like Whitbeck, suggests that we need to explore frameworks beyond the individual rights model to guide our discussion about research priorities and the application of childbirth technologies.

Certainly influential in the debate about the use of these technologies has been the legal issues that they have raised. In her chapter, Clayton describes a set of legal questions surrounding when the state or doctors may permissibly interfere with a woman's choice. Throughout her discussion she focuses on three aspects of the law. The first is the presence of immunity rights, that is the extent to which the law bars the state or doctors from intervening in individuals' choices. The second is the definition of entitlement rights, that is the extent to which the law forces the state or doctors to enable individuals to act upon their choices. The third is when the law permits individuals' desires to be overridden.

The law traditionally has emphasized the individual rights model. The law's fundamental premise is that patients should be allowed to make their own health-care decisions. But the rights actually ensured by the law are limited. Indeed, the only option that the law of informed consent protects is the decision not to get treatment. Clayton notes there is never a suggestion that a patient has a right to get therapy that her physician does not want to provide. In fact, the law has a limited commitment in practice to enable patients to proceed by their own rights. She argues that patients' choices are limited in another important way by the law. They may be forced to undergo invasion of their privacy and bodily integrity if these intrusions are viewed by the law as necessary to avoid harm to others. Indeed, she further argues that women are not just self-contained patients whose choices are subject to the law's usual ambivalence to protecting patient autonomy. Women's capacity to procreate raises special legal problems, one set turning on women's personal interest in decisions about whether or not to procreate, and the other on the interests of the fetus, whether or not the conception was intended.

The next chapter takes the approach of a discipline whose emphasis is on the consequences of the technologies from the point of view of the individual. Adler and her colleagues, working from a social/psychological perspective, consider the multiple sources of stress and conflict that surround the use of reproductive technologies, and their implication for the psychological health and well-being of women. Adler and her colleagues review a variety of technologies associated with reproduction, with a special focus on in vitro fertilization (IVF) and genetic screening. They emphasize that understanding the impact of the new technologies requires studying the stresses involved in the decision-making process as well as in the various procedures themselves. Although there is little evidence that significant psychopathology results even with adverse outcomes, women undergoing these procedures often do experience negative emotion and distress. Such responses deserve attention and often can be ameliorated by psychological intervention.

Adler and her colleagues suggest that, given the potential stresses involved in the application of these technologies, it is critical that women understand the risks involved. Abstract probabilities often are hard for individuals to understand and evaluate, and biases such as the availability heuristic can distort perceptions. In the case of IVF, these biases seem to increase estimates of success, whereas in the use of diagnostic screening they may increase estimates of complications. In either case, distortions can increase distress. Unrealistically positive expectations could contribute to a desire to proceed with treatment that the woman might otherwise decline, or could heighten disappointment after failure. Excessively negative expectations could lead to unnecessary apprehension about the procedure or to a decision not to avail oneself of a useful technology.

Finally, Rapp takes an anthropologist's perspective on the use of reproductive technologies and uses as her example the social impact and cultural interpretation of prenatal diagnosis in the context of genetic counseling. Based on anthropological fieldwork in New York City, Rapp interprets genetic counseling sessions using a language-based perspective.

Thus, she helps inform our understanding of the impact of technologies as they are influenced by characteristics such as class, ethnicity, race, and gender. These variables deeply affect clients' communication choices and the context in which meanings are actively and interactively produced. They also influence how the outcomes of technologies are understood and the ambiguities of choice. Rapp highlights the variability in the meaning of disability for different ethnic and cultural groups and argues that the impact of the diagnosis from a genetic test, and decisions about courses of action, is profoundly different as a consequence.

Throughout her analysis, she describes the discourse of genetic counseling as caught in a potential contradiction. Developed to provide pregnant women and their families with more choices, genetic counseling also inadvertently and unselfconsciously replicates and extends a social hierarchy that limits choices, and within which it is embedded. Counselors, like other health-care professionals, are limited by their own communication resources. A different language is only one concern, but many others are salient. For example, some types of patients cannot understand the mathematics of risk appraisal. Even if they could, as Adler and her colleagues point out, some are too stressed at the time to understand. The opportunity provided by the choice depends on how one interprets disability as well as the family's needs and values.

REFERENCES

Annas, G. J. (1986). Pregnant women as fetal containers. *Hastings Center Report, 16,* 13–14.

Fries, J. F. (1980). Aging, natural death, and the comparison of morbidity. *New England Journal of Medicine, 303,* 130–135.

Gallagher, J. (1989). Fetus as patient. In S. Cohen & N. Taub (Eds.), *Reproductive laws for the 1990's* (pp. 185–236). Clifton, NJ: Humana Press.

Hubbard, R. (1990). *The politics of women's biology.* New Brunswick, NJ: Rutgers University Press.

Robertson, J. A. (1989). Reconciling offspring and maternal interests during pregnancy. In S. Cohen & N. Taub (Eds.), *Reproductive laws for the 1990's* (pp. 259–276). Clifton, NJ: Humana Press.

2 The History of the Relationship Between Women's Health and Technology

Nancy Schrom Dye
Vassar College

Technological intervention is important to any historical consideration of women's health. Effective contraception, the control of puerperal sepsis, and the capability to manage obstetrical complications and gynecological pathology surgically along with other technological developments, have had definite impact on the quality of women's lives.

It would be easy to fashion a historical narrative about women's health in America with technology at the heart of the story. Such a history would touch upon many milestones: the invention of obstetrical forceps, the medical discovery of ergot, the first successful cesarean section, the invention of the vaginal speculum, the perfection of gynecological surgery for the repair of vesicovaginal fistulae and perineal lacerations, the introduction of obstetrical anesthesia, the adoption of antisepsis, asepsis, and, later, antibiotics to control infection, and blood transfusions to treat hemorrhage. The story would end with the chemical control of fertility and the recent technological capabilities for extrauterine gestation.

All of us are familiar with the outlines of this narrative, and with the assumption upon which it rests—namely, that there is a direct causal relationship between technological development and improvements in women's health over time. But shaping the story of technology and women's health in such linear, progressive fashion is misleading. In point of fact, the relationship between women's health and technology has been rarely, if ever, clear-cut, in part because the development of new technologies and decisions about their use always have been embedded in social and cultural contexts, and in part because not all technological intervention has carried benefits for women. Two historical examples—the first dealing with fertility

11

decline and contraceptive technology, the second dealing with 19th-century gynecological practice — help illustrate the ways in which technology, cultural attitudes toward women, and social choices about health care have intersected.

Over the course of the 19th century, American fertility declined by approximately 50%. Whereas the average American woman in 1800 bore 7.4 children, her counterpart in 1900 bore 3.56 children (Degler, 1980). This dramatic drop in fertility may well have had more impact on women's health than any other development. But no major technological innovations accompanied this decline in the birth rate. Personal determination to limit family size led many Americans to control fertility through a combination of methods that had long been available: abortion, periodic sexual abstinence, and barrier contraceptives. At the same time, dominant cultural values about woman's role made the development of new, more effective means of birth control very difficult (Degler, 1980; Gordon, 1974; Mohr, 1984). Most doctors, for example, disapproved of family limitation because they adhered to the cultural belief that women's purpose in life was to bear children. The medical profession made up an influential and vocal wing of a conservative coalition that managed to make contraception and abortion illegal in the United States late in the 19th century (Mohr, 1984; Reed, 1978). The research that ultimately resulted in highly effective hormonal means of contraception did not flourish until well into the 20th century, long after the demographic transition from natural birth cycle to planned family size had taken place (Reed, 1978). Technology, then, was largely incidental to this shift, and conflicting cultural values about fertility limited technological development (Reed, 1979).

A second example that helps illuminate the relationship between technology and culture concerns the emergence of gynecology as a discrete field of medical knowledge in the mid-19th century. Gynecology took shape as a medical specialty at a time when Americans were exceedingly concerned about gender differences. It is to the middle decades of the 19th century that historians trace the development of modern sex roles and definitions of "masculinity" and "femininity" (Smith-Rosenberg, 1985a, 1985b; Welter, 1966). In particular, Americans came to view women — at least White, urban, middle-class women — as innately delicate and passive (Welter, 1966). At the same time, American cultural ideas about female sexuality were contradictory. Much 19th-century writing depicts women, paradoxically, as at once devoid of sexual interest and entirely sexual, beings whose purpose could be defined solely in terms of reproduction. In fact, Americans sometimes referred to women simply as "the Sex." Doctors reflected these new concerns about sex differences in their often singleminded focus on female reproductive organs as the key to women's health (Smith-Rosenberg, 1985a, 1985b; Smith-Rosenberg & Rosenberg, 1973). As one doctor stated at mid-century, it is "as if the Almighty, in creating the female sex, had taken the uterus and built up a woman around it" (Smith-Rosenberg & Rosenberg, 1973, p. 334).

Heightened attention to sex differences may well have created the cultural climate in which a specialty devoted to the ills of women could take root. And the notion that women were innately weaker and sicklier than men underlay the medical belief that women's debilities could be traced to their always-capricious uteri and ovaries. This conviction, in turn, led to doctors' increased willingness to remove those organs surgically as a way to restore health to women patients. By the 1860s, for example, many doctors looked favorably upon bilateral oophorectomy of normal ovaries—the so-called Battey's operation—as an acceptable treatment for an extensive list of gynecological, neurological, and psychological symptoms (Longo, 1979). During the mid-19th century, then, the female life cycle itself became medicalized—menstruation, conception, pregnancy, lactation, and menopause became defined as processes worthy of medical scrutiny—and women became the objects of special medical intervention (Smith-Rosenberg & Rosenberg, 1973). These facts help explain why women today are more often patients than men, and why they continue to be the focus of contraceptive research and development. In this example, cultural beliefs about women encouraged the development of new technologies. At the same time, cultural values related to female modesty and decorum sometimes limited the use of those technologies, and propriety, not efficacy, determined the ways in which innovations such as the vaginal speculum or obstetrical anesthesia were adopted (Donegan, 1978; Duffy, 1964).

Social class also has played a role in determining various technologies' use. Early 20th-century doctors, for instance, often ordered Wasserman tests for clinic populations, but rarely did so for their private patients. On the other hand, early in the 20th-century, upper-class women stood a significantly greater chance of being delivered by cesarean section than poor women (Hawks, 1929). The relationship between technology and women's health, then, always has been complex, mediated by cultural and social factors that have sometimes inhibited and other times encouraged technological development.

There is another important respect in which the history of women's health and technological intervention cannot be couched as a straightforward narrative of progress. In late 20th-century America, we are accustomed to a system of health care that relies on intensive diagnostic and therapeutic technologies, and that rapidly incorporates technological innovation. Before the last two decades of the 19th century, however, this was not the case. No technological imperative dominated the medical treatment of women, especially in childbirth. Indeed, most 19th-century doctors were reluctant to employ many of the technologies available to them. A historical account of women's health and technological intervention must come to terms with the shift from a medical culture that employed technology sparingly to one in which technology has been a dominant force. How and why did this transformation come about? Did it result in improved health for women? These are central questions for a historical investigation of the relationship between technology and women's health that can be illuminated best by examining the history of childbirth management in 19th- and early 20th-century America.

Most of the technologies we associate with childbirth were introduced in America between 1750 and 1850. American physicians began to use forceps in the 1760s. During the same time period they became familiar with the art of pelvimetry. A New York physician outlined the properties of and specified the dosage for ergot in 1807. In 1809, Ephraim McDowell performed the first oophorectomy, although he did not publish an account of it until some years later. Laparotomy was essential to further developments in obstetrical and gynecological surgery, most important for the cesarean section, an operation first performed successfully in the United States in 1827. The use of chloroform and ether for pain relief in labor dates to the late 1840s. And in 1852, J. Marion Sims published his successful technique for repairing vesicovaginal fistulae (Donegan, 1978; Leavitt, 1986; Wertz & Wertz, 1977).

How did the new technologies affect women's health in 19th-century America? A detailed answer to this question is impossible. Our knowledge of maternal mortality and morbidity for any time before the 20th century is sparse and fragmented, as is our information about the frequency of various obstetrical complications, gynecological maladies, or the female incidence of rickets, tuberculosis, and syphilis (Leavitt, 1986; Shorter, 1982). Without answers to such basic questions, it is impossible to assess with any precision the impact of technological intervention. The fact that medical practice was almost entirely unregulated also complicates the matter. These difficulties are illustrated by the varying historical interpretations of the impact of obstetrical forceps on women's health. The traditional argument is that forceps saved an untold number of lives by sparing women the trauma and infants the certain death of craniotomy (Thoms, 1933). This interpretation makes sense in theory, but the instrument's actual impact on women's health was not necessarily positive. Some historians argue that forceps actually harmed more women than they helped. The incorporation of forceps into medical practice coincided with a rise in the incidence of puerperal sepsis, the most common cause of maternal death. More infection may have been the direct result of more instrumental intervention (Bogdan, 1987; Leavitt, 1983; Leavitt, 1986).

To be sure, examples of doctors who misused forceps are easy to find in 19th-century medical literature, and it is even easier to find published diatribes against instrumental obstetrics. As one 1836 medical guide cautioned, forceps were "instruments of cruelty," but "many of our man-midwives resort to instruments on every slight emergency, using the forceps to expedite a lingering labor" (Hersey, 1836, p. 220). Much such rhetoric, particularly in the first half of the 19th century, was that of alternative practitioners—botanics, homeopaths, and the like—who were critical of regular physicians' growing hold on American medicine. Such rhetoric also contains a critique of American society generally, in which childbirth served as a metaphor to express the writers' dismay that the city was replacing traditional rural life, and that "unnatural" urban, commercial values were eclipsing the simple ways of nature (Comfort, 1845; Hersey, 1836; Skinner, 1850).

Medical case notes, doctors' correspondence, and transcripts of medical society meetings tell a different story. Although some doctors did not hesitate to bleed parturient women, administer ergot, or resort to forceps, far more appear to have been cautious about birth technology. Anesthesia was the most commonly employed obstetrical technology after its introduction at mid-century, but not uncommonly physicians stated that they rarely if ever administered it (Duffy, 1964). The same held true for forceps. Many practitioners prided themselves on using the instruments rarely or not at all. Only 80 cesarean operations were performed in the half-century between 1827 and 1878; it was the rare physician who witnessed, let alone performed, such surgery.

The records of two Massachusetts physicians suggest that frequent intervention in labor was the exception rather than the rule. John Metcalf (1824–1832) attended 84 labors between 1830 and 1832. He never employed forceps or ergot, although he bled one patient and considered using ergot on several occasions. After one breech stillbirth, he asked himself:

> whether I might safely have used more force in my attempts at extraction after the child's hips had passed than I did. But all directions in the books as to the amount of force that may be safely and judiciously used are so vague and indefinite (as they must necessarily be) that a junior member of the Faculty . . . had better (if he must err) err upon the safe side. (p. 71)

Invariably, his approach was "to wait awhile and see what nature would do" (p. 38).

Metcalf (1824–1832) was a novice physician at the time he kept this notebook, and it is possible that as he gained experience he felt more secure about intervention. George Snow (1865–1875), on the other hand, was an experienced doctor who practiced obstetrics among a predominantly working-class population in Newburyport, Massachusetts, and who attended 313 births between 1865 and 1875. He occasionally administered ether (usually to treat eclamptic convulsions), made only two references to ergot, attempted one craniotomy and one version, and ruptured membranes once ("[Thought] it would make labor faster, but [it] didn't," he commented. "Think it retarded the labor. Meddlesome midwifery is bad."). He induced labor twice, also in cases of eclampsia, and used forceps five times. In a sixth case, he "urged the use of instruments," but his patient "objected so strongly that I yielded to her wishes."

The catchphrase in 19th-century obstetrics was "watchful expectancy." Doctors often watched a long time without intervening. A young New York physician was not unusual in his management of severe labor in 1842. His patient, an Irish woman with a contracted pelvis, suffered the "most severe labor I have witnessed . . . very little progress made, so much so that I thought it would be expedient to use the forceps, but finally concluded to trust to nature" (Midwifery Manuscript, 1842–1843). Trusting to nature in this case resulted in a stillborn infant, puerperal fever, and a vesicovaginal fistula. A few months later, faced with a similar case, the same doctor decided to use his instruments, although he waited through more than 50 hours of active labor before doing so (Midwifery Manuscript, 1842–1843).

What explains this caution? Part of the reason lies in the inadequacy of medical education, which provided very little clinical training (Leavitt, 1983, 1986). As one doctor who began his practice in 1846 reminisced, he attended more than 700 births in the first 13 years of his career, but used forceps only three times. "I was shy of using forceps," he recalled, "having too much trouble making them lock, not having then learned the trick of depressing the handles. . . . I learned how nature, if given time, would overcome what seemed insurmountable obstacles" (Clark, 1891, pp. 778–780).

Then, too, pregnancy and birth were still largely unknown processes. Pregnancy was difficult to diagnose and impossible to monitor directly. The physiology of labor was understood at best imperfectly. Many doctors may have hesitated to interfere in processes they did not understand, especially when interference clearly courted disaster. Physicians were well aware, for example, that the use of high forceps often resulted in the death of an infant and a severely lacerated mother. Some judged them "always injurious" and eschewed their use (Boston Society for Medical Improvement, 1855). And although they did not agree upon the etiology, many doctors observed a clear connection between intervention and infection. As one physician summarized his case for noninterventionist obstetrics, during his first 12 years in practice, he attended nearly 500 births without once using forceps. Although some of those labors had been very tedious, none resulted in perineal rupture or fistula. In more recent years, he had attended more than 1,000 cases, but had used forceps only rarely. Only two of his patients had died, and he believed that "more of his patients had lived than if he had used forceps frequently" (Worcester Society for Medical Improvement, 1879).

Most important in explaining doctors' hesitation to employ technology was the fact that they, like other Americans, felt considerable ambivalence about the ideal relationship between art and nature. Because childbirth was believed to be a physiological rather than a pathological process, and because it was both a natural and a cultural event, it was at once within and outside the purview of human agency. The debate over nature versus art permeated obstetrical literature for the entire century (Dye, 1987).

Nineteenth-century physicians could not fail to be impressed by the efficacy of birth technologies. One medical student captured something of the awe that must have accompanied successful technological intervention in his 1843 description of a difficult labor. The doctor, he recorded, applied the forceps and delivered the infant, "much to the gratification of himself and attending students . . . and to the infinite delight of the mother and gratification of her friends" (Midwifery Manuscript, 1842–1843). But despite such admiration, most doctors insisted that they did not "meddle" with nature. Instead, they saw themselves as observers of and assistants to the natural processes of birth.

Doctors also believed that they had the responsibility of instructing their female patients to live in accordance with nature's laws. Samuel Bard (1808), author of the first American obstetrics text, set the tone. The practitioner who "meets with most occasion for the use of instruments," he declared in his *Compendium of the Theory and Practice of Midwifery,* "knows least of the powers of nature, and he who also boasts of his skill in the application of forceps is a very dangerous man" (p. 9). Bard went on to state that interference was necessary in no more than four or five times in every 2,000 births. Indeed, the need for instruments was probably considerably less in America, where there were fewer "crooked" women who suffered from pelvic deformity (Bard, 1808). Worcester, Massachusetts doctors echoed the same themes as late as 1879, when they debated how often forceps should be used. Those who rarely employed forceps believed their success was due to their willingness to "leave cases to nature," whereas those who intervened more frequently conceded that reliance on instruments led doctors to "undervalue the process of nature" (Worcester Society for Medical Improvement, 1879).

Despite the proliferation of birth technologies, then, American doctors often were cautious about intervention. Their conservatism was based in the belief that nature was fundamentally benign. Left to its own devices, nature almost always would achieve a good outcome in childbirth.

In the decades after 1880, medical consensus on the relation of nature to art, and the conception of nature as fundamentally benign, rapidly broke down. During the same years, doctors' stance toward technological intervention underwent radical change. Increasingly, doctors believed that nature's outcomes simply were not good enough. Many agreed with their colleague E. H. Grandin (1893), who stated that "no longer should the guess work, the trusting-to-nature of obstetrics of the past be tolerated" (p. 493). Then, too, doctors began to regard labor as a pathological, invariably dangerous process, and to view nature as inherently destructive. As Joseph DeLee (1920), the preemininent obstetrician of the early 20th century, stated, labor was a "decidedly pathologic process" (p. 39). Accordingly, their responsibility as physicians came to involve intervening as much as necessary to protect mother and infant from the innately harmful effects of parturition.

The decades around the turn of the 20th century witnessed a major upturn in technological intervention. Not uncommonly, physicians used forceps in as many as 20% of their cases (Corson, 1897; Miller, 1917). New methods of inducing labor by mechanical and chemical means found acceptance during these years, as did surgical techniques for incising the cervix to speed labor and methods for performing internal version. The long-neglected operations of symphesiotomy and pubiotomy found new favor. Most important, the cesarean section became a viable, increasingly popular delivery method. Even self-defined conservatives intervened far more than doctors throughout most of the 19th century. W. C. Danforth (1922), for example, believed that "a watchful conservatism, allowing the forces of Nature to accomplish delivery if possible, with careful operative interference at once upon proper indication remains the safest standard of obstetrical practice" (p. 611). In 500 cases of labor, he used forceps 98 times (19.6%) and performed nine versions, and eight cesarean sections (Danforth, 1922).

By the 1920s, doctors' new faith in technology and their corresponding misgivings about the efficacy of nature led many to employ interventions such as prophylactic forceps or podalic version that were designed to shorten or even eliminate the second stage of labor (Bill, 1922; DeLee, 1916, 1920; Potter, 1918, 1921). Others envisioned technologies that would do away with labor altogether (Humpstone, 1921; Lull, 1927; Tate, 1922). Doctors' new belief that technology should protect mothers and infants from nature's baneful effects (Joseph DeLee's prophylactic forceps operation, e.g., was designed to protect against nature), their new eagerness to intervene in the birth process, and their faith in the power of technology to render gestation and birth observable, predictable, and controllable embody the principles and practices that have dominated childbirth management in modern America.

The trend toward operative obstetrics and the reasons underlying it are well illustrated by the history of the cesarean operation in the late 19th and early 20th centuries. Before the 1880s, hysterotomy was invariably a desperate operation that carried a maternal mortality of well over 50% (Harris, 1879). Even in cases of severe pelvic deformity, doctors almost always elected to perform craniotomy rather than subject a woman to the dangers of what was widely regarded as the "most dangerous operation in surgery" (Harris, 1879, p. 82). In the early 1880s, however, several developments transformed cesarean section into a viable operation.

In 1882, the German surgeon, Max Sanger, introduced the technique of suturing the uterus after delivery—an innovation that lowered the incidence of postoperative hemorrhage. At the same time, doctors adapted antiseptic and aseptic techniques to obstetrics, thereby dramatically lowering the puerperal sepsis rate. Most doctors' antiseptic and aseptic techniques were imperfect at best, and puerperal morbidity was common—infection remained the most frequent cause of maternal death until the introduction of sulfonamides in the late 1930s. But antisepsis and asepsis provided many doctors with a new—and often false—sense of security. As one practitioner declared in 1893, "The boldness in operating and in reasoning about operations which grew out of the successes made possible by [antisepsis] led men to throw off the shackles of the past" (Noble, 1893, p. 208). Finally, reinterpretation of the statistics of cesarean section convinced many physicians that the risks of infection and shock could be lowered to acceptable limits if the operation were performed early in labor (Harris, 1879, 1881).

In the early 1880s, cesarean section found acceptance only for cases of severe pelvic contraction. But the surgery rapidly gained ground. By 1890, supporters maintained that properly performed, cesarean section posed no more risk to women than oophorectomy or craniotomy. Others were more extravagant, claiming that "the cesarean section done by the expert before or early in labor is scarcely more dangerous than the average of labors as at present conducted in our great cities" (Noble, 1893, p. 210). By the turn of the century, cesarean section had eclipsed all other obstetrical surgeries for a growing number of complications, including malpresentations and placenta praevia. It clearly had become the operation of choice for cases of contracted pelvis. What was more, the success of the operation encouraged the routine making of pelvic measurements and the more pelvimetry doctors performed, the more contracted pelves they found. In the 1880s, doctors believed that pelvic deformity was very rare in the United States, but few took pelvic measurements. By 1900, the incidence of reported pelvic contraction had skyrocketed to more than 11% of women in some patient populations (Dobbin, 1897). The growing trend toward routine pelvimetry meant that many women who once would have delivered spontaneously were now identified during pregnancy and scheduled for operative delivery.

The surgery also gained support for relative cephalopelvic disproportion, as doctors began to perform cesarean section on anatomically normal women who carried large fetuses (Voorhees, 1908).

Cesarean section remained exceedingly hazardous in the first decades of the 20th century: Most published series for individual operators reported maternal mortality between 10% and 20%, whereas community studies found death rates considerably higher (Moran, 1905; Parke, 1915). Nevertheless, many doctors had come to believe that the operation was safe. The key to resolving the seeming contradiction lies in doctors' newfound faith in technology and in their new emphasis on specialization. Physicians acknowledged that cesarean death rates remained high, but argued that the operators, not the technology, were to blame. Too many general practitioners and surgeons attempted the operation for improper indications. Too many women became infected and exhausted during "tests of labor" or in the care of generalists or midwives. Obstetricians urged that the performance of cesarean section be limited to specialists, in whose hands the technology could achieve perfection (Allen, 1909; Lull, 1927).

Another key to understanding the rapid acceptance of cesarean section lies in changing medical valuation of the fetus (Shorter, 1982). Herein lies a critical shift in obstetrical consciousness that also helps explain modern reliance on technological intervention. Before the last decades of the 19th century, doctors had only one obstetrical patient, the mother. By the 1880s, however, doctors had begun to stress their responsibility for two lives; some began to consider the needs of the mother and the needs of the child separately. The late 19th-century debate over the comparative efficacy of craniotomy and cesarean section reflected this new concern for infant life. Enthusiastic cesareanists admitted that the surgery often was undertaken in the interest of the child, and argued that cesarean section rendered embryotomy an unjustifiable procedure under any circumstances. Critics maintained that cesarean advocates were too willing to risk maternal life (Busey, 1894; DeLee, 1901; Edgar, 1893; Jaggard, 1884). Then, too, doctors increasingly described labor as a violent process (DeLee, 1920). Technology, in other words, especially the cesarean operation, could rescue infants from the trauma of natural labor. And as the number of contracted pelves declined over the course of the 20th century, cesarean section was performed increasingly for fetal rather than maternal indications.

During the 1920s, the trend toward operative obstetrics reached its peak, and the rate of cesarean section continued to increase. American obstetricians first began to voice the possibility that cesarean section might replace spontaneous delivery in virtually all labors. Cesarean birth, they argued, offered painless childbirth for women and greater safety for infants. As Joseph DeLee stated in 1921, "Many women are ready to undergo the slightly increased risk of cesarean section in order to avoid the perils and pain of even ordinary labor. I am confident that if women are given only a little encouragement in this direction, demand for cesarean section will be overwhelming" (Holmes, 1921, p. 299). Routine cesarean section performed by obstetricians in hospitals could tame the innately destructive processes of natural childbirth by eliminating labor altogether. Such technological rationalization of the birth process could render parturition entirely predictable and systematic. By the 1920s, then, the technological course of 20th-century childbirth management was set.

What can the history of the modern cesarean operation and the general trend toward operative obstetrics tell us about the relationship between technological intervention and women's health? The most obvious conclusion is that the upsurge in intervention did not ameliorate the most pressing of women's health problems: the risk of dying in childbirth. The death rates associated with cesarean section continued to decline during the 1920s. By the latter part of the decade, experienced surgeons published figures for maternal deaths that ranged from 2% to 5% (Lull, 1929; Montgomery, 1927). But national maternal death rates remained flat from 1900 to 1935, despite the increasing sophistication of birth technologies. Each year, approximately 20,000 women lost their lives giving birth – a maternal death rate of about 6.8 per 1,000 live births (Woodbury, 1936). About 40% of maternal deaths were due to puerperal sepsis – a fact that strongly suggested intervention often contributed to maternal death (Adair, 1927; Woodbury, 1936). Maternal death rates in cities, where women were much more likely to give birth in hospitals and under the care of physicians, were persistently higher than rural rates. In 1915, the urban maternal death rate stood at 64 per 10,000 live births. In 1932, the urban rate stood at 74 maternal deaths per 10,000 births.

These figures gave rise to intense public and medical concern about maternal mortality. Obstetricians' response to this concern was contained within the framework of their newfound faith in technology. Some leading obstetricians condemned the *furor operandi* that characterized the medical management of childbirth. But the solution, they maintained, was not to abandon surgery, but to bring about higher standards of practice and professional accountability so that unqualified practitioners would cease practicing obstetrics (Antler & Fox, 1976). The other part of obstetricians' program for reducing maternal mortality was to continue to work toward perfecting birth technologies so that no complication of parturition could evade technological scrutiny and remedy. Accordingly, obstetrical literature throughout the early 20th century was devoted almost entirely to accounts of new surgical incisions, instruments, techniques, and anesthetics. Despite technological advances, however, maternal mortality did not begin to decline until the introduction of sulfonamides late in the 1930s.

During the same years that the medical management of childbirth became dominated increasingly by technology, social welfare reformers and public health workers emphasized the socioeconomic aspects of maternal mortality in the United States. Although middle- and upper-class women were likely to die in childbirth due to technology, lower-class women were likely to die due to poverty. And Black women were the highest risk group, with the data suggesting that they were nearly twice as likely to die in childbirth than White women. In 1915, the aggregate maternal death rate per 10,000 live births stood at 61. In 1932, the figure was 63. Black women's rates in 1915 were 106 deaths per 10,000 live births. In 1932, the Black death rate stood at 98 per 10,000 births (Adair, 1935). Poverty and maternal death also were correlated positively (Bolt, 1934; Woodbury, 1936).

Those who emphasized the socioeconomic causes of maternal death stressed that many women died in childbirth not for want of advanced technology, but for want of basic health care. Poor women also were more likely to suffer from diseases such as tuberculosis that increased the dangers of parturition. The incidence of contracted pelvis was much higher among Black women than White, the result of early childhood rickets. All of these facts meant that impoverished women were in special need of prenatal supervision during pregnancy and careful attendance during labor, but they were far less likely than middle-class women to have access to such care. The organizations that were established to provide maternal care to impoverished women, most notably the Maternity Center Association, established in New York City in 1918, and the Frontier Nursing Service, established in eastern Kentucky in 1925, provided impressive documentation that careful prenatal care and skilled assistance during labor and delivery could reduce maternal mortality dramatically (Dublin & Corbin, 1930; Dye, 1983; Pickett, 1928).

Surveys of maternal and infant mortality through the 1930s consistently found that only a minority of American women had access to prenatal care and, of those, only a small fraction received high quality care (Adair, 1935). Accordingly, public health workers, members of women's clubs, and government officials concerned with maternal welfare concentrated on broadening access to health care. They pushed for federal appropriations for maternal and infant welfare programs along the line of the programs set in motion by the 1921 Sheppard–Towner Act, which funded state maternal and infant health projects. Through the U.S. Department of Labor Children's Bureau, reformers worked to document the extent of maternal and infant mortality, and the connection between death and poverty, to perfect the American system of collecting vital statistics, and to increase public awareness of the importance of good maternal health care.

The technological orientation of obstetrics and the socioeconomic orientation of the maternal welfare movement represented two approaches to the pressing problem of puerperal death in the early 20th century. The socioeconomic approach has been largely preventive in orientation, whereas the approach of professional obstetrics has been curative. The focus of the one has been broad-based, the focus of the other more on employing technologies to meet the immediate medical needs of an individual patient. For the most part, the two approaches have run along separate tracks. To be sure, prenatal supervision became a mainstay of obstetrics. But many American women still lack access to such care. Indeed, the approach embodied in the programs put forth by maternal and infant welfare workers in the early 20th century represents a road not taken in 20th-century health care. Social choices about the distribution of health-care resources and cultural faith in technology, then, help explain why American childbirth management and women's health care generally remain characterized by a very high level of technological intervention.

REFERENCES

Adair, F. (1927). Maternal mortality: The risk of death in childbirth from all diseases caused by pregnancy and confinement. *American Journal of Obstetrics and Gynecology, 13,* 113–116.

Adair, F. (1935). Maternal, fetal, and neonatal morbidity and mortality. *American Journal of Obstetrics and Gynecology, 29,* 384–394.

Allen, L. M. (1909). A plea for the more frequent performance of the cesarean section. *American Journal of Obstetrics and the Diseases of Women and Children, 49,* 189–201.

Antler, J., & Fox, D. M. (1976). The movement toward a safe maternity: Physician accountability in New York City, 1915–1940. *Bulletin of the History of Medicine, 50,* 569–595.

Bard, S. (1808). *Compendium of the theory and practice of midwifery.* New York: Collins.

Bill, A. (1922). The choice of methods for making labor easy. *American Journal of Obstetrics and Gynecology, 3,* 65–71.

Bogdan, J. (1987). In P. Eakins (Ed.), *The American way of birth* (pp. 50–103). Philadelphia: Temple University Press.

Bolt, R. A. (1934). Maternal mortality study for Cleveland, Ohio. *American Journal of Obstetrics and Gynecology, 27,* 309–13.

Boston Society for Medical Improvement. (1855, October). *Proceedings of the Boston Society for Medical Improvement.* Boston: Countway Library of Medicine.

Busey, S. M. (1894). Craniotomy upon a living fetus is not justifiable. *American Journal of Obstetrics and the Diseases of Women and Children, 17,* 176–193.

Clark, J. S. (1891). Fifty years' experience in obstetrics. *American Journal of Obstetrics and the Diseases of Women and Children, 24,* 778–789.

Comfort, J. W. (1845). *Thomsonian practice of midwifery, and treatment of complaints peculiar to women and children.* Philadelphia: Aaron Comfort.

Corson, E. R. (1897). Some clinical jottings on five hundred cases of labor. *American Journal of Obstetrics, 35,* 175–196, 364–392.

Danforth, W. C. (1922). Is conservative obstetrics to be abandoned? *American Journal of Obstetrics and Gynecology, 3,* 609–616.

Degler, C. (1980). *At odds; women and the family in American from the revolution to the present.* New York: Oxford University Press.

DeLee, J. B. (1901). Three cases of cesarean section, and a consideration of the indication for craniotomy. *American Journal of Obstetrics and the Diseases of Women and Children, 44,* 454–475.

DeLee, J. B. (1916). Progress toward ideal obstetrics. *American Journal of Obstetrics and the Diseases of Women and Children, 73,* 407–415.

DeLee, J. B. (1920). The prophylactic forceps operation. *American Journal of Obstetrics and Gynecology, 1,* 34–44.

Dobbin, G. W. (1897). The frequency of contracted pelves in the obstetrical service of the Johns Hopkins Hospital. *American Journal of Obstetrics and the Diseases of Women and Children, 36,* 145–163.

Donegan, J. (1978). *Women and men midwives: Medicine, morality, and misogyny in early America.* Westport, CT: Greenwood.

Dublin, L., & Corbin, H. (1930). A preliminary report of a study of the records of the Maternity Center Association of New York. *American Journal of Obstetrics and Gynecology, 20,* 877–881.

Duffy, J. (1964). Anglo-American reaction to obstetrical anesthesia. *Bulletin of the History of Medicine, 38,* 32–44.

Dye, N. S. (1983). Mary Breckinridge, the Frontier Nursing Service, and the introduction of nurse-midwifery in the United States. *Bulletin of the History of Medicine, 57,* 485–507.

Dye, N. S. (1987). The medicalization of birth. In P. Eakins (Ed.), *The American way of birth* (pp. 21–46). Philadelphia: Temple University Press.

Edgar, J. C. (1893). Embryotomy, its prognosis and limitations. *American Journal of Obstetrics and the Diseases of Women and Children, 27,* 496–509.

Gordon, L. (1974). *Woman's body, woman's right.* New York: Penguin.

Grandin, E. H. (1893). The relative value of certain obstetrical operations (embryotomy, cesarean section, symphysiotomy). *American Journal of Obstetrics and the Diseases of Women and Children, 27,* 492–496.

Harris, R. J. (1879). Lessons from the study of the cesarean operation in the City and State of New York, and their bearing upon the true position of gastro-elytrotomy. *American Journal of Obstetrics and the Diseases of Women and Children, 12,* 82–91.

Harris, R. J. (1881). Special statistics of the cesarean operation in the United States, showing the successes and failures in each state. *American Journal of Obstetrics and the Diseases of Women and Children, 13,* 341–361.

Hawks, E. M. (1929). Maternal mortality in 582 abdominal sections. *American Journal of Obstetrics and the Diseases of Women and Children, 18,* 392–406.

Hersey, T. (1836). *The midwife's practical directory, or, woman's confidential friend . . . the whole designed for the special use of botanic friends in the United States* (2nd ed.). Baltimore: Author.

Holmes, R. W. (1921). The fads and fancies of obstetrics: A comment on the pseudoscientific trend of modern obstetrics. *American Journal of Obstetrics and Gynecology, 2,* 225–237, 297–307.

Humpstone, P. O. (1921). Cesarean section versus spontaneous delivery. *American Journal of Obstetrics and Gynecology, 1,* 987–989.

Jaggard, W. W. (1884). Is craniotomy upon a living fetus a justifiable operation? *American Journal of Obstetrics and the Diseases of Woman and Children, 17,* 1131–1141.

Leavitt, J. W. (1983). "Science" enters the birthing room: Obstetrics in America since the 18th century. *Journal of American History, 70,* 218–304.

Leavitt, J. W. (1986). *Brought to bed; childbearing in America, 1750–1950.* New York: Oxford University Press.

Longo, L. (1979). The rise and fall of Battey's operation: A fashion in surgery. *Bulletin of the History of Medicine, 53,* 244–267.

Lull, C. (1927). Indications and technic of cesarean section. *American Journal of Obstetrics and Gynecology, 13,* 633–641.

Lull, C. (1929). Cesarean section; a review of 109 cases. *American Journal of Obstetrics and Gynecology, 27,* 403–408.

Metcalf, J. (1824–1832). Manuscript, Harvard University School of Medicine, Countway Library of Medicine, Boston.

Midwifery Manuscript, New York Asylum for Lying-In Women. (1842–1843). New York Academy of Medicine, New York.

Miller, G. B. (1917). A review of 300 obstetrical cases in private practice. *American Journal of Obstetrics and the Diseases of Women and Children, 75,* 798–808.

Mohr, J. (1984). Patterns of abortion and the responses of American physicians, 1790–1930. In J. W. Leavitt (Ed.), *Women and health in America* (pp. 117–123). Madison: University of Wisconsin Press.

Montgomery, T. (1927). The morbidity and mortality of cesarean section. *American Journal of Obstetrics and Gynecology, 13,* 610–617.

Moran, J. F. (1905). Indications for cesarean section: Report of two cases; recovery. *American Journal of Obstetrics and the Diseases of Woman and Children, 51,* 320–324.

Noble, C. P. (1893). The cesarean section and its substitutes. *American Journal of Obstetrics and the Diseases of Women and Children, 27,* 340–347.

Parke, W. E. (1915). The cesarean operation; its wider applications; with report of cases. *American Journal of Obstetrics and the Diseases of Women and Children, 72,* 281–289.

Pickett, A. (1928). A study of the results of prenatal care vs. no prenatal care; based on over 3,000 cases in the obstetrical department at the Louisville City Hospital. *Kentucky State Medical Journal, 26,* 52–56.

Potter, I. W. (1918). Version, with a report of two hundred additional cases since September, 1916. *American Journal of Obstetrics and the Diseases of Women and Children, 77,* 215–220.

Potter, I. W. (1921). Version. *American Journal of Obstetrics and Gynecology, 1,* 560–573.

Reed, J. (1978). *From private vice to public virtue; the birth control movement and American society since 1830.* New York: Basic.

Reed, J. (1979). Doctors, birth control, and social values, 1830–1970. In M. J. Vogel & C. E. Rosenberg (Eds.), *The therapeutic revolution: Essays in the social history of medicine* (pp. 47–61). Philadelphia: University of Pennsylvania.

Shorter, E. (1982). *A history of women's bodies.* New York: Basic.

Skinner, G. W. (1850). *Nature defended, and the abuses of custom exposed: Being an argument advocating the claims of female midwifery.* Newburyport, MA: Author.

Smith-Rosenberg, C. (1985a). The hysterical woman: Sex roles and role conflict in nineteenth-century America. In C. Smith-Rosenberg (Ed.), *Disorderly conduct: Visions of gender in Victorian America* (pp. 197–216). New York: Knopf.

Smith-Rosenberg, C. (1985b). Puberty to menopause: The cycle of femininity in nineteenth-century America. In C. Smith-Rosenberg (Ed.), *Disorderly conduct: Visions of gender in Victorian America* (pp. 182–196). New York: Knopf.

Smith-Rosenberg, C., & Rosenberg, C. E. (1973). The female animal: Medical and biological views of woman and her role in nineteenth-century America. *Journal of American History, 60,* 332–356.

Snow, G. (1865–1875). Obstetrical Casebook, Newburyport, Massachusetts. Harvard University Medical School, Countway Library of Medicine, Boston.

Tate, M. A. (1922). A method of delivery in normal cases. *American Journal of Obstetrics and Gynecology, 3,* 61–65.

Thoms, H. (1933). *Chapters in American obstetrics.* Springfield, IL: Thomas.

Voorhees, J. D. (1908). Disproportion between the fetal head and the maternal pelvis and its management. *American Journal of Obstetrics and the Diseases of Women and Children, 57,* 519–527.

Welter, B. (1966). The cult of true womanhood. *American Quarterly, 18,* 151–174.

Wertz, R. W., & Wertz, D. C. (1977). *Lying-in: A history of childbirth in America.* New York: Free Press.

Woodbury, R. M. (1936). Infant mortality in the United States. *Annals of the American Academy of Political and Social Science, 188,* 94–106.

Worcester Society for Medical Improvement. (1846–1888). *Proceedings of Worcester [Massachusetts] Society for Medical Improvement.* Worcester, MA: American Antiquarian Society.

<table>
<tr><td>3</td><td>Pregnancy-Inducing Technologies:
Biological and Medical Implications</td></tr>
</table>

Sam Thatcher
Alan DeCherney
Yale University

The theme . . . is not the advancement of science as such; it is the advancement of science as it affects human beings.
  —From a foreword to a later printing of *Brave New World* by A. Huxley

On July 25, 1978, an uneventful delivery of baby girl Brown marked the birth of a new reproductive technology that has revolutionized the therapy of the infertile couple and caught the interest and imagination of the ethicists, the press, and the general public. Rather than the result of a precisely planned scientific experiment, this birth was the cumulation of a sound knowledge of reproductive science, a human malady in need of a therapy, and 10 years of trial and error. Less than a decade later, a vast, clinically oriented science has grown around in vitro technologies and human reproduction. Although initially used as a method to bypass blocked fallopian tubes, in vitro technologies have become the final common path for the treatment of infertility. The combined procedure of stimulation of follicle growth and maturation, follicle puncture and oocyte capture, insemination in vitro, and placement of the conceptus directly into the uterine cavity enables a bypass of an array of both defined and undefined blocks to fertility. As such, in vitro techniques are now being used for treatment of endometriosis, endocrinopathy, cervical factor, male factor, immunologic, and unexplained infertility, when less invasive techniques have failed.

Because of in vitro fertilization (IVF), a vast array of other, both more and less invasive, technologies have arisen that rely on the lessons learned from IVF. IVF has enabled a much more detailed understanding of the science of reproduction, which in turn has provided additional therapeutic options to the more than 5 million infertile couples in the United States. In April 1987, the Fifth World Conference on In Vitro Fertilization and Embryo Transfer (IVF/ET) was held and an international collaborative report of 55 of 120 registered centers presented (Cohen, Mayaux, & Guihard-Moscato, 1987). Detailed information was available on 2,339 pregnancies conceived from 1979 to 1985 of which 70% resulted in delivery of liveborn infants or ongoing pregnancies. During 1988, the U.S. Registry of in vitro fertilization-embryo transfer reported of its then 135-member clinics performing 22,649 ovarian stimulation cycles with 16% resulting in a clinical pregnancy and 12% in a live delivery. Of the clinics, 93% had at least one delivery and 3,427 babies were born. The following description uses the Yale experience, with IVF/ET as a basis, to present the new technologies for "inducing" pregnancies.

The process of IVF/ET can be divided into four essentially technical components: (a) augmentation of folliculogenesis to increase the number of preovulatory follicles, and thus "eggs," available for recovery, (b) capture (recovery, retrieval) of these oocytes, (c) fertilization and initial growth of the conceptus in the laboratory, and (d) replacement of the cleaving conceptus (preembryo) into the uterus. Each step is a point of potential failure and a separate technology has arisen around each. Each technology has created new therapeutic options.

AUGMENTATION OF FOLLICULOGENESIS

Induction of ovulation is a term used to describe administration of exogenous hormonal agents to induce (promote) ovarian follicle growth and ovulation. This modality has been used in the past in anovulatory women to correct disorders of the hypothalamic-pituitary-ovarian axis with the goal of the ovulation of a single egg. The terminology has been borrowed, but the application is somewhat different for IVF/ET patients, most of whom do not have ovulatory disorders. In fact, successful stimulation for IVF/ET involves suppression of the normal regulatory mechanisms for follicular growth. Here the goals are neither induction of the growth of a single preovulatory oocyte nor its ovulation, but stimulation of multiple follicles along a preovulatory path. Recovery is planned near enough to ovulation to allow full intrafollicular development of the oocyte, but before follicular rupture (ovulation). The rationale for this is that, up to four conceptui, the pregnancy rate is directly proportional to the number of concepti replaced (Speirs, Lopata, Gronow, Kellow, & Johnston, 1983). Number of concepti replaced is obviously related to the number of oocytes collected. However, as presented in the following, it is not just the quantity of oocytes that is important, but their quality.

A relatively small number of agents has been used in almost unlimited varieties of dosages, and schedules, in an attempt to produce "proper" stimulation and recovery. The mainstay of stimulation protocols relies on human menopausal gonadotropin (hMG) (Pergonal®), which is a mixture of human luteinizing hormone (LH) and follicle stimulating hormone (FSH), in equal concentrations, clomiphene citrate (Clomid®, Serophene™), which is a nonsteroidal antiestrogen, or a combination of the two. Promising results have been obtained from selected patients when purified FSH (Metrodin®) is added to, or used as a substitute for, hMG. A limited number of centers use the natural cycle in preparation for IVF/ET. Although the egg from these cycles potentially is the healthiest, pregnancy rates are usually lower.

At Yale (Laufer et al., 1983) we use 225 iμ (3 ampoules) of hMG injected intramuscularly each day from Days 3 to 8 of the cycle, at which time daily estradiol and ultrasound measurements are made to determine follicle number, size, and growth. Injections are given at home, usually by the male partner, after conferring with the IVF nurse practitioner. Starting on Day 8, each patient is reviewed in a daily conference, when a decision is made on the amount of hMG to be used that evening. Once two follicles reach at least 15 mm and the estradiol level is greater than 400 pg/ml, which is about twice the usual preovulatory level, 10,000 iμ of human chorionic gonadotropin (hCG) is injected. This agent acts as an artificial LH surge, promoting the completion of the first meiotic division of the oocyte, and begins the conversion of the follicle transformation into the corpus luteum. Some centers use the endogenous LH surge to time the oocyte recovery, but this has not been shown to improve the success of the cycle and often makes surgical scheduling more difficult. The hCG injection is given 36 hours before the scheduled recovery. If a cycle fails to reach 400 pg/ml of estradiol by Cycle Day 12, or if there is more than a 30% drop in estradiol on the morning after hCG, the cycle is abandoned. A major cause of drops in estradiol levels, and of abandoned cycles, is the interference by natural LH surges and unplanned prerecovery ovulations. Several new regimens using compounds, either similar to the hormone secreted from the hypothalamus (gonadotropin releasing hormone, GnRH), which causes the release of LH, or steroid agents which suppress ovarian function, have been used in attempts to prevent unwanted LH surges.

Other new developments involve programmed stimulation regimens, which, using hormonal manipulation of the cycle before the IVF/ET cycle, allow a recovery day to be scheduled several months in advance. Previously, exogenous ovulation induction protocols, using high doses of exogenous gonadotropins, were associated with severe ovarian hyperstimulation. The careful monitoring of follicle growth and estrogen secretion, together with follicle aspiration, has made this a rare complication of IVF.

Tremendous effort has been applied in attempts to identify the "good egg." Even in the most synchronized cycles, oocytes are recovered at different levels of maturity (Laufer, DeCherney, Haseltine, & Behrman, 1984). Eggs, judged morphologically to be immature, or postmature, have less chance of producing a pregnancy, but overall we have little ability to assess developmental potential. The oocyte, because of its relatively rudimentary nature, is notoriously difficult to study. Therefore, efforts have been directed to the study of the more dynamic preovulatory follicle. It appears that in vitro estrogen production by the follicle cells (DeCherney, Tarlatzis, & Laufer, 1985) may be one indicator of follicle health. The nucleotide cAMP, the so-called second messenger, has a pivotal role in the expression of the cellular response to gonadotropins. It has been shown that this compound also may inhibit oocyte maturation and lower levels of cAMP in follicular fluid may indicate that the oocyte is more likely to be mature, fertilize, and cleave (Tarlatzis et al., 1985).

CAPTURE OF OOCYTES

The LH surge (hCG injection) causes a loosening or separation of the oocyte and its surrounding cumulus cells from the follicular wall. An oocyte is obtained by puncture and aspiration of follicular fluid from the preovulatory follicle. Classically, follicular puncture was performed under direct visualization at laparoscopy. Most centers now use an ultrasound guided approach, either by abdominal ultrasound and capture through the filled urinary bladder (transvesical), or more often, vaginal ultrasound and capture through the posterior vaginal fornix (transvaginal) (Russell, De-Cherney, & Hobbins, 1987). Overall pregnancy rates are essentially the same, regardless of the method of capture.

The benefit of the transvaginal ultrasound is that general anesthesia is not needed and there are no incisions other than small puncture sites in the vaginal wall. Transvaginal capture is possible in some patients in whom laparoscopy is impossible because of inaccessibility of the ovaries with adhesions. In other patients, laparoscopy is indicated because of the position of the ovary. A small subset of patients may have such extensive adhesive disease that a laparotomy is necessary in preparation for future IVF/ET cycles (DeCherney, Tarlatzis, Laufer, & Naftolin, 1985).

CULTURE TECHNIQUES

Follicles are aspirated into 10 to 20 ml plastic collection tubes, transported to the culture laboratory in a mobile incubator, and examined with a dissecting microscope for presence of oocytes. The oocytes then are transferred to small dishes containing culture medium and stored in an incubator at 37°C (98.6°F). Insemination is not performed immediately, in that it appears that fertilization and cleavage rates are improved after a delay of 6 hours for mature, and 24 hours for immature, oocytes. During this incubation period a semenanalysis is performed on freshly collected semen. The sample is centrifuged allowing a separation of the sperm from the seminal fluid. The seminal fluid is removed from the top of the tube and the sperm, concentrated into a pellet in the bottom of the tube, are covered with media. During the next hour, the sperm "swim up" into the overlying media, allowing isolation of the most motile and probably healthiest sperm. Usually between 100,000 and 500,000 sperm per oocyte are used.

At one time it was thought that the concentration of sperm around the oocyte was critical. Now it appears that concentration is of little significance over 50,000 and polyspermy, penetration of the oocyte by more than one sperm, is not increased with high sperm concentrations. Polyspermy still represents a significant problem, occurring in 5% to 15% of fertilizations. It seems that immature and postmature eggs are more vulnerable to polyspermy, but precise correlations are difficult.

Treatment of male factor infertility is often more difficult both to diagnose and to treat, with success rates often low. By removal of seminal fluid, selection of the most motile sperm, and direct application of these to the egg, some of the factors involved in male infertility can be eliminated, offering new promise in the treatment of male infertility. Still, a major point of failure in IVF therapy for male infertility is penetration of the egg and in its investments by sperm. Research is underway on several possible ways to bypass artificially the need for sperm penetration of these barriers.

The zona pellucida, a protein-rich transparent halo around the egg, is important in sperm recognition and blocking fertilization by more than one sperm, but it also can form an impenetrable barrier. Weak enzymes or acids that can cause dissolution of this barrier have been used experimentally in microscopic amounts for removal of this block. Sperm also have been injected by micromanipulation through the zona pellucida, either directly into the oocyte or between the oocyte membrane and the zona pellucida. So far, the success with these procedures is low and, in general, the success rates of IVF/ET for male factor are the lowest of all indications.

An additional value of IVF is that it may represent the ultimate diagnostic test of the sperm's capacity to fertilize. Couples who have had repeated cycles in which there has been no fertilization overall have a dismal prognosis of achieving a pregnancy. In cases of suspected male infertility, it is common to have frozen donor sperm available if fertilization does not occur after 24 hours. When indications coexist in the woman for IVF, some cycles are managed entirely with donor sperm. And in those cases where there is no female indication for IVF, therapy is better relegated to donor insemination cycles.

A variety of less invasive techniques has been developed to overcome the functional blocks to the meeting of the egg and sperm. The most widely employed of these is intrauterine insemination (IUI). Theoretically, direct placement of sperm into the uterine cavity can bypass the occasionally "hostile" cervical environment. This adverse cervical environment for the sperm may be a result of sperm antibodies in cervical mucus that elicit an immunologic reaction and reduce sperm motility and/or viability. A sensitive assay is now available that can test for these antibodies that may be present in either the male or female partner.

Semen cannot be instilled directly into the uterus, except in very small quantities, without the risk of violent uterine contractions and even shock. Before IUI is performed, sperm are separated from the remainder of the semen by a technique very similar to the one described earlier. This has the additional advantage of removing sperm from antibodies that may exist in the seminal fluid. IUI also may have an indication in cases where the sperm count is low (oligospermia) or sperm motility is decreased (asthenospermia). A benefit theoretically is derived from reducing attrition, occurring with migration of sperm through the vagina and cervix, thus providing increased numbers of sperm closer to the site of fertilization. It is unknown whether this technique may be bypassing an important step in sperm maturation, because success rates with IUI are disappointingly low. Small trials also have been performed on instilling sperm directly into the abdominal cavity and into close proximity to the tubal ostium via a catheter through the vagina. The numbers of cases are still too small to make a statement on the effectiveness of this technique.

TRANSFER OF THE CONCEPTUS

After 24 hours of incubation, cultures are inspected for fertilization and cleavage and the time of transfer is set, which is 44 to 48 hours after recovery. Extensive work has failed to give a precise answer on the best time for transfer. If transfer is delayed, the viability of the conceptus is impaired due to the yet undefined requirements for culture. If the culture time is advanced, the uterus is less well prepared for nutrition of the conceptus. Generally the two- to eight cell stage is considered optimum. The conceptus at this stage usually is referred to as an embryo, but by strict definition the conceptus is not an embryo until formation of the germ layers about 14 days later. Perhaps preembryo or conceptus are better terms, but the term embryo is firmly entrenched in the current literature.

Technically, the transfer procedure is the easiest step in the IVF/ET process. It is accomplished by placing the conceptui and a very small quantity of medium in a narrow gauge plastic catheter and passing this through the internal cervicas os into the uterine cavity. Some centers use plastic or metal introducers to facilitate passage of the catheter through the cervix, but regardless, the procedure is most often painless and requires no anesthesia. The patient then rests undisturbed for several hours after the transfer and is allowed to go home, generally able to resume normal activities.

A popular alternative therapy to IVF/ET for couples when tubal factor has been excluded, is gamete intra-fallopian tube transfer (GIFT). Oocytes are collected at laparoscopy, mixed in the laboratory with sperm, and placed in the uterine tube while the patient is still under anesthesia. This may have theoretical, if not ethical, advantages, but it requires the general anesthetic of laparoscopy and success rates have not been proven conclusively superior to IVF/ET. In an attempt to find the proper timing and environment for the optimal developmental advantage for the conceptus, multiple variations of the GIFT and IVF/ET protocols have been developed. We are trying a new procedure where, rather than transferring the embryos into the uterus, we are placing them into the fallopian tubes via laparoscopy 48 hours after a transvaginal recovery. Although this has the disadvantage of two surgical procedures, it offers the positive benefits of confirmation of fertilization and cleavage and placement of the conceptus into the tube, where it would be at this stage of development in a spontaneous pregnancy.

Limited trials have begun on two other techniques that allow IVF, but minimize exposure of the conceptus in culture. Both techniques, pronuclear stage transfer (PROST) and zygote intra fallopian tube transfer (ZIFT), are performed on the stages after fertilization, but before division of the conceptus.

IVF/ET OUTCOME

It has been estimated in a general population of women having regular intercourse, that 60 of 100 ovulatory cycles will show evidence of pregnancy. Of this 60, 25 will become clinical pregnancies with 3 subsequently aborting (Miller et al., 1980). Given that in an IVF cycle there are multiple eggs recovered and fertilized, our success rates are still disappointingly low. Many centers report pregnancy rates in excess of 20% per transfer, but generally live birthrate seldom exceeds 15%. Caution must be used in interpretation of the success of individual programs due to variation in manner of reporting. Often biochemical or subclinical pregnancies are included in statistics based on transfers, and not cycles started or ovum captures attempted. Also certain subgroups, such as male factor infertility, may be excluded.

Because recovery, fertilization, and cleavage rates are in excess of 75%, most failures of IVF/ET probably occur after the point of transfer. The most important barrier to IVF/ET success, and the area least amenable to study, is implantation and early development. There is concern that an asynchrony of the ovarian and uterine cycles may result from ovulation induction. Some centers routinely use progesterone to supplement the ovarian production and support the endometrium, but the results of studies on the efficacy of progesterone are inconclusive.

THE NEW REPRODUCTIVE TECHNOLOGIES AND THE RISK OF MALFORMATION

A major concern of society and science has been the chromosomal integrity and the risk of anomalous development in babies conceived in vitro. At present it seems that the risk for congenital malformation and chromosomal anomalies is no greater, and possibly less, than for natural pregnancies in the general population (Cohen et al., 1987). With regimens that stimulate the growth of more than one follicle, whether or not this stimulation is associated with IVF/ET, there appears to be an increased risk of spontaneous abortion. Certainly, not all oocytes contained in the ovary have the same developmental potential. It may be that there is an inherent defect in the oocytes before the stimulation and in vitro processes begin. Still, the risk of the birth of a child with chromosomal or developmental anomaly appears low.

CRYOPRESERVATION

Recent advances are making cryopreservation of embryos both feasible and practical. Because no advantage is gained from transferring more than four conceptui per cycle — and more than four per cycle are often obtained — these "spares" can be frozen and transferred in subsequent cycles. Cycles in which exogenous stimulation regimens have been used for increasing the yield of oocytes may provide a uterine environment that is less conducive to implantation. If transfer of conceptui is postponed until the proper time in a natural cycle, the uterus may be more properly prepared for successful implantation. Perhaps in the future, more attention can be paid to maximizing the uterine environment in cycles that may be programmed precisely for this purpose. Distributing conceptui between recovery and "thaw" cycles can diminish the risk of multiple gestation when more than four conceptui are replaced, as well as decrease the number of recovery cycles.

TOMORROW

A totally new science is developing around micromanipulation of the conceptus. By removing a single totipotential cell from the two to eight cell stage ("embryo" biopsy), it may be possible to perform multiple screens for chromosomal and biochemical disorders. The conceptus could be transferred to the uterus at this point. This may allow diagnosis much before it could be made with chorionic villus biopsy or amniocentesis.

The in vitro manipulation of reproduction is certainly a vanguard of today's medicine and science. IVF has had a tremendous impact on our understanding of fertility and will remain a milestone for future development. However, it is important to emphasize that scientists and physicians working in this field are never far away from the complex ethical and moral considerations that accompany their work.

REFERENCES

Cohen, J., Mayaux, M. J., & Guihard-Moscato, M. L. (1987, April). *Pregnancy outcomes after in vitro fertilization: A collaborative study on 2,342 pregnancies.* Paper presented at the Fifth World Congress on In Vitro Fertilization and Embryo Transfer, Norfolk, VA.

DeCherney, A. H., Tarlatzis, B. C., & Laufer, N. (1985). Follicular development: Lessons learned from human in vitro fertilization. *American Journal of Obstetrics and Gynecology, 153,* 911–923.

DeCherney, A. H., Tarlatzis, B. C., Laufer, N., & Naftolin, F. (1985). A simple technique of ovarian suspension in preparation for in vitro fertilization. *Fertility and Sterility, 43,* 659–661.

Laufer, N., DeCherney, A. H., Haseltine, F. P., & Behrman, H. R. (1984). Steroid secretion by the human egg-corona-cumulus complex in culture. *Journal of Clinical Endocrinology and Metabolism, 58,* 1153.

Laufer, N., DeCherney, A. H., Haseltine, F. P., Polan, M. L., Mezer, H. C., Dlugi, A. M., Sweeney, D., Nero, F., & Naftolin, F. (1983). The use of high-dose human menopausal gonadotropin in an in vitro fertilization program. *Fertility and Sterility, 40,* 734–741.

Miller, J. F., Williamson, E., Glue, J., Gordon, Y. B., Grudzinskas, J. G., & Sykes, A. (1980). Fetal loss after implantation: A prospective study. *Lancet, 1* 554–556.

Russell, J. B., DeCherney, A. H., & Hobbins, J. C. (1987). A new transvaginal probe and biopsy guide for oocyte retrieval. *Fertility and Sterility, 47,* 350.

Speirs, A. L., Lopata, A., Gronow, M. J., Kellow, G. N., & Johnston, W. I. (1983). Analysis of the benefits and risks of multiple embryo transfer. *Fertility and Sterility, 39,* 468–471.

Tarlatzis, B. C., Laufer, N., DeCherney, A. H., Polan, M. L., Haseltine, F. P., & Behrman, H. R. (1985). Adenosine 3', 5'-monophosphate levels in human follicular fluid: Relationship to oocyte maturation and achievement of pregnancy after in vitro fertilization. *Journal of Clinical Endocrinology and Metabolism, 60,* 1111–1115.

<table>
<tr><td>4</td><td>Autonomy, Choice, and the New
Reproductive Technologies:
The Role of Informed Consent
in Prenatal Genetic Diagnosis</td></tr>
</table>

4   Autonomy, Choice, and the New Reproductive Technologies: The Role of Informed Consent in Prenatal Genetic Diagnosis

Ruth Faden
Johns Hopkins University

AN INTRODUCTION TO INFORMED CONSENT

▷An *informed consent* may be defined as an autonomous action by a subject or a patient that authorizes a professional either to involve the subject in research or to initiate a medical plan for the patient (or both). Based on an analysis of autonomous action we have defended elsewhere, this definition can be expanded as follows: An informed consent is given if a patient or a subject with (a) substantial understanding and (b) in substantial absence of control by others (c) intentionally (d) authorizes a professional to initiate either a medical plan or research involvement, or both (Faden & Beauchamp, 1986).

Although the breadth of this chapter does not permit careful examination of each of these conditions, one of these conditions, substantial understanding, warrants further discussion. As a practical matter, it is virtually impossible in most circumstances for the condition of substantial understanding to be satisfied absent extensive, effective communication between the potential patient and her health-care providers. By effective communication I mean what I, and others, have referred to elsewhere as shared understanding (Faden & Beauchamp, 1986; Katz, 1984). That is, the health professional seeking authorization and the patient from whom authorization is being sought share an understanding of the situation. Each attaches the same meaning to the messages exchanged such that they understand each other's intentions and beliefs relevant to the consent solicitation, although they may not necessarily agree as to those beliefs.

An important part of this shared understanding involves a mutual appreciation of not only the medical interventions under consideration — the treatment options, the alternatives, the implications for the patient if she does or does not have specific interventions — but also the role of the patient in medical decision making. To borrow a phrase from Stephen Bochner (1983), what is needed is a shared understanding of the culture of the consent solicitation; most particularly, that the reason consent is being solicited is because the patient has a central role in reaching a decision as to which interventions, if any, should be instituted and which rejected. That central role is captured by the fourth condition of informed consent enumerated previously — authorization of treatment or research.

This analytic definition of the term informed consent as autonomous authorization reflects the historical goal of informed consent in medical care and in research — that is, the purpose behind the obligation to obtain informed consents — which is to enable potential subjects and patients to make autonomous decisions about whether to grant or refuse authorization for medical and research interventions (Faden & Beauchamp, 1986). The implicit normative position is that, in most circumstances of informed consent, absent this express autonomous authorization from the patient or subject, the physician or researcher has no moral warrant to proceed.

It should be emphasized that this account of informed consent has nothing to do with compelling patients to be sole or isolated decision makers, or with compelling patients to take responsibility for substantive decisions they would rather relegate to others. It is inherent in the understanding of informed consent that one option that a patient can elect is to have other people make the medical decision for her. This is not a popular construal of what is meant by informed consent, but it is certainly logically consistent with the concept. In a similar vein, nothing about informed consent requires abandonment of the patient, or absence of compassion, or absence of caring, or absence of involvement with the patient or the decision-making process. Nor is informed consent incompatible with models of shared decision making between provider and patient currently being advocated (Katz, 1984; President's Commission, 1982). Indeed, the historical relationship between the two — informed consent and shared decision making — is quite intimate.

The institution of informed consent emerged in response to the extreme imbalance in the way in which decisions were made in medicine, serving as an important constructive and symbolic force in righting this imbalance and improving proportionality in relations between doctors and patient. Informed consent continues to serve these substantive and symbolic functions, for the following reasons. Intrinsic to the concept are the notions of authorization and moral warrant — that is, there are certain circumstances in medicine (and in research) in which the moral authority to go forward rests, in the end, with the patient. This is not to say that under informed consent it is the patient's responsibility to work through complex issues entirely alone, that unless the patient bears the burdens of decision making in isolation, without the involvement and caring of others, it is not the patient's decision. As noted previously, there are no such requirements. However, what the concept of informed consent does put before us, always, is the recognition that in certain consequential contexts in medicine, the ultimate moral authority for legitimizing decisions rests with the patient. Informed consent does require that the patient be the center, the nexus, of the decision-making process, even as this process appropriately may involve health-care providers, family, counselors, friends, and others.

Under what circumstances do professionals have a moral obligation to obtain informed consents? That is, under what circumstances are professionals unjustified in intervening without an express patient or subject authorization? In clinical medicine, this remains a hotly contested issue. Informed consent, and the underlying moral principle of respect for patient autonomy, are relative newcomers to traditional medical ethics. Historically, medical ethics has been dominated by a commitment to the principle of medical beneficence — a principle that obligates physicians to further the medical best interests of their patients. Although in recent years informed consent has achieved substantial standing in moral thinking about medicine, there is empirical evidence that in practice informed consents, in the sense of autonomous authorizations defined earlier, are neither frequently solicited nor frequently obtained by physicians (Fisher, 1983; Lidz & Meisel, 1982). Both implicit and explicit conflicts between the principles of medical beneficence and respect for patient autonomy account in part for this discrepancy. Most relevant to our present concerns is the view that the resources in professional time needed to obtain informed consents (e.g., resources needed for meaningful patient education) are in many instances better spent producing direct patient benefits in the form of patient care.

Insofar as a consensus has emerged, the proper role for informed consent in clinical medicine can be described as follows: All other things being equal, informed consents should be obtained for research or experimental interventions (therapeutic as well as nontherapeutic), for innovative interventions, for interventions that carry with them substantial or unknown risks, and in situations of choice between substantially different medical plans. Also, all other things being equal, informed consents need not be obtained for routine interventions that pose little or no risk to the patient and that are not part of a research protocol. These general areas of agreement obviously leave unresolved whether informed consent should be obtained in many specific medical situations.

Medical genetics can be understood as a subspecialty of medicine, with genetic counseling functioning as the patient education arm of medical genetics. Although the connections between medicine and medical genetics are quite strong, medical genetics has a very different moral tradition. A relatively new enterprise, medical genetics almost from its inception has adopted as its primary moral principle respect for the autonomy of the client or patient. This position is evidenced in genetics in a thoroughgoing commitment to the ideal of nondirective counseling in the provision of genetic information and in the convention of obtaining informed consent prior to all diagnostic genetic testing.

In part, this commitment to respect for autonomy in genetics can be explained by the fact that, at least until recently, medical genetics has not been as much in the business of producing the traditional "medical benefits" of therapy and cure as in providing information of relevance to highly personal, nonmedical decisions about parenting and abortion, decisions for which geneticists could claim no special "medical" expertise. In the absence of any strong role for a principle of medical beneficence, informed consent, as well as other moral rules grounded in respect for autonomy, have evolved a firm grip on professional ethics in genetics.

HISTORY OF INFORMED CONSENT

I have already mentioned that informed consent is a relative newcomer to traditional medical ethics. Indeed, the current controversy about informed consent is only about 30 years old (*Salgo v. Leland Stanford Jr. University Board of Trustees,* 1957). Informed consent first appeared as an issue in American medicine in the late 1950s and early 1960s. Prior to this period, we have not been able to locate a single substantial discussion in the medical literature of consent and patient authorization.

Among scholars of the history of informed consent, there is some debate as to whether there was any meaningful role for patient authorization and decision making prior to this period (Katz, 1984; Pernick, 1982). However, there is reason to believe that whatever the general status of patient authorization, women patients were seen as less capable than men of making reasoned decisions about medical treatment and thus were more likely than men to be bypassed in treatment decisions. An example of this is the following case, which is illustrative of several cases we identified in reviewing case reports in the *Boston Medical and Surgical Journal* published in the 19th century (between 1829 and 1837): A "very heavy" woman had fallen and severely fractured both bones of her right leg. A question arose regarding the necessity of amputation. The *Journal* reported: "Dr. W. therefore resolved to take the responsibility of allowing the limb to remain, without suggesting to the patient the question of amputation; and this opinion was concurred in by Dr. S." The patient was an adult who was described as "of much fortitude, and a strong religious confidence." Nonetheless her physician explicitly assumed decisional authority.

The key questions for our purposes is where informed consent came from and why it took on the force that it did beginning about 30 years ago. The most immediate and prominent influences were doubtlessly case law and a revitalized interdisciplinary medical ethics. The emerging legal doctrine of informed consent — the term was coined in case law in 1957 (*Salgo,* 1957) — must be credited with first bringing the concept of informed consent to the attention of the medical community. In this case, a patient, after suffering permanent paralysis as a result of a translumbar aortography, sued his physician for negligence in its performance and in failing to warn him of the risk of paralysis. Numerous legal cases followed *Salgo.* However, within short order, informed consent was lifted from this narrow legal base by a new medical ethics and placed in the center of a debate about decisional authority and the doctor–patient relationship, a debate still underway.

Many hypotheses could be invoked to explain why and how case law and medical ethics came to address informed consent in medical care beginning in the late 1950s, and why and how law and ethics influenced each other. Perhaps the most accurate explanation is that law and ethics, as well as medicine itself, were all affected by issues and concerns in the wider society about individual liberties and social equality, made all the more dramatic by increasingly technological, powerful, and impersonal medical care. Although this thesis would be difficult to sustain without situating it in the context of a careful and extensive sociohistorical analysis of the period, it seems likely that increased legal interest in the right of self-determination and increased philosophical interest in the principle of respect for autonomy and individualism were but instances of the new rights orientation that various social movements of the last 30 years introduced into society.

Prominent among these social movements is of course the women's movement, many of whose central concerns involved medical care and informed consent issues — reproductive rights, abortion, and contraception. Indeed, among the first areas where informed consent provisions were adopted as a legislative remedy to prevent abuses of individual rights was in sterilization, with the promulgation of federal regulations and state laws designed to reduce the numbers of forcible or coercive sterilizations of vulnerable and easily exploited women — most notably women of color and women with cognitive disabilities (*Relf v. Weinberger,* 1974; *Stump v. Starkman,* 1978; *Walker v. Pierce,* 1977).

CONSENT AND GENETIC DIAGNOSIS

The centerpiece of the recent explosion in knowledge of genetics is the newfound ability to map and determine the fine structure of human genes. With this ability comes the theoretical capacity to develop genetic tests to determine susceptibility to a wide range of diseases, eventually perhaps to all diseases with some genetic component.

This testing can be performed well in advance of the development of disease symptoms, including in utero. Thus, one of the key characteristics of this new technology is that identification does not depend on gene expression: Any cellular tissue removed for testing any time after conception will suffice.

To date, the bulk of our experience with genetic testing has focused, with the important exception of some newborn screening, on reproductive issues — the identification of disease in fetuses and the identification of carrier status in adults. (Carrier status testing, among other things, enables prospective parents to make more informed reproductive decisions.)

By comparison with our current experience, the new technology will increase dramatically the numbers of diseases that can be identified prenatally, while at the same time permitting identification of disease risk, not merely carrier status, in adults and children.

It is important to clarify one distinction that will differentiate among the new genetic tests. Some susceptibility tests identify genes that by themselves are necessary and sufficient conditions for a person's developing a specific disease; that is, the tests will identify "disease-causing" genes. A perfected test for Huntington's disease would fall under this category. Other susceptibility tests identify genes that do not by themselves cause disease but whose presence indicates that a person is susceptible to developing a disease, so-called "susceptibility-conferring" genes. This latter type of susceptibility test identifies only whether an individual or fetus is at some specified increased risk of suffering from or developing a disease, and not whether the person will with certainty suffer from the condition.

Among the most promising diseases for the development of genetic tests of the increased risk, susceptibility-conferring variety are: Type I diabetes, malignant melanoma, breast cancer, Alzheimer's disease, manic depression, colon cancer, and certain forms of heart disease. For example, in the case of Type I diabetes, it is thought that the predictive value of the genetic test will be at best one in four. That is, out of every four individuals or fetuses identified by the test to have a genetic predisposition to diabetes, one will actually develop the disease — the other three will not.

With a few exceptions, it generally is recognized that the availability of large numbers of efficient, feasible genetic tests to be applied postnatally is anywhere from 2 to 10 years off. There is also a growing belief that for the foreseeable future our capacity to identify disease susceptibility will outstrip our ability to intervene effectively. Thus, in many instances, the most immediate application of genetic testing will be in reproductive planning — using genetic information to avoid the birth of susceptible offspring. These developments raise many morally and politically problematic issues, if for no other reason than that prenatal testing necessarily implies the option of aborting fetuses found to be affected or at risk. Included among these issues are several substantive consent issues, that can be summarized as follows.

Issue 1: What Problems of Autonomy, Personal Values, and Decision Making Are Raised by Genetic Knowledge Applied to Fetal Testing?

At the personal level, genetics increasingly will confront prospective parents, and especially mothers, with draconian type decisions regarding how far they are willing to use abortion in their search not merely for the perfect baby, but for the perfect offspring. Virtually all our experience to date has been with the use of selective abortion to prevent the birth of fetuses who at birth will suffer from a disabling condition or a clinically significant disease.

What is unique and overwhelming about the new age of fetal tests is that we now will have to make decisions about not only whether we want to raise infants with Down's syndrome, or spina bifida, or even cleft palates, but also whether we want to have children who will be healthy at birth, and perhaps for decades to come, but at some point later in life will develop (or are at increased risk of developing) a serious disease — such as breast cancer, heart disease, schizophrenia, or Huntington's disease. Of increasing concern is the use of genetic technologies in prenatal testing to determine the physical characteristics of the fetus. This is being done most often by couples desiring a child of a specific sex, who are willing to terminate a pregnancy if the fetus is of the unwanted gender. It must be decided on the policy level whether this is an allowable use of developing technologies.

These sorts of decisions expand the boundaries of quality of life considerations — issues that are already very vexing in prenatal diagnosis. The new fetal diagnostics will compel an examination of very fundamental psychological and philosophical issues about the meaning and characteristics of human life, issues that will have to be examined with a reframed understanding of that old psychological chestnut — individual differences.

Data from our research on prenatal screening suggest that White, middle-class, pregnant women are more likely to view as justifiable the abortion of fetuses who after birth would have cognitive rather than physical disabilities (Faden et al., 1987). Perhaps analogous views will develop about the relative propriety of aborting fetuses that later in life will develop cognitive diseases — Alzheimer's, Huntington's, depression — as opposed to the physical diseases of cancer, diabetes, or angina. Perhaps these views already exist, perhaps not. Rapp (chapter 9) suggests that these views are not shared across ethnic and class groups.

In the short term, there is an immediate need to develop efficient techniques to assist prospective parents in coping with these new options, helping them to clarify their own values so that they will be able to make autonomous decisions as to which tests they choose to have and what they will do with the results. We have become persuaded in our own work of the relevance of contemporary risk, choice, and action theory in assisting individuals in making informed decisions about whether to consent to, or refuse, genetic testing. For example, that risk properties can have a dramatic effect on behavioral preferences regarding abortion was demonstrated to us very graphically in our study cited earlier. Forty-six pregnant women out of 200 said they would have an abortion if there was a 100% chance that the fetus had a neural tube defect, but not if there was a 95% probability—a clear illustration of what Tversky and Kahneman (1974, 1981, 1984) call the certainty effect.

Issue 2: Should Women Be Permitted to Make These Kinds of Choices?

Thus far, I have been assuming that as these new technologies for prenatal diagnosis become technically available, they will be made available to prospective parents who then will be encouraged to make their own, increasingly difficult, decisions about both whether to consent to testing and whether to have a selective abortion. As I noted earlier, this assumption is certainly consistent with the ethics of clinical genetics. Indeed, historically, the policy option of prohibiting the use of technologies for fetal testing has been advocated only by those with the most conservative positions on abortion. However, as the possibilities for genetic testing increase, some suspect that support for banning fetal applications of these tests will also increase.

Such an outcome is consistent with the Supreme Court's recent ruling giving to the states greater latitude in the regulation of abortion. Both in the public and private sectors there is currently serious consideration being given to withholding the application of certain genetic technologies to fetal testing. The de facto result of such a policy would be to restrict the range of options available to prospective parents regarding the use of abortion in matters of reproductive choice.

Issue 3: Should Women Be Compelled to Submit to Testing?

The flip side of this policy debate is the argument that for certain conditions not only should prenatal genetic or neonatal testing be available, but also it should be mandatory. That is, it is being argued on the one hand that for certain conditions parents should be denied access to testing technologies, whereas for other conditions parents should be compelled to use testing technologies, generally through the conduct of a public health-screening program. In both instances, there is no role for maternal consent or authorization. Key examples currently include prenatal maternal serum alphafetoprotein screening for neural tube defects and Down's syndrome, and neonatal screening for phenylketonuria and sickle cell. For morally relevant reasons, thus far the consensus of opinion and public policy has been that, with the exception of screening for syphilis, maternal consent should be required for prenatal screening programs, but not for neonatal screening programs (Acuff & Faden, in press). However, there are indications that this consensus of opinion is beginning to break down around the issue of prenatal screening for antibodies to the HIV virus, where increasingly there are calls for mandatory HIV testing of all pregnant women (Faden, Geller, & Powers, in press).

Issue 4: What Is the Role for Maternal Consent When Fetal Therapy Is Possible?

Questions of the proper role of maternal consent for fetal testing are perhaps most dramatic when fetal therapy is possible to modify the condition for which the fetus could be tested. Many supporters of maternal rights to refuse prenatal and neonatal testing balk at the prospect of permitting women to refuse interventions that demonstrably could benefit their fetuses. The complex legal and ethical issues raised by this scenario are discussed in depth elsewhere in this volume (see chapters 5, 6, & 7). I wish here to make only one point. Although it is possible to view this situation as a paradigm for examining the complex relationship between women's rights to bodily integrity and the rights of fetuses to protection, it is important not to let intriguing theoretical issues sidetrack us into thinking that the interests of pregnant women are at war with those of their fetuses. In general, there is a very close correspondence between the interests of pregnant women and fetuses, and it seems reasonable to expect that in most cases pregnant women are supportive of anything that can be done to improve prospects for their babies. Indeed, it seems likely that, as a practical matter, most women not only will not refuse fetal testing when fetal therapy is possible, but also will actively seek and support such testing.

CONCLUDING COMMENTS

Consent issues do not begin to exhaust the moral issues raised by the new genetic technologies. Indeed, the most pressing issues do not involve so much questions of consent but questions of social justice. For example, one issue that does not have much to do with consent but is very central and in need of development is how advances in genetic testing and prenatal diagnosis will affect the way society values persons with disabilities, as well as societal obligations to those with disabilities. In this context, the role society plays in defining disabilities and in making living with disability easier or harder becomes paramount. Also relevant is the social context in which prospective parents have to make decisions about fetal testing and abortion. To connect this theme with the theme of consent, how free are parents to make these decisions if they live in communities with inadequate social and medical services for raising a child with a disability?

Equally troubling is the gap in access to prenatal testing and genetic technologies between the privileged and the poor, a gap that is expected to widen as new and more expensive technologies emerge. One potential outcome of this gap is the possibility that children with disabilities will be born in increasingly disproportionate numbers to disadvantaged as opposed to privileged women, with predictable, negative implications for allocation of resources to assist those with disabilities.

Finally, there is an even more fundamental question of allocation of resources raised by these new technologies. Not only are sizable numbers of women disenfranchised from prenatal diagnostic technology, they and their children are disenfranchised as well from basic medical care. It is morally questionable, at best, to pour resources into new diagnostic technologies for the fetus when millions of women and children are denied access to even the most rudimentary forms of medical care. Too narrow a focus on the admittedly intriguing issues raised by the new technologies risks blinding us to our as yet unfulfilled obligations to many millions of women, children, and persons with disabilities.

REFERENCES

Acuff, K., & Faden, R. R. (in press). A history of prenatal and neonatal screening programs. In R. R. Faden, G. Geller, & M. Powers (Eds.), *AIDS, women and the next generation.* New York: Oxford University Press.

Bochner, S. (1983). Doctors, patients and their cultures. In D. Pendleton & J. Hasler (Eds.), *Doctor–patient communication.* London: Academic.

Faden, R. R., Chwalow, A. J., Quaid, L. K., Chase, G. A., Lopes, C., Leonard, C. O., & Holtzmann, N. A. (1987). Prenatal screening and pregnant women's attitudes toward abortion of defective fetuses. *American Journal of Public Health, 77,* 288–290.

Faden, R. R., & Beauchamp, T. L. (1986). *A history and theory of informed consent.* Oxford, England: Oxford University Press.

Faden, R. R., Geller, G., & Powers, M. (Eds.) (in press). *AIDS, women and the next generation.* New York: Oxford University Press.

Fisher, S. (1983). Doctor talk/patient talk: How treatment decisions are negotiated in doctor–patient communication. In S. Fisher & A. D. Todd (Eds.), *The social organization of doctor–patient communication.* Washington, DC: Center for Applied Linguistics.

Katz, J. (1984). *The silent world of doctor and patient.* New York: Free Press.

Lidz, C., & Meisel, A. (1982). *Informed consent and the structure of medical care.* In President's Commission for the Study of Ethical Problems in Medicine & Biomedical & Behavioral Research, *Making health care decisions* (Vol. 2, pp. 317–410. Washington, DC: U.S. Government Printing Office.

Pernick, M. S. (1982). *The patient's role in medical decision making: A social history of informed consent in medical therapy.* In President's Commission for the Study of Ethical Problems in Medicine & Biomedical & Behavioral Research, *Making health care decisions* (pp. 1–35).

President's Commission for the Study of Ethical Problems in Medicine & Biomedical & Behavioral Research. (1982). *Making health care decisions.* Washington, DC.

Relf v. Weinberger, 372 F. Supp. 1196 (D.D.C. 1974).

Salgo v. Leland Stanford Jr. University Board of Trustees, 317 P.2d 170, 181 (Cal. App. 1957).

Stump v. Starkman, 435 U.S. 349 (1978).

Tversky, A., & Kahneman, D. (1974). Judgment under uncertainty: Heuristics and biases. *Science, 185,* 1124–1131.

Tversky, A., & Kahneman, D. (1981). The framing of decisions and the psychology of choice. *Science, 211,* 453–458.

Tversky, A., & Kahneman, D. (1984). Choices, values and frames. *American Psychologist, 39,* 341–350.

Walker v. Pierce, 560 F.2d 609 (4th Cir. 1977).

5

Ethical Issues Raised by the New Medical Technologies

Caroline Whitbeck
Massachusetts Institute of Technology

I begin by setting the discussion of medical technology and women's health in its larger context, and then discuss ethical issues raised by various types of technology. Consider first the modern tendency to think of everything as a potential resource. To regard everything, even ourselves, as a potential resource is implicitly to regard all possible goals or ends as on a par. Therefore, efficiency—that is, the efficient use of resources in the pursuit of goals—is taken implicitly as the primary value. The determination of goals or ends appears as a matter of personal taste. Respect merely reflects one set of tastes, tastes that may obstruct the efficient pursuit of other goals.

The general tendency to regard everything as a potential resource has been criticized by thinkers like Martin Heidegger who label it "technological thinking," and by others, like Virginia Held and Robert Bellah, who call it "economic ideology," or the "ideology of economic man." Describing the tendency as "economic" in some sense is less confusing, for three reasons: first, because consideration of efficiency is regularly linked to the economic category of productivity; second, because technological innovation may be motivated by attitudes of reverence for nature and for life; and third, because the tendency to view everything as a potential resource often is carried to extremes in matters that have no connection with technology. For example, the tendency is very much in evidence in contemporary legal circles where proponents of so-called "law and economics," like U.S. Court of Appeals Judge, Richard Posner, advocate eliminating inefficient adoption agencies and legalizing the sale of babies.

However, if the ideology of economic man, the tendency to treat everything, including ourselves, as a potential resource, is a peculiarly modern tendency, it has its precursors in ancient thought. Women and subject people throughout history often have been treated as mere resources. The present situation that encourages both sexes to think of *themselves* as well as others as resources for the achievement of their goals may look like comparative liberation when measured against the patterns of domination sanctioned by the earlier patriarchal ideologies of the Classical and the Judeo-Christian traditions.

What are the central features of those earlier patriarchal ideologies? Both Judeo-Christian and Classical sources for so-called "Western thought" assumed it proper for the man to dominate the woman, and for the men of the reference culture to dominate slaves and barbarians. We find that view exemplified in many Biblical stories in which men are commended, or at least exonerated, for using their daughters, sisters, and wives as resources even when the men gave those women to other men for their sexual use (e.g., *Genesis,* 12:11-16, 26:7-10, & 19:180). It found influential expression in Saint Paul's message that woman is not created in the image of God as man is, and that although man was not created for woman, woman was created for man, and finds her place in the order of things because, as mothers, women are necessary to the existence of men (1 *Corinthians,* 11:7-12; also *Ephesians,* 5:22-24, & *1 Timothy,* 2:12-15).

A similar theme is worked out in detail in Aristotle's thought and raised to the level of metaphysics where the supposed natural subjugation of women by men is mirrored in what Aristotle postulated as the relation between matter and form, namely that matter seeks to be subjugated by form (*Physics, 192a, 20-24*).

The female body always has been at risk. Traditional patriarchal ideology sanctioned the oppression of women and modern individualistic ideology puts women at special risk both because of women's special involvement with childbearing and because economic ideology obscures the continued existence of the oppression of women. The continued existence of attitudes that foster the oppression of women in the United States today is shown dramatically in the enormous size of the pornography industry—it is larger than the film and record industries combined. The recent epidemic of anorexia and bulimia among girls and women gives evidence of the extent to which some women have internalized the culture's destructive attitudes concerning the female body.

Applied ethics, no less than other areas of modern thought, has been shaped by economic ideology. It shares with the rest of modern thought the tendency to represent people as ahistorical beings, social atoms, whose morally relevant characteristics are limited to the possession of rights and the capacity to make contracts, whose relationships are assumed to be contractual or quasi-contractual, and whose moral deliberations can be understood on the model of market calculations. According to this individualistic ideology, injustice is a matter of "discrimination." The difference between discrimination and oppression is not a difference of degree or severity: The two concepts form a part of very different conceptual frameworks. The impulse to degrade women to which the pornography industry panders cannot be subsumed under the category of discrimination because the problem is not that gender has been taken into account when it should not have been. The problem is that pornography centrally involves the commodification of women's bodies and frequently takes the degradation of women as its explicit theme. If the only issues of injustice that we can recognize are those that fit the category of discrimination, we miss many of importance.

Economic ideology that sanctions treating everything as a resource has limited the range of issues that can be represented adequately in the medical ethics literature. As a result, many important ethical issues have been neglected. The concept of a moral right (or a moral obligation or a moral rule) and the concepts of costs and benefits (or "utilities") are the ethical concepts that are reconciled most readily with the individualistic model of the person assumed in economic ideology.

Cost-benefit analysis requires that costs and benefits be subject to arithmetic operations such as addition. Therefore, the use of such techniques restricts our attention to those consequences that can be quantified and subject to arithmetic operations. Many morally important consequences, such as loss of integrity, for example, do not have this character and so are not considered as costs. Although cost-benefit, risk-benefit, and decision analysis—techniques that all are taken from market economics—are used increasingly in medical decision making, contemporary medical ethics has been influenced most by the patient rights movement that in turn was influenced by the consumer rights movement. As a result, the concept of a moral right or obligation (instead of a benefit or 'utility') has predominated in the medical ethics literature. The statement of a moral right or a moral obligation specifies a rule of behavior; that is, it specifies what acts are required, permitted, or forbidden. So, for example, a person's right to life makes it morally impermissible for others to kill that person and the obligation to tell the truth forbids lying. Although the focus on isolated acts that is fostered by the reliance on the concepts of rights obligations and moral rules is sometimes appropriate, in other matters questions of character, or of relationship, are also of importance.

The influence of the patient rights movement has led to an emphasis on ethical issues in medicine that can be understood in terms of rights and obligations of key actors. Those issues in turn often are interpreted as turning on the correct ordering of those rights and obligations and, perhaps, other values. Only a small number of ethical issues, however, can be expressed adequately in terms of the rights model. As examples of those that can, we have the question of whether, and under what circumstances, considerations of health risk to others outweigh considerations of liberty and self-determination of the individual and so justify putting that person in quarantine, or the question of when, if ever, the value of the growth of scientific knowledge takes precedence over the patient's right to privacy. However, many other moral questions call for consideration of such things as moral responsibilities, relationships, character, and integrity and cannot be expressed in terms of rights, obligations, and moral rules, or in terms of costs and benefits.

Discussions of informed consent, truth telling, confidentiality, and the allocation of scarce resources dominate the medical ethics literature. One reason for this is that the first three topics lend themselves to expression in terms of rights, obligations, and moral rules, and questions of the allocation of scarce resources is often handled in terms of costs and benefits.

Consider what the customary focus on informed consent in the use of medical technology does and does not do for us in illuminating ethical issues. Informed consent for treatment does constitute a minimal ethical requirement, however. As I have discussed elsewhere (Whitbeck, 1981), health is a fundamental element of human well-being. It is necessary to the fulfillment of many moral responsibilities (and hence, the maintenance of moral integrity) and is necessary for the attainment and enjoyment of many other elements of well-being. Therefore, it is clear if people are to have any control over their lives, they must be informed fully about health risks and in particular those associated with the application of a medical technology. Abuses in the form of disregard for a person's right to know the risks of treatment are still common, and many patients still are informed inadequately about medical alternatives. For example, it is still common (especially in states without relevant legislation) for a woman with breast cancer to be scheduled for a radical mastectomy without having received information about alternative treatments. Furthermore, patients often are told that there are no known risks associated with some procedure when it would be truer to say that the magnitude of certain risks is unknown because there have not been systematic studies of those risks. For example, although some are urging that ultrasound imaging be used routinely in pregnancy, there have been no systematic studies of even the acute effects of low-dose pulsed ultrasound and long-term effects virtually have been ignored (Statmeyer & Christman, 1982).[1]

---

[1]Routine testing has continued to have its advocates, even after a panel of experts convened by the National Institutes of Health recommended that the use of ultrasound for fetal diagnosis be limited to 28 medical indications and discouraged routine use of ultrasound testing in pregnancy. For example, Dr. W. Desmond McCallum, director of Stanford Medical

Although it is of some moral value, the requirement of informed consent often functions merely to limit the circumstances under which people have been treated as resources to those under which they have consented to be so treated. The requirement of informed consent does not aid the examination of particular designs and applications of technology to discover whether they promote or restrict opportunities for people to be more than resources, to experience meaning in their lives, and to participate in their own maturation.

Recognition of the limitations of the concept of informed consent is reflected in the shift from informed consent to shared decision making in *Making Health Care Decisions,* the 1982 report of the President's Commission for the Study of Ethical Problems in Medicine and Biomedical and Behavioral Research. The rule of informed consent requires only the recognition of the patient's right of veto over a major procedure that the provider has presented to the patient as an alternative. In contrast, shared decision making requires participation of the patient in setting the goals and methods of care and, therefore, in formulating the alternatives to be considered. This participation requires that patient and practitioners engage in complex communication.

The focus on shared decision making requires abandonment of the assumption, which is common in the medical ethics literature, that for most medical decisions there is an answer to the question, "Who should decide?" That is, who owns the decision. The case of a man whose daughter had been killed suddenly in an automobile accident illustrates this point. Immediately upon hearing of her death, the distraught father was asked for permission to use some of his daughter's organs for transplant. He responded by punching the physician who asked him. Later he regretted both hitting the physician and denying permission. He felt that he should have been approached differently, and that in his predictably sensitive state, he should have been given more of an opportunity to rise to the occasion and make a decision that was in keeping with his daughter's memory. This example highlights the ludicrousness of reducing the standards for ethical decision making in medicine to identifying the person who should have "the final word" in a given matter, and giving him or her the final word. Often what is required is sensitive communication that enables participants to come to terms with grim realities and to take part in making decisions—decisions that are quite unlike ordinary consumer decisions—in ways that will be consistent with the total configuration of their values and relationships. The

Center's obstetric ultrasound laboratory, argued for routine use saying, "There is no other test that gives as much information for the money spent as does ultrasound" (McLaughlin, 1984, p. 8).

process of sharing decision making is more complex than that of getting informed consent. Shared decision making takes account of risks to moral integrity as well as to life and property.

The moral requirement of truth telling understood merely as neither lying nor withholding "the facts," like the requirement of informed consent, although valid as a moral requirement, does not express what is most needed. Enabling patients to understand their situation requires more than neither lying nor withholding facts. It requires skills such as those that Patricia Benner eloquently described in her important 1984 work on nursing practice, *From Novice to Expert*. For example, she discussed the coaching function in nursing, the task of "making culturally avoided aspects of an illness approachable and understandable" (p. 89). When a medical condition or an application of medical technology has not been made understandable in this sense, the patient has been told the truth in only the most meager sense, and does not yet have a basis for acting and for participating in crucial decisions.

In addition to considering patient rights and calculating the mortality risks and other quantifiable costs of various courses of action, we need to ask how the application of medical technologies influences individuals, families, communities, and societies. The people who are affected include those who refuse as well as those who use the technologies and those who might use the technology but do not have access to it. The effect on people includes the effect on their character, their integrity, and their relationships, as well as their life expectancy or health status. Being faced with more decisions may mean only having more occasions for regret as *Sophie's Choice* illustrates. You may recall that in the story of Sophie's choice, concentration camp guards forced Sophie, in the presence of her two children, to choose which to send to the gas chamber on penalty of having them both killed. The choice was devastating to her moral integrity in a way that her daughter's death itself would not have been.

The moral devastation to Sophie did not involve her having made the wrong decision—on any plausible representation of risks and probabilities, the son, who was older, stood a better chance of survival. The moral aspect of Sophie's devastation is unintelligible from the point of view of a rights-based ethics.

Our use of technology to make health care more efficient and effective often has distracted attention from the issue of whether the conditions under which people are forced to make decisions about the application of technology puts them at risk for betraying those who are closest to them.

Many thinkers in the last decade have questioned the individualistic assumptions of the economic ideology, and a significant minority of writers on ethical theory have taken the concepts of responsibility, relationship, moral integrity, community, character, virtue, and story as key moral notions. These concepts at best are irrelevant and perhaps unintelligible from the point of view of economic ideology. Consideration of the influence of technologies on human relationships, character, integrity, and so forth takes as its starting point the recognition of the social nature of human life and the dynamic character of the moral self. The inadequacy of current approaches to applied ethics that are consistent with economic ideology is a topic that I have discussed at length elsewhere (Whitbeck, 1983, 1985, 1988). From the early 1970s, John Ladd (1970, 1975, 1976, 1979, 1982) developed a systematic philosophical investigation of the language of (prospective) responsibility. Although this is not the place to discuss in detail the responsibility approach that I find adequate for framing ethical issues raised by technology, I point out a few features of this "ethics of responsibility" to forestall misinterpretation. First, although responsibility is taken as the central ethical concept, this approach does have a place for consideration of rights and of quantifiable benefits (utilities). Second, the ethics of responsibility is applicable to many issues raised by medical technology that are at once public and private because, unlike the approach to ethics that arises from economic ideology, the ethics of responsibility does not assume a split between the ethical categories that are applicable to public and to private matters. In both these respects the ethics of responsibility differs from the "ethics of care" described by Carol Gilligan and others (Gilligan, 1982). The ethics of care applies to dealings with one's intimates. Work on the ethics of care is helpful in showing how many moral concerns are inexpressible in terms of rights and obligations alone, but does not provide a framework that is adequate to express the many moral issues raised by technology that concern responsibilities for the well-being of anonymous others.

The overview of ethical issues that I offer is indebted most deeply to the empirically based critiques of specific medical technologies in the women's health literature. These studies concern issues that are at once public and private. They illuminate the particular responsibilities that are at issue for women of various backgrounds and circumstances in dealing with medical technology. These critiques often explicitly object to treating lives and bodies as commodities—that is, to treating lives and bodies as resources to be bought and sold. They show how to raise ethical issues without conceding the assumptions of economic ideology.

I wish to reject both the assumption that technology per se is bad and the assumption that technology can solve perennial human problems and make it unnecessary to deal with human vulnerability, suffering, and death. Instead, I begin with the assumption that technology always exchanges one set of problems and vulnerabilities for another, and ask for particular applications of technology, "What are the vulnerabilities that are reduced and how do these compare with the risks and vulnerabilities that they introduce or increase?" Because of the previous bias in favor of issues that can be expressed readily in terms of rights and obligations, and those outcomes that can be quantified like profits—outcomes such as risk of mortality, days of morbidity, and cost in dollars—I focus on the question: What are the effects on human relationships, on character and moral integrity, and on families and communities that result from applications of the technology we are considering?

The focus on this question is found in the work of many women-centered studies of particular medical technologies designed for use in human birth and reproduction. Many of the essays collected in *The Custom-Made Child* (Holmes, Hoskins, & Gross, 1981b), *Birth Control and Controlling Birth* (Holmes, Hoskins, & Gross, 1981a), *Test-Tube Women* (Arditti, Klein, & Minden, 1984), and *Embryos, Ethics and Women's Rights* (Baruch, d'A-mado, & Seager, 1988), are notable for such an emphasis. One illustration of this sort of work, for those of you who may be accustomed to thinking of moral issues in medicine in terms of informed consent, truth telling, confidentiality, and the allocation of scarce resources, is Barbara Katz Rothman's (1986) study of the influence of amniocentesis on the relationship between a woman and her fetus and later her child, which she reported in her book, *The Tentative Pregnancy, Prenatal Diagnosis and the Future of Motherhood*. She explicitly focused on the relationship of a woman to her fetus as the first phase of the relationship of a mother to her child. She found that:

A diagnostic technology that pronounces judgment halfway through Pregnancy makes extraordinary demands on women to separate themselves from the fetus within. Rather than moving from complete attachment through the separation that only just begins at birth, this technology demands that we begin with separation and distancing. Only after an acceptable judgment has been declared, only after the fetus is deemed worthy of keeping, is attachment to begin. (p. 114)

I began with the observation that the supposed value-neutrality of economic ideology actually makes efficiency the primary value and, by treating everything else as a potential resource, devalues it. But, if I reject value-neutrality as illusory,[2] what alternative values do I find implicit in

---

[2]The illusion of value-neutrality of an ideology is particularly dangerous as a component of ideology because the function of ideology is to provide justification for certain social practices and claims to authority at the expense of others. It is also useful, if less urgent, to recognize the values that underlie scientific investigation. Typically, at a minimum, the investigation is based on the judgment that something is worth knowing, that it is important to investigate some question. It would be arbitrary to classify those investigations that are judged important because of their anticipated importance for the investigator's career as value-neutral, although

women-centered critiques of technology? What values provide an appropriate standard for understanding the ethical issues that do not lend themselves to formulation in terms of rights and obligations or cost-benefit calculations? If the commodification of life, which appears only natural according to economic ideology, is morally suspect, what are the alternatives? A full answer would require more than the length of this essay, but we need some answer, an answer that is more than a general statement about respect and valuing life, an answer that can provide a basis for judging the larger implications of technologies and applications of them.

As a start, I want to ask how technologies affect families. My concern is not with the composition of the family but with its capacity to perform certain functions. As sociologist Elise Boulding (1978) pointed out, there is considerable variation around the world about what households are considered standard — matrilineal, partrilineal, polyandrous, polygamous — but within any society many live in households that are not considered standard. Throughout the world "up to one-third of women are either never married or widowed, many of them with children . . . and their needs contribute to the creation of alternative patterns" (Boulding, 1978, p. 7). By "family" or "familistic households" Boulding meant:

> any household grouping which involves adults and children in continuing commitment to each other over time. There may be one, two or more adults, in couples or singly or in combination of the two. They may be heterosexual, gay or celibate, with from zero to many children. (The possibility of children is important to the concept of family, but a certain percentage of households remain childless in every society.) What makes the household a family is that each member will care about each other member and be available in time of need with no expiration date on that availability. This includes a commitment to sharing the experience of facing death. (p. 9)

I concur with Boulding (1978) that "the living throbbing human being" never quite fits the social prescription, whatever that social prescription may be, and that families, and the religious and secular communes that have served as alternative, familistic households, provide the social and spiritual resources for dealing with the uniqueness of each person, so that each can mature into a full person, or as she put it, "pursue the task of individuation in community" (p. 9).

It is against the background of such reflections on the nature of the relationships and families that we can view the larger implications of the application of medical technology and judge whether a particular applica-

---

the values that underlie these investigations are different from considerations of the social value of research. Notice that to suggest that scientific investigation typically reflects value judgments is not to suggest that the investigation is biased in favor of a particular outcome.

tion of technology is, in the fullest sense, responsible. Notice the features of Boulding's (1978) account. She does not propose some family structure as the standard. She discusses the function of families—both standard and nonstandard—by the norms of the particular culture in which they exist. Her account is applicable cross-culturally and in particular it is applicable to the many subcultures in the United States. Nonetheless Boulding's account bears the marks of its cultural origins. To take the maturation of each person, much less the individuation of each person, as a goal assumes both the value of the individual and the essential place of human relationships in the life of the person, and articulates this assumption in a way that is necessarily culturally marked. It is unavoidable that any articulation of standards should be culturally marked, although many scholars are embarrassed by the recognition of cultural influence in their own work. Without the articulation of alternative standards we are likely to adopt the assumptions of the prevalent ideology. Furthermore, if alternative standards that are used are not articulated fully and held open to criticism then the limitations of those standards will be harder to recognize and for that reason all the more dangerous.

Women-centered critiques have shown that although technologies give us control over certain matters, they require something of us beyond their expense and their side effects. They require that we make explicit decisions where formerly we made none. As a result, they change our responsibilities. Furthermore, as I argued earlier, the requirements for ethical decision making do not reduce to finding the person who should have the final say and giving him or her the final say, but typically require complex communication among many people. New technologies often place burdens on families to engage in new and unfamiliar negotiations with one another and the primary decision maker(s) bear the primary responsibility not only for the decision, but also for conducting those negotiations.

The technologies that we are considering have afforded women some new options, but in our individualistic society often have led to sanctioning the abdication of responsibility on the part of other individuals and society at large, and so have resulted in saddling women with responsibility that is out of proportion to their new control. For example, modern contraception has made a major difference not only in a woman's capacity to control her fertility, but also in her perceived obligation to do so. It is now possible for a husband to blame his wife for getting pregnant without having discussed the matter with him, despite his willing participation in intercourse and his failure to have taken any contraceptive measures himself. Similarly, the availability of modern contraception and of legal abortion have lessened some men's perceived responsibility for impregnating a woman and for the well-being of the resulting child. If we take the ethical issues posed by contraception to be confined to mortality risks, the risk of failure, the effects on emotional and physical well-being, difficulty of use, and the cultural and personal acceptability of each of these, we will miss how technology is affecting the kinds of people we become and the strength of the kinds of families and communities and families we form.

If we examine the response to the AIDS epidemic we find evidence both of the tendency to transfer to women responsibilities that are out of proportion to their ability to control the outcome, and the tendency to disregard the health risks to women. It is notable that the main effort to curtail the AIDS epidemic among heterosexuals is a campaign aimed at individual women, and that women are encouraged to insist on a measure — the use of condoms — that gives uncertain protection of the woman from infection. Although HIV has been isolated from many body fluids, only semen and blood have been implicated directly in transmission (Friedland & Klein, 1987), although transmission by breast milk is likely. (The question of the transmission by vaginal fluid is complicated by the presence of menstrual blood or smaller, and often undetected, quantities of blood at other times in the menstrual cycle.) There are documented cases of the infection of women through donor insemination as well as from blood transfusion showing that infected blood and semen by themselves may transmit the infection (Stewart et al., 1985). Condoms often leak or fall off. Although one can become pregnant for only a few days each month, condoms as a method of birth control have an "actual" (i.e., best observed) failure rate of about 10%.[3] There is no similar safe period in which a woman is immune to infection. Furthermore, women who are at greatest risk for HIV infection are least able to insist on the use of condoms by their sex partners (see Norwood, 1987).

Both the popular and technical literature on AIDS have obscured the health risks to women, although the proportion of women among people with AIDS (PWA) is growing rapidly. The weight of expert opinion predicts that the proportion of PWA in various demographic categories will resemble the present pattern in New York City. Recent trends in New York City show a dramatic increase in the number of women being diagnosed with AIDS (Twersky, Whitbeck, & Hattis, 1989).

Many women with AIDS (or with HIV infection) were infected by heterosexual intercourse. (For example, spring 1990 figures for Boston show that half of the women with AIDS in Boston contracted the infection through heterosexual intercourse [Gardner, 1990].) Nonetheless, many

---

[3]That is, the most favorable results observed with condom use found that 10% of the women using this method become pregnant each year. Even with ideal, not observed, use there is a failure rate of about 2%. This is called "the theoretical failure rate."

continue to question whether there will be a heterosexual epidemic because there may be little transmission from women to men through heterosexual practices.

The misrepresentation of AIDS in the United States as a disease of homosexuals and drug users misrepresents the risks to women in two ways: First, it underestimates the risks to women of heterosexual intercourse by ignoring the large proportion of women who have been infected through that route. Second, it overestimates the risks to lesbians, whose practices seem to be among the least likely to transmit HIV infection. A true representation of the epidemic in the United States it that it has been a disease of men and is becoming a disease of women and their children.

If we turn to the technologies used for the induction of pregnancy and in childbirth, we again find that many issues are not expressible in terms of biological risks and informed consent. Women often find themselves being treated as mere material when what they had sought was the very active role of a mother. A woman in labor often finds herself largely ignored in favor of the fetal monitor that is attached to her and that prevents her from taking a physiologic birthing position.[4] She experiences abandonment by the people who surround her, including her husband. The wife of a spinal cord-injured man, whose ovulatory cycle is controlled by drugs to time her ovulation to fit the schedule of the veterinarian who flies in to inseminate her, finds herself confused by her rage. After all, she does want a child and her husband is so pleased that in spite of his disability he may be able to father a child. If we question the assumption that everything may be regarded appropriately as a resource and that the only ethically relevant question is whether those involved are so in sympathy with the goal to be achieved that they consent to be treated as resources, then we will be able to understand the anger and confusion experienced by these women.

Pregnancy induction, unlike the usual means of conception, requires a conscious decision and some measure of resolve to become a parent. Therefore, the children conceived in these ways must be wanted. Prima facie it is good for the children to be wanted. However, the matter is not simple. For example, Alice Miller (1981), in her influential work *The Drama of the Gifted Child,* lists among the different reasons that people may have for wanting children: "I want to have someone whom I can completely possess, and whom I can control [unlike my own parents]; someone who would stay with me all of the time" (p. 79).

---

[4]The fetal monitor is a technology that I have discussed elsewhere (Whitbeck, 1988). It has become widely used in hospitals in spite of a lack of evidence that it improved outcome, even in high-risk births. Now there is not only evidence that it does not improve outcome (Luthy, Stenchever et al., 1987), but in a paper published in March 1990 in the *New England Journal of Medicine,* Kirkwood K. Shy and others showed that its use is associated with 2.9-fold increase in the incidence of cerebral palsy.

Another reason that a woman might wish to have a child is that she, at least unconsciously, believes St. Paul's message that she is innately inferior to a man and achieves worth only by producing (male) offspring. Such examples should warn us that children may be wanted for many reasons, reasons that are likely to lead to the deformation instead of the development of the child and the family. The fact that a child is wanted does not settle the issue of whether it is responsible to have that child, or to use technology to conceive it.

The costs to people and to their relationships of repeatedly trying and failing to bear children must be considered. Methods that require the application of high technology seem to take a psychological toll on the couple involved. The extent of the toll is illustrated by the term *IVF psychosis,* used by the staff of some IVF clinics. They developed this pejorative label to describe the distraught and hostile behavior of couples who have tried and failed to become pregnant by IVF. As expected, the information given to a couple who are asking about the procedure does not include information about behavior typical of couples who try but fail to have a child by this means, or about the staff's label for that behavior. I told this to the husband in a successful IVF couple who was a speaker with me at another conference and who was expressing his anger at feminists who attacked the procedure. I told him about the term IVF psychosis and asked him if he had been informed of the emotional risks and risks to his relationship with his wife before undertaking IVF. His answer was "We were crazy before we went for IVF." His remark shows the importance of examining all methods of pregnancy induction rather than focusing attention on IVF alone. The battery of tests and procedures that are part of an advanced infertility workup presents many of the same sorts of risks to relationship as does IVF. Once a couple has sacrificed much of their privacy, as well as time, money, and comfort to undergo these procedures, the pressure to vindicate the sacrifice with an eventual "success" may create overwhelming pressure to try IVF.

As I mentioned earlier, the individuals and families that are affected by a new technology are not only those who use the technology, but also those who refuse the technology and those who do not have access to it. As Marsha Saxton (1984) has argued, prenatal diagnosis is likely to have a large effect on the lives and relationships of those who do not use them. In her article, "Born and Unborn: The Implications of Reproductive Technologies for People with Disabilities," she argued that the possibility of preventing certain disabilities through the abortion of affected fetuses may create the pressure to do so and increase our culture's myths and fears about the disabled (in Arditti, Klein, & Minden, 1984).

The greatest number of disabilities come from accidents, not birth defects, and in the United States where the protection of children from accidents still is left largely to the resources of parents, poor children are much more likely than the children of the privileged to be disabled through accident. As the privileged now make more use of prenatal diagnosis as well, this technology may contribute to diminishing concern with the problems faced by the disabled on the part of those who often have the greatest ability to make their concerns influential. The point of these remarks is not that we should deny access to prenatal diagnosis to the privileged, but that it is important to be aware of the danger that the application of technology may make us as a society more callous to the needs of the disabled, and lose sight of our problems of social justice.

I have argued that the prevalent ideology of our society, economic ideology, is likely to blind us to certain sorts of ethical issues raised by the application of new medical technologies. The received ideology distorts many ethical issues, especially issues that involve women and other oppressed groups. In its criticisms of reproductive technology, women-centered studies have provided an essential supplement to the customary focus on issues of informed consent, truth telling, confidentiality, and the allocation of scarce resources. They have supplied important alternative standards against which to judge the wisdom of applying particular technologies. Health and safety risks of new technologies, as important as they are, do not exhaust the risks that must be considered when making responsible decisions about the application of technology. In addition to calculating health and safety risks and ensuring that full information is given about these risks, it is important to understand the effects of new technologies upon human relationships, and the ability of families and communities to foster the maturation of their members.

ACKNOWLEDGMENTS

Some of the research for this chapter was supported by Grant No. 94159 from the National Science Foundation.

I thank Jana Sawicki for comments on an earlier draft of this chapter.

REFERENCES

Arditti, R., Klein, R. D., & Minden, S. (1984). *Test-tube women*. Boston: Pandora.
Baruch, E., d'Amado, A., & Seager, J. (Eds.). (1988). *Embryos, ethics, and women's rights: Exploring the new reproductive technologies*. Binghamton, NY: Haworth.
Benner, P. (1984). *From novice to expert: Excellence and power in clinical nursing*. Reading, MA: Addison-Wesley.
Boulding, E. (1978). *The family as a· way into the future* (Pendle Hill Pamphlet No. 222. Wallingford, PA: Pendle Hill Publishers.
Friedland, G. H., & Klein, R. S. (1987). Transmission of the Human Immunodeficiency Virus.

The New England Journal of Medicine, 317(18), 1125-1135.

Gardner, K. A. (1990). *Resources for HIV+ women in Boston.* Unpublished bachelor of science thesis in biology and women's studies, Massachusetts Institute of Technology, Cambridge.

Gilligan, C. (1982). *In a different voice: Psychological theory and women's development.* Cambridge, MA: Harvard University Press.

Holmes, H. B., Hoskins, B., & Gross, M. (1981a). *Birth control and controlling birth, women-centered perspectives.* Clifton, NJ: Humana.

Holmes, H. B., Hoskins, B., & Gross, M. (1981b). *The custom-made child?, women-centered perspectives.* Clifton, NJ: Humana.

Ladd, J. (1970). Morality and the ideal of rationality in formal organizations. *The Monist, 54* (4), 488-516.

Ladd, J. (1975). The ethics of participation. In J. R. Pennock & J. W. Chapman (Eds.), Participation in Politics: NOMOS XVI (pp. 98-125). New York: Atherton-Leiber.

Ladd, J. (1976). Are ethics and science compatible? In H. T. Engelhardt, Jr. & D. Callahan (Eds.), *Science, ethics, and medicine* (pp. 49-78). Hastings-on-Hudson: The Hastings Center.

Ladd, J. (1979). Legalism and medical ethics. In J. W. Davis, B. Hoffmaster, & S. Shorten (Eds.), *Contemporary issues in biomedical ethics* (pp. 1-35). Clifton, NJ: Humana.

Ladd, J., (1982, May). The distinction between rights and responsibilities: A defense. *Linacre Quarterly,* pp. 5-11.

Luthy, D. A., Shy, K. K., van Belle, G., Larson, E. B., Hughes, J. P., Benedetti, T. J., Brown, Z. A., Effen, S., King, J. F., & Stenchever, M. A. (1987). A randomized trial of electronic fetal monitoring in preterm labor. *Obstetrics and Gynecology, 69* (5), 687-695.

McLaughlin, L. (1984, February 12). Doctor defends ultrasound pregnancy testing. *The Boston Globe,* p. 8.

Miller, A. (1981). *The drama of the gifted child.* New York: Basic.

Norwood, C. (1987). *Advice for life.* New York: Pantheon.

President's Commission for the Study of Ethical Problems in Medicine & Biomedical & Behavioral Research. (1982). *Making health care decisions.* Washington, DC.

Rothman, B. K. (1986). *The tentative pregnancy, prenatal diagnosis and the future of motherhood.* New York: Viking.

Saxton, M. (1984). Born and unborn: The implications of reproductive technologies for people with disabilities. In R. Arditti, R. D. Klein, & S. Minden (Eds.), *Test-tube women* (pp. 298-312). Boston: Pandora.

Shy, K. K., Luthy, D. A., Bennett, F. C., Whitfield, M., Larson, E. B., van Belle, G., Hughes, J. P., Wilson, J. A., & Stenchever, M. A.. (1990). Effects of electronic fetal-heart monitoring, as compared with periodic auscultation, on the neurologic development of premature infants. *The New England Journal of Medicine, 322,* 588-593.

Statmeyer, M. E., & Christman, C. L. (1982). Biological effects of ultrasound. *Women and Health, 7* (3, 4), 65-81.

Stewart, G. J., Tyler, J. P. P., Cunningham, A. L. et al. (1985). Transmission of human T-cell virus type III (HTLV-III) by artificial insemination by donor. *Lancet, 2,* 581-584.

Twersky, F., Whitbeck, C., & Hattis, D. (1989). *Exposures of health care workers to HIV— Factors affecting occupational risks in San Francisco, Boston, and New York* (Report No. CTPID 89-5). Cambridge: Massachusetts Institute of Technology, Center for Technology, Policy & Industrial Development.

Whitbeck, C. (1981). A theory of health. In A. C. Caplan, H. T. Englehardt, Jr., & J. J. McCartney (Eds.), *Concepts of health and disease: Interdisciplinary perspectives,* (pp. 611-626). Reading, MA: Addison-Wesley.

Whitbeck, C. (1983). The moral implications of regarding women as people: New perspectives on pregnancy and personhood. In W. B. Bondeson, H. T. Engelhardt, Jr., S. F. Spicker,

& D. Winship (Eds.), *Abortion and the status of the fetus* (pp. 247–272). Dordrecht, Holland: D. Reidel.

Whitbeck, C. (1985). Why the attention to paternalism in medical ethics? *Journal of Health Politics, Policy and Law, 10*(1), 181–187.

Whitbeck, C. (1988). Fetal imaging and fetal monitoring: Finding the ethical issues. *Women and Health, 13*(1, 2), 47–57.

6

Women's Reproductive Rights: The Impact of Technology

Sheryl Ruzek
Temple University

Birth and birth technologies are important in all societies. Although professional expertise and new technologies are sought to improve the safety and comfort of birth for both mothers and children, these goals take on very different meanings in different societies and even between many groups in complex industrial societies. National health policies reflect larger societal values regarding social inequities. Policies vary enormously in the extent to which they perpetuate or seek to reduce inequities in life chances that vary by social class, race, and ethnicity during pregnancy, birth, and the neonatal period. In Western Europe and the Scandinavian countries that have socialized health-care systems and social policies designed to reduce social inequities, access and equity in birth-related services are dominant social and ethical issues. In the United States, dominated by fee-for-service medicine where services are rationed on the basis of ability to pay, the social and ethical issues surrounding birth that now receive the greatest attention are those embedded in a highly individualistic "health rights" model.

This chapter addresses some of the social and ethical issues surrounding birth that are related to the individual rights model. Other moral and ethical issues are raised about how resources are allocated for medical research and services in relation to the burden of birth-related mortality and morbidity in the United States. Attention is directed also to how some birth technologies become accepted as the standard of care without regard to scientific evidence of safety or efficacy, or their social and psychological consequences. Finally, it is suggested that in the United States we need to explore moral frameworks beyond the individual rights model to guide our decisions about research priorities and the application of childbirth technologies.

65

THE EMERGENCE OF THE "COMPETING INDIVIDUAL RIGHTS" MODEL OF BIRTH

On May 4, 1987, I attended the "Forum on Reproductive Laws for the 1990's" in New York. The Forum, sponsored by the Rutgers University School of Law and Institute for Research on Women, represented the culmination of over 2 years of research and deliberation on the part of more than 25 leading scholars and health-rights activists in the field of reproductive health. In the filled-beyond-capacity conference room, I was chilled by the turn discussion of reproductive health issues has taken. Less than a decade ago, forums on childbirth and childbirth technology focused on the rights of women to be involved in decisions about their care, and debates raged over "rooming-in," licensing of midwives, and the superiority of the home or the hospital as a birthplace (Ruzek, 1978). The current discourse pits birthing women against their babies and puts obstetricians in the role of adjudicating disputes over whose "interest" should come first.

Janet Gallagher (1987a, 1987b), one of the Forum member speakers, emphasized how the steadily increasing focus on the concept of the "fetus as patient" has led to demands by some doctors and lawyers that pregnant and laboring women be subjected to physical regulation, forced surgery, detention, and to criminal and civil punishment for behavior deemed dangerous to the fetus. Some judges have ordered cesarean sections performed despite women's refusal and other women have been taken to court for refusing surgical procedures to prevent miscarriage and for taking nonprescription drugs. These actions, which have consumed a large amount of space in the *Hastings Center Report,* involve questions of civil rights, ethics, the adequacy of our scientific knowledge base regarding childbirth technologies, and allocation of resources.

Doctors and hospitals have taken very drastic actions such as forced cesarean sections to get women to comply with medical advice largely out of fear of malpractice suits. Although I concur with Gallagher that lawsuits should not be permissable where treatment has been refused, I believe that we must look more critically at how childbirth procedures are defined by doctors and the courts as "necessary." And, we must ask what, as a society, is necessary and appropriate to provide to improve maternal and child health outcomes.

ON WHAT DO WE BASE A "STANDARD OF CARE"?

We have good reason to be skeptical about the necessity or even the safety and efficacy of many childbirth technologies. As Barbara Katz Rothman (1986) pointed out, "obstetrics has too long a history of errors in management for us to be certain that obstetricians always *know* the best interests of the fetus" (p. 25). Rothman's strong stand against allowing medically and legally ordered procedures to be done against a woman's will rests on historical facts. She drew our attention to the danger of accepting the concept of forced treatment by asking us to consider scenarios of 25 years ago. Had this concept been operative, how would we now view women's refusal to take DES to prevent miscarriage and refusal to limit weight gain to under 13 pounds — both "standard practices" of the time that have since been discredited as harmful?

Today, electronic fetal monitoring, episiotomy, cesarean section for an ever-growing array of conditions, and in-hospital delivery are defined as the "standard of care." Even if all women were willing to accept and receive these procedures, many cannot pay for them.

Between 1978 and 1984, there was a one-third increase, or an additional 9 million Americans, who had no health insurance (Hugh, Johnson, Rosenaum, & Butler, 1987). Recent research from the National Medical Expenditure Survey (NMES) reported by the National Center for Health Services Research and Health Care Technology Assessment (1989) reveals that lack of insurance is by no means a "welfare problem" alone. More than three quarters of the 37 million Americans who have no private insurance, Medicaid, or other public or private insurance are workers and their dependents. Workers earning $5 or less an hour (well above the minimum wage) are over three times more likely to be uninsured than persons earning over $5 an hour. Their income, however, makes them ineligible for Medicaid or other public insurance. Lack of insurance is more prevalent among Blacks (22%) and Hispanics (32%) compared to Whites (12%); adults under 24 years of age are especially likely to be uninsured. The growing segment of the population without health insurance lacks access to basic health care including maternity care. There is growing concern over the consequences of lack of medical care and declining living conditions in this group. The effect on maternal and child health indicators is only beginning to emerge.

Between 1955 and 1985, the United States infant mortality ranking among 20 industrialized nations declined from 6th place to 18th. In the United States, the overall infant mortality rate was 10.6 per 1,000 live births compared to 6.0 in Japan, the country with the most favorable rate (Hugh et al., 1987). A persistently high prevalence of low-birthweight births and high mortality rates among older infants has contributed to this decline in relative international standing. But the aggregate data obscure many significant differences in infant mortality by race and region. These are difficult to analyze because differences often are confounded by socioeconomic status differentials.

Overall, the infant mortality rate for Black infants (18.2 in 1985) continues to be twice that of White infants (9.3) (National Center for Health Statistics, 1987). Among Native Americans, infant mortality varies from community to community; some groups have very low rates whereas others have rates approaching twice the national rate. Rates for other groups (Hispanics and Asian Americans) are difficult to interpret because of problems of classification; recent research suggests that published rates may underestimate infant mortality from 28% to 61% (U.S. Department of Health & Human Services, 1990).

It is critical to note geographical variations in survival rates of infants. For example, from 1983 to 1984, infant mortality increased in 6 of the 22 largest American cities: Washington DC, Detroit, San Antonio, Milwaukee, Boston, and Cleveland (Hugh et al., 1987). The rate in Washington, DC climbed to 20.8 in 1986 and likely is increasing. There is widespread belief that infant mortality and morbidity associated with crack and cocaine use is on the rise. Although national data are not yet available, there are growing reports of dramatic upswings in infant mortality in large inner cities. Speaking at Meharry Medical College in 1989, U.S. Secretary of Health and Human Services Louis Sullivan reported a 50% increase in infant mortality in Washington, DC during the first 6 months of the year. He attributed this increase to drug use among mothers (Butler, 1989).

Given the distribution of risk, the burden of infant mortality and morbidity in the United States, our allocation of scarce resources for childbirth-related research and medical services seems grossly misplaced. In July 1987, the National Commission to Prevent Infant Mortality was established formally by Congress to "develop a national strategy for reducing infant mortality in the United States" (Brown, 1988, p. 308). The results of such efforts remain to be seen. As Yankauer (1990) noted, "The elevated infant mortality of Blacks has been a rallying cry of social reformers during (the 1960s through 1980s); yet outcries and the sporadic actions that spawned new programs for limited periods of time seem to have had no effect" (p. 654). Perhaps we must ask if the birth technologies themselves, which are a growing economic burden, are in fact effective as well as accessible.

SOME PATTERNS IN BIRTH TECHNOLOGY ADOPTION

It seems critical and timely to raise issues about how and why particular technologies and not others come to be regarded as the standard of care. Are standard childbirth technologies necessary and efficacious and do they make good use of scarce societal resources? Or might other technologies, overall, produce better outcomes for mothers, babies, families, and society?

In an era of ever-increasing specialization, it is tempting and certainly easier to focus narrowly on a single technology or two. But if we do this, particularly in the area of childbirth technology, we will overlook recurring patterns in technology adoption and the social consequences of resource allocation. To illustrate the problem, in her study of labor induction, British sociologist Ann Cartwright (1979) asked: "How did it happen that a procedure which had not been carefully evaluated, which involved considerable costs and hazards, and was disliked by childbearing women, came to be used so widely and accepted uncritically?" (p. 161). If the question is posed this way, without reference to other technologies, the implication is that the situation is an anomaly, something out of the ordinary. If instead we look across a wide array of childbirth technologies, it is clear that most have been adopted without close scientific scrutiny. The lack of scrutiny is disturbing particularly with respect to what is and is not evaluated in terms of cost effectiveness and health benefits relative to health risks, issues we shall return to later.

There is considerable debate over how medical technologies actually are adopted, in stages (Banta & Behney, 1981; McKinlay, 1981) that follow some predictable order or in a more interactive manner, following a course specific to the ways in which the sciences, academic medical centers, clinical medicine, drug and device industries, the state, and sometimes repressed interest groups such as health consumer groups interact in a given time period (Bell, 1986; Waitzkin, 1979). An interactive model appears far more accurate to describe the adoption of childbirth technologies because it allows us to consider the history not only of "promising" technologies, but others that fail to "progress" through what are conceptualized as rationally ordered stages of development.

When proponents of rational-conceptual models of technology adoption present evidence that adequate clinical testing often is not done before widespread diffusion and adoption occur (Banta & Behney, 1981; Banta & Thacker, 1979), it raises serious questions about how particular technologies become the standard of care. To understand fully how some technologies but not others become the standard of care, it is instructive to consider physician resistance to technology abandonment as well as adoption.

The road from "promising report" to "standard procedure" (McKinlay, 1981) in childbirth is especially urgent to examine because it is on the basis of medical-legal judgments of technologies being standard that women increasingly are asked, expected, or at times forced to give up their constitutional and ethical rights to autonomy, including the right to refuse treatment (Annas, 1982, 1986; Gallagher, 1987a, 1987b; Hubbard, 1982; Mackenzie & Nagel, 1986; Rothman, 1985, 1986). How is this knowledge base of "expert opinion" constructed?

We would hope — and certainly the public expects — that new technologies are evaluated critically on scientific grounds. We would also hope that technologies that offer little benefit relative to cost would be eliminated quickly before they are widely used. In practice, obstetrical technologies commonly are adopted and only later evaluated for efficacy and safety relative to benefits (Young, 1982). And, the relationship between scientific evidence and continued medical use are not well coordinated in the United States compared to countries that have socialized health-care systems structurally capable of implementing policies of technology adoption and abandonment such as the United Kingdom, Sweden, and Finland (Banta, Behney, & Willems, 1981).

For practitioners, keeping up with the technical aspects of rapidly changing technologies is a difficult task, but assessing the overall efficacy of technologies is even harder. Research reports are scattered in an ever-growing array of specialized journals. Differences in study design and subjects make it difficult to compare the results of different investigators. Because single studies are rarely definitive, overall assessment must be made on the basis of the "weight of evidence" culled from numerous sources (Ruzek, 1983). But who is responsible for amassing this evidence, and how does this evidence affect clinical practice if one practices in a fee-for-service system without systematic monitoring?

The federal government has shown some concern over this issue, partly in relation to cost-containment and partly because of a perceived interest as the funder of most large-scale research through the National Institutes of Health (NIH). The U.S. Congress Office of Technology Assessment and the NIH Consensus Conference programs both have been conceptualized as ways to pull together and make sense out of the confusing bits and pieces of evidence that are published. The Consensus Conference program was viewed specifically as a kind of "science court" in which scientists could weigh the available evidence and make recommendations to practitioners. But to reach the science courts, a medical issue must be defined as a genuine controversy by scientists and medical experts and conference recommendations are in the end just that—recommendations (Mullen & Jacoby, 1985; Perry & Kalberer, 1980).

Two birth technologies that have been subjected to the greatest scientific scrutiny over the past decade are electronic fetal monitoring and cesarean section—both procedures that are expensive, require in-hospital supervision by obstetrical specialists, and reduce the power of the woman giving birth relative to physicians and other technical experts. These technologies have been the subject of several technical reports that, far from being definitive, raise serious questions about how we, as a society, choose to reduce maternal and infant mortality and morbidity, the ostensible purpose for which investments in expensive technologies might be justifiable. Here, some of the key features of assessments of these and other childbirth technologies are highlighted.

Electronic Fetal Monitoring

Banta and Thacker's (1979) U.S. Congress Office of Technology Assessment Report on the costs and benefits of electronic fetal monitoring (EFM) revealed that of the hundreds of items that had appeared in the medical literature on EFM, there were only four randomized, controlled clinical trials reported and none of these trials showed definitive benefits relative to risks and costs. In a 1982 review article on EFM, Haverkamp and Orleans pointed out that the alleged benefits of EFM have not been well established, particularly relative to costs, although some clearly high-risk situations may benefit.

Some of the debate on the use of EFM centers on what constitutes evidence of benefit and definitions of high-risk groups. Because the proportion of neonates who potentially could benefit by reduction in mortality and morbidity as a result of EFM may be small, research on efficacy is difficult to conduct. The sample size needed to show significant benefit is a major obstacle. It was calculated that to do a study of the difference in perinatal death rates between full-term, low-risk monitored and unmonitored women, one would have to analyze 180,000 women in each group (Haverkamp & Orleans, 1982). The size of the sample needed to detect statistically significant differences between the two groups reflects the low incidence of situations in which EFM even theoretically might be of benefit. Haverkamp and Orleans cogently argued that this, in itself, "casts doubt on the need for universal use of EFM . . ." (p. 121).

Despite the ambiguous benefits of EFM relative to costs, routine monitoring of all labors is standard in many hospitals. In the March 1986 issue of *Clinical Obstetrics and Gynecology,* J. Milton Hutson and Roy H. Petrie wrote of EFM:

> Today the obstetrician managing the fetus during labor must realize the limitations, accuracy, and prognostic significance of these methods of clinical fetal assessment. These known limitations must be incorporated into the final evaluational equation to avoid unnecessary intervention or to prevent the progression of a remedial pathological condition to an irreversible state. (p. 104)

They go on to note numerous electrical and mechanical artifacts and hazards of direct (internal) fetal heart monitoring, doppler ultrasound (external) fetal heart rate monitoring, and uterine activity monitoring. Also mentioned are the high false-abnormal rate of monitoring, the limitation of the woman's activity when monitored from the time of hospital admission until delivery, the negative reaction of women to the electrode placement and monitoring output, and malfunctions in the equipment. After all of this their conclusion is particularly interesting. They stressed that fetal heart rate (FHR) monitoring has "helped change obstetrics from an art to a science over the past 25 years. The correlation of FHR pattern and the fetal physical state now can be based on a rational understanding of the physiological mechanisms present" (p. 112).

Without being able to present scientific evidence of benefit, Hutson and Petrie (1986) nonetheless asserted that monitoring "should" prevent intra-partum fetal death and "should" decrease intrapartum fetal morbidity—in short, a "hope and a prayer" (p. 112). What EFM "does best," however, according to them, is "allows the prediction of a normal outcome" (p. 112). If the most clearly established benefit of FHR monitoring is predicting normal outcome, it seems imperative to allow women to determine whether or not they wish to subject themselves to the risk of internal monitoring to be reassured of the likelihood of a normal outcome.

But women routinely are monitored electronically—and often coerced into it—ostensibly for their baby's "safety." Despite the number of studies that have failed to show that EFM reduces perinatal mortality or the incidence of neurologic developmental disorders, approximately 75% of all births in the United States use EFM. The most recent study published not only failed to show any improvements in perinatal outcomes among infants born prematurely who underwent EFM, but also indicated that EFM was associated with a threefold risk of cerebral palsy compared to periodic auscultation by a nurse (Shy et al., 1990). How long this ineffective technology will be used will be shaped by the sociopolitical process; it is not by any means simply a matter of scientific evidence.

Cesarean Section

Some childbirth technologies that are well established rather than new are defined as the standard of care for an ever-increasing proportion of the childbearing population. In fact, we are close to the point where virtually every pregnant woman could be defined as high risk by someone's criteria. One birth technology that has undergone a dramatic increase in use is cesarean section. Helen Marieskind, who was commissioned by the U.S. Department of Health, Education, & Welfare Office of Planning and Evaluation to compile an encyclopedic volume on cesareans in 1979, reported that until the early 1970s, only 3% to 5% of babies born nationwide were delivered by cesarean section. By 1980, 15% to 17% of all births were by cesarean. In the United States today, approximately 22.7% of all births are by cesarean; in many hospitals the rate is much higher (Placek, Taffel, & Liss, 1987). In an examination of 1986 hospital data in California, cesarean section rates varied widely by payment source. Women with private health insurance had the highest rates (29%), whereas women covered by Kaiser-Permanente, the state's largest hospital-based HMO, had about the same cesarean section rate (20%) as women who self-paid (19%). Women covered by California's Indigent Services program had a rate of 16% — just over half that of privately insured women (Stafford, 1990a).

 Although many professionals believe that the rise in cesarean sections is improving birth outcomes, it is a cause for concern on the part of many others because of the physical, financial, and psychological costs. The maternal mortality rate is four times higher than in vaginal delivery, and at least one third of all cesarean patients have some postoperative infection. Almost all patients report discomfort from abdominal and intestinal pain, as well as depression and exhaustion. Many women report feelings of guilt, inadequacy, regret, hostility toward the infant, and other psychological effects. Respiratory distress syndrome and hyaline membrane disease are the major risks to the infant (Guillemin, 1981). Guillemin pointed out that data on fetal mortality by mode of delivery are scarce and difficult to interpret, because it is often impossible to determine if mortality was due to the delivery mode or the underlying condition.

The financial costs associated with the increased cesarean rate are staggering. The direct cost of a cesarean delivery is about three times that of a vaginal delivery. In addition, the woman's loss of productivity, the cost of hiring household help or relying on friends and relatives to care for other children, and intensive care for infants born prematurely must be added to the overall cost (Guillemin, 1981). Stafford (1990b) estimated that if California private insurers, smaller HMOs, and MediCal had had the same cesarean section rate as Kaiser-Permanente, they would have performed 22,500 fewer procedures in 1986 alone. This would have saved $57 million. Reducing the rate, however, will not be easy to accomplish.

Marieskind (1979, 1982) presented numerous explanations for the dramatic increase in cesarean rates, including fear of malpractice suits and the "repeat cesarean" policy, despite evidence that vaginal delivery is possible for some women in subsequent births. She noted that obstetrical training, which emphasizes surgical deliveries and fails to provide training in low technology approaches, plays a role in its growth. The increase is related also to the belief that a superior outcome can be obtained with the use of EFM, which results in a higher number of cesarean deliveries. Changing definitions of indications for the procedure add, too, to the increase. There has been a steady increase in the number of women defined as suffering from cephalopelvic disproportion and fetopelvic disproportion, a catch-all category that includes "failure to progress" or "prolonged" labor – vague, nondiagnostic indications for cesarean section.

This surgery now is used routinely for breech presentation in 60% to 90% of breech cases in many hospitals. Although there are data to support a superior outcome from cesarean breech delivery for very small or very large babies, Marieskind (1979, 1982) argued that it is impossible to know if the seemingly superior outcome is related to the surgical intervention per se or if it is the result of comparing cesarean breech outcomes with outcomes of vaginal breech deliveries performed by practitioners who increasingly are untrained and unskilled at such deliveries. This hypothesis is plausible in light of favorable data on breech vaginal delivery obtained at sites where cesarean section is seldom used (in midwife deliveries and in many European countries).

Another contributing factor Marieskind (1979, 1982) cited is the changing characteristics of childbearing women to include more older women and primigravidas. Women in these categories, both of which have higher risk of cesarean section, have been undergoing increased and repeat sections. Although some of the increase is due allegedly to the increased birthweight of babies, there are not data supporting a significant change in birthweight. However, low-birthweight babies increasingly are delivered by cesarean section. The medical management of women with serious medical conditions (e.g., diabetes, lupus, and chronic hypertension) often involves birth by cesarean section. This procedure is used also to protect babies from complications resulting from vaginal exposure to active Herpes II.

Marieskind (1982) suggested that the data on rising cesarean sections are consistent with the argument that economic incentives contribute to the cesarean section rate. What is involved is a complex interaction of economic factors that can exert influence on both physicians and hospitals to take the more profitable surgical approach. Although she concluded that cesarean section is a useful and essential part of obstetrical practice, its benefits should have been examined carefully before it was so widely adopted. In her view, "It should not be necessary to come later and assess the merits and consequences of a practice when it is already widespread, entrenched and affecting over 600,000 women and babies every year" (p. 194).

Jeanne Guillemin (1981), the Boston College sociologist who served on the NIH Consensus Task Force on Cesarean Childbirth (which recommended more judicious use of cesarean delivery), noted that the work of the committee focused almost exclusively on the clinician's rationale for relying increasingly on the cesarean procedure. She emphasized that a complicated interplay between four categories of influence – professional authority, hospital resources, health policy, and public opinion – have resulted in increased cesarean delivery rates. Ironically, heightened public conscious-

ness of reproductive options — coming largely from biomedical researchers — outstrips real scientific understanding of the stages of pregnancy, fetal growth, or the onset of labor. She pointedly emphasized that:

> As is common at the frontiers of medical research, diagnostic tests are far
> more refined than applicable therapies are — or ever may be . . . In this phase
> of misalignment . . . Cesarean delivery, an innovation only because it is
> occurring more often, has become an imperfect solution for a broad range of
> potential mishaps. (p. 15)

Guillemin (1981) also raised concerns about the accuracy of data on
which pronouncements of minimal maternal mortality and morbidity risks
and infant morbidity risks are based. The complex organization of many
hospitals makes accurate reporting of deaths that occur after transfer to
intensive care units, after discharge, or after readmission, difficult to
obtain. Although there is not much documented proof that cesarean
delivery has reduced infant morbidity, cases of iatrogenic prematurity in
elective cesareans illustrate at least one liability related to the increase in this
technology.

Maternal morbidity, mentioned cursorily in reports of increased cesarean
delivery, remains largely uninvestigated. The emotional and physical anguish of mothers after cesarean birth has been noted by childbirth educators
and some psychologically oriented nursing researchers who report difficulties in parenting following the procedure (Mercer, 1977).

The growth of support groups for mothers who have had cesarean
deliveries in many cities throughout the United States indicates that there
are consequences and problems associated with this technology that are not
adequately factored into the risk–benefit equation. In 1982, the Cesarean
Prevention Movement (CPM) was founded and now has 1,500 members in
the United States, Canada, Australia, Mexico, Puerto Rico, India, and New
Zealand. When CPM founder Esther Booth Zorn appeared on *Hour
Magazine* in April 1986, 1,000 letters requesting help poured in within a
week. More typically, CPM receives about 150 inquiries asking how one can
know if one really needs a cesarean, ways to avoid one, and ways to find
knowledgeable, supportive practitioners (Nelson, 1987).

Cesarean delivery is a standard of care for which the elasticity of demand
is enormous. Cesarean delivery rates in England, France, Norway, and the
Netherlands are a small fraction of those in the United States (Chalmers,
1979). One of the highest rates of cesarean section worldwide is found in
Brazil (Janowitz, Nakamura, Lins, Brown, & Clopton, 1982). One study of
12,512 women in nine hospitals in southern Brazil showed that approximately 75% of all deliveries to private patients were by cesarean whereas
40% of public-private insured patients and less than 25% of indigent

patients were delivered by cesarean. Examination of medical records showed that medical indications could not explain these variations and financial considerations play an important role in these practices. In 1986, the World Health Organization (WHO) proclaimed, "There is no justification for any region to have a Cesarean rate higher that 10–15%" (Nelson, 1987). Our current obstetrical practices seem to be moving us well beyond this upper end rate of surgical deliveries in the United States.

Numerous observers cite the growing public demand for "perfect" babies as an indication for cesarean delivery, a technology in which obstetricians seem to place magical faith to produce perfect products. Pamela Summey's (1986) research on ideology and obstetrical care reveals an array of nonmedical factors that enter into the decision over whether or not to do cesareans. Physicians with the highest rates present cesarean delivery as the ultimate in a good doctor–patient relationship. One obstetrician interviewed told her:

> We do a lot of Cesareans because we really care about our patients and are involved in their deliveries. If you know a patient well, take care of her during her pregnancy, you are much more likely to do a Cesarean than for a patient whom you don't know and don't care much about. (p. 193)

Others report doing cesareans for no apparent indication other than bad previous outcomes completely unrelated to method of delivery. Summey concluded, "The ideology linking Cesareans to better babies continues to guarantee the autonomy of obstetricians and their dominance over birth" (p. 194).

Ironically, the fear of lawsuits leads doctors to perform more tests, diagnostic procedures, and cesareans than in the past — driving up both the risks and costs of care. A 1983 survey of members of the American College of Obstetricians and Gynecologists (ACOG) revealed that obstetricians increased prenatal testing by as much as 76.2% and electronic fetal heart monitoring by 82.3% specifically because of fear of a lawsuit (ACOG, 1985). In her study of cesarean sections in the United States, Marieskind reported that, "When questioned, physicians freely agreed 'off the record' that fear of a suit prompted Cesareans . . . Physicians said that a Cesarean is 'defensive medicine' and that even if the baby was 'less than perfect,' if a Cesarean had been done they were covered" (O'Reilly, Eakins, Gilfax, & Richwald, 1986, p. 199). Despite physicians' beliefs in cesarean as defensive medicine, reviews of cesarean-related lawsuits between 1970 and 1976 indicate that most of the suits were actually for malpractice associated with cesarean surgery rather than for failure to perform it. Thus physicians who do cesareans actually may increase their likelihood of being sued and increase their indemnity claims as well. The findings of a National

Association of Insurance Commissioners study of closed malpractice insurance claims from July 1975 to June 1976 showed that 9.5% of the 637 claims against obstetrician-gynecologists were related to cesarean sections and resulted in indemnity payments of $2,596,564. In comparison, the 7.8% of claims brought related to vaginal delivery resulted in a total indemnity of only $798,138 — less than a third the amount paid for cesarean-related claims (Marieskind, 1979).

As concern grows over excessive cesarean section rates, efforts to control their rise are being explored. Consensus development conferences and continuing medical education do not appear successful. External review of obstetric practices, public dissemination of cesarean rates, and changes in hospital and physician reimbursement are being tried but results have not been evaluated (Stafford, 1990b).

Episiotomy

While debate continues over the efficacy and safety of newer techniques such as EFM, other older technologies routinely are used with equally little evidence of benefit relative to costs or risks. Thacker and Banta (1982) argued that episiotomy, the surgical enlargement of the vaginal orifice during labor and delivery, another routine procedure, has not received adequate scrutiny in the United States. Rates for this surgery vary widely by country and by regions and birth sites within countries. In the Netherlands, where home delivery is common, episiotomy is performed in only 8% of all deliveries, whereas in the United States, episiotomy was performed in 64.2% of all vaginal deliveries in 1978. In large university-affiliated medical centers, rates are often above 90% for primigravidas, indicating routine use.

Although episiotomy is said to prevent third-degree lacerations, pelvic relaxation, and damage to the head of the fetus, there has been little study of benefit relative to risks and/or costs. Thacker and Banta (1982) argued that available data do not indicate a clear benefit in terms of decreased numbers of lacerations. The role of episiotomy in preventing serious pelvic relaxation has not been studied adequately. Although clinical experience indicates that there are cases where episiotomy may be indicated, for example when the fetus is large and labor is prolonged, this does not justify routine episiotomy.

Prior to 1982, no published study specifically addressed the risks or side effects of episiotomy (Thacker & Banta, 1982). Several studies of episiotomy have appeared recently. Reading et al. (1982) documented women's perceptions of episiotomy-related pain. Harrison, Brennan, North, Reed, and Wickham (1984) reported in the *British Medical Journal* the results of a randomized clinical trial of 181 primigravid women delivered vaginally in

Dublin. Women were randomized to undergo episiotomy or not unless it was considered "essential" during delivery. Although perineal tears occurred in a substantial proportion of the women who did not receive episiotomies, assessments of perineal pain, bruising, swelling, and healing and records of analgesics showed that those who did not receive episiotomies and sustained second-degree tears fared no worse than women who had routine episiotomies. Only 8% of the women randomized not to have episiotomies finally were judged to need them. Thus the episiotomy rate was reduced from 89% in the preceding 6 months in the same hospital to only 8%. The investigators question the value of routine episiotomy.

If episiotomy is not necessary as a routine procedure, might there be technologies to reduce the proportion of women who "need" it? For some time midwives and some childbirth educators have advocated perineal massage to soften the tissues and increase the muscle tone. Thus far, only one study of the effectiveness of perineal massage has appeared in the literature. Avery and Burket (1986) reported that women who practice perineal massage have a lower rate of episiotomy than those who do not massage.

How the concept of standard of care makes it difficult to research the efficacy of childbirth technologies is well illustrated in the case of perineal massage. Patricia Mynaugh (personal communication, March 1, 1987), a nursing professor at Thomas Jefferson Medical College in Philadelphia, started to conduct a randomized trial to evaluate the effectiveness of massage in reducing the episiotomy rate. Half of the childbirth education classes were to include perineal massage instruction; the other half would not. Her research design had to be changed at the insistence of the Human Subjects Committee in the large urban teaching hospital (which attracts an affluent clientele). The committee argued that it was not ethical to "deprive" half of the patients the standard of care. Mynaugh resorted to comparing the effectiveness of two methods of teaching perineal massage, an issue that begs the real question. In this case, perineal massage instruction had become rather casually the standard of care by virtue of the nurses receiving the approval of the medical staff to instruct women in the procedure in their classes using a written handout.

Are Safety and Efficacy "Knowable"?

The willingness of hospital officials to define a simple, low-technology procedure as the standard of care might be viewed as appealing in some respects, however it is disturbing to see how the application of the standard of care concept to avoid malpractice claims makes it difficult, if not impossible, to gather scientifically sound evidence on the safety and efficacy of childbirth technologies. Parallel to the difficulty Mynaugh faced doing perineal massage research, Banta and Thacker (1979) reported that one of the reasons so few randomized trials were done of EFM was that physicians refused to participate and "deny" their patients (those randomly assigned as controls) what they considered the "best" medical care available. If by definition whatever is newest is best, we never will be able to research the safety and efficacy of birth technologies adequately and thus we never in fact will know what is best.

Although randomized controlled clinical trials must be undertaken judiciously, there are some who feel that "leaving therapy to chance" is incompatible with the ethics of the doctor–patient relationship. University of Kansas philosopher Don Marquis (1983) went so far as to argue that, "If this problem cannot be resolved, then either a key procedure for achieving scientific knowledge in medicine must be given up or unethical behavior by physicians must be tolerated (p. 40).

Thus far the childbirth technologies discussed are physician-controlled surgical procedures. We now consider two birth technologies that are client centered, involve less prestigious health-care providers, and involve what might be termed "lower technology" approaches to maximizing maternal and child health. These two technologies, out-of-hospital birth and prenatal care, have generated considerable research over the past decade. Yet these technologies have not been developed, disseminated, researched, and debated nearly to the extent that fetal monitoring and cesarean birth have been. They certainly have not gone from being promising reports to the proposed standard of care. The first, out-of-hospital birth, in fact has been bitterly opposed and the second, prenatal care, remains neglected for social groups in greatest need and most likely to benefit from it.

Out-of-Hospital Birth

Out-of-hospital birth gained major proponents in the United States during the early 1970s with the support of an uneasy alliance between the women's health and natural childbirth movements. Consumer movements for the humanization of birth, associated with low-technology, out-of-hospital birth, in-hospital, family-centered alternative birth centers, and free-standing birth centers are the antithesis of the high-technology, mechanized and medicalized birth that dominates the United States today.

These alternative birth practices have grown steadily but are used in a small proportion of all births. In 1968, alternative birth centers (ABCs) were officially endorsed first by ACOG, the Nurses Association of ACOG, the American Association of Pediatricians, and the American Nurses Association. Hospitals, in an effort to maintain their private-pay clientele willing and able to shop around for such services, responded. In 1975, three such birth centers were in operation in California. By 1979, there were 70 in the United States and the numbers continued to grow. Concomitant with the growth of ABCs was a more radical approach to providing birth care — the freestanding birth center (FSBC). In 1975 there were only four in the entire United States. Eakins (1986) reported that by 1981 there were over 150 FSBCs in 28 states. Although FSBCs currently provide birth services to less than half of 1% of all American births, they represent an important countertrend to consider because they indicate considerable dissatisfaction with standard obstetrical care on the part of a knowledgeable segment of the population.

Eakins (1986) reported that women who chose out-of-hospital birth in California were less interested in having comforts of home than avoiding the stark and regimented hospital environment. Many reported extremely negative previous experiences in hospital care. The two major themes that emerged as rationales for giving birth out of hospital were fear of harm to the baby as a result of hospital procedures and a desire to maintain the view that pregnancy is not a disease.

The overall outcome of out-of-hospital birth is difficult to analyze because aggregate data obscure very significant differences between planned and unplanned, voluntary and involuntary out-of-hospital birth outcomes. Data from the Birth Cohort File from the California Department of Health Statistics in 1977 show that ethnicity is associated with medical outcomes. Babies in all California minority groups born out of the hospital had lower birth weights than those born in the hospital. For example, the percentage of low-birthweight infants — 2,500 g or less — was more than 50% higher for Hispanic babies born out of the hospital than for those born in the hospital. For Black babies, it was almost one third higher. For White babies, the opposite was found; the average birth weight of White infants born outside the hospital was higher than for those born in the hospital (Eakins, 1986).

Data on in- and out-of-hospital death rates are particularly difficult to compare. Those who are in most regards low risk and choose out-of-hospital birth are largely White, middle- or upper-class women. Low-income Black and Hispanic women are less likely to choose out-of-hospital birth than to be forced into it out of economic necessity or disruptive life events. Not surprisingly, morbidity and mortality are far lower for the lower risk, voluntary, out-of-hospital participants than for the higher risk, nonvoluntary participants (Eakins, 1986).

There has been considerable controversy over the weight of evidence of safety from the United States and Europe. Research suggests that for low-risk, prepared women, there is no evidence of significant excess risk in home birth over hospital delivery if hospital backup is available (Campbell & Macfarlane, 1986; Hines, Bergeisen, & Allen, 1985; Hoff & Schneiderman, 1985; Tew, 1985). The largest study to date of freestanding birth center births in the United States (11,814 women admitted for labor and delivery to 84 centers) showed extremely favorable birth outcomes. There were no maternal deaths, a 4.4% cesarean section rate, and intrapartum and neonatal mortality rate of 1.3 per 1,000 births (Rooks et al., 1990).

Out-of-hospital birth is a technology largely chosen by educated White women who really have choices. Many women have limited access to care and these are women who often are at greatest risk of having poor birth outcomes. Research on freestanding birth center and midwifery care for such women is sorely needed.

Prenatal Care

Prenatal care (medical, nutritional, and social support) remains the most underresearched birth technology, except for midwifery care. Both are especially salient to low-income and minority women who have high rates of infant mortality and low-birthweight babies. Two thirds of all deaths in the neonatal period occur among infants born at 2,500 g or less and the risk of mortality increases with lower weights. Low-birthweight infants are five times more likely than normal weight infants to die later in the first year and those who survive are more likely to have neurodevelopmental handicaps (Wallace, 1988).

A recent study of birthweights of White compared to Black babies in different Chicago neighborhoods showed that the proportion of low-birthweight babies rose for both Blacks and Whites as census tract median income rates fell. Neonatal mortality was twice as high for Blacks as for Whites (16 compared to 7/1,000) and Blacks had over twice the proportion of low-birthweight births (14% compared to 6%). The risk of low birthweight among Blacks remained essentially double that of Whites across all maternal income, education, and age groups, although the risk to Blacks appeared to be eliminated among those residing in census tracts with median family incomes over $40,000 per year (Collins & David, 1990).

A time-series study of births from 1968 to 1988 in New York City estimates that if trends in the rate of low birthweight continue along the upturn discernable since 1984, the rate of low birthweight among Blacks in 1990 will exceed the rate of 22 years ago, reversing the substantial improvement achieved between 1968 and 1984 (Joyce, 1990).

Although the WHO Perinatal Study Group concluded in 1983 that there was no scientifically established benefit of prenatal care per se (Fraser, 1983), more recent studies suggest otherwise for women at greatest risk. In 1985, the Institute of Medicine (IOM) Committee to Study the Prevention of Low Birthweight (the major cause of infant mortality and morbidity) concluded that "the overwhelming weight of the evidence is that prenatal care reduces low birthweight. The IOM has estimated that even with substantial additional expenditures in enhanced prenatal care, the overall savings involved in preventing low birthweight in the United States could be $12 million to $28 million (p. 229).

The recommendations of the IOM Committee regarding how to reduce low birthweight remarkably were oriented toward social and behavioral aspects of pregnancy and health. Their major recommendations included giving increasing prominence to certain elements of prenatal care, many of which are relatively low in technological complexity. They emphasized tailoring prenatal care to meet the widely varying needs and risk profiles of individual pregnant women, including access to programs aimed at smoking reduction, better nutrition, and stress alleviation. The Committee also recommended providing low-income, high-risk women with transportation to enable them to use prenatal services and urged legislation to assure women maternity leave to reduce stress related to work and economic insecurity. The IOM Committee noted the need for federal leadership in setting professional practice standards, improving provider information, and changing reimbursement practices.

Although the IOM group based recommendations in part on scientific evidence, the recommendations go beyond those that can be made on a narrow cost-benefit analysis of specific technologies. Commenting on the controversies surrounding the continuance of the Women's, Infants, and Children's Supplemental Food Program (WIC) and expanded prenatal care based on recent evaluation research findings, Alfred Yankauer (1984), editor of *The American Journal of Public Health,* argued that cost-benefit factors are not the only issues that warrent consideration in continuing WIC and other health-welfare programs. He pointed out that:

> The United States is virtually unique among its peer countries in failing to provide family allowances and in regarding many child health and welfare services — which consensus considers basic to life in a complex industrial society — as amenities to be purchased only by those who can afford to do so. Instead of squarely facing the issue of government responsibilities to support a floor of equity in access to essential services, we seem to need other reasons before taking action. . . . Paradoxically, our generosity of heart relative to very costly services is the reverse of our position in relation to basic and less costly services. (p. 1148)

In recent research reports and debates over the methodology used in evaluating services such as WIC and expanded prenatal care (see, e.g., Kotelchuck, 1984; Kotelchuck, Schwartz, Anderka, & Finison, 1984; Rush, 1984; Schramm, 1985; Showstack, Budetti, & Minkler, 1984; Stockbauer, 1987; Yankauer, 1984), there is no evidence of harm or danger to women or infants related to the interventions. Yet it is striking to see how far more evidence of both efficacy and cost-effectiveness are demanded of WIC and expanded prenatal care than of EFM, cesarean section, episiotomy, and other surgical interventions that carry substantial risks. The rules of evidence appear to be applied differently to interventions that are popular among practitioners compared to interventions only begrudgingly provided to women and children at greatest risk for birth complications and problems (Ruzek, 1980).

This reality remains hidden from public debate in part because of the trend toward specialization with focus on narrow, single issues when assessing technologies. Those issues that command media attention and academic research and debate are also those viewed as being on the forefront of scientific medicine. It is always more interesting and exciting to focus on these emerging issues than to grapple with basic problems in maternal and child health that are not solved easily by high technology approaches or measured easily in scientific studies. Discourse that frames social and ethical issues strictly in an individual rights model primarily on the frontiers of new reproductive technologies also diverts our attention from fundamental problems in birth associated with social inequities.

REFRAMING SOCIAL AND ETHICAL ISSUES: BEYOND AN INDIVIDUAL RIGHTS MODEL

Conceptualizing and debating issues in a competing individual rights model is destined to be divisive and unproductive in a sphere of life in which community, common shared interests, and social well-being are of paramount importance. Indeed, Dan Beauchamp (1988) viewed disregard for public health as a serious threat to democracy itself. It is time to ask where an individual rights model has taken us and where it could lead us. Conflicts between providers and recipients of medical services have reached a level where defensive medicine and malpractice claims feed on each other in a vicious cycle that benefits no one, especially not families. Given this history, how can we conceivably benefit by expanding the individual rights model by arguing for a doctrine of individual responsibility that obligates women to accept medical intervention, sometimes against their will?

Perhaps it is time to accept the reality that some mistakes and errors of judgment inevitably will be made — by individual pregnant women and by medical experts. Most women, most of the time, are likely to act in the best interest of the unborn child to the best of their ability. That may be the best for which we can hope. Rather than seeking legal avenues for coercing women to accept treatments they refuse, might we find that spending time, energy, and resources providing basic care to women who currently do not have access to basic health services would be a better allocation of resources for society as a whole? Might large-scale feeding programs and income redistribution make greater contributions to improving birth outcomes than expensive medical machines and procedures? If so, how do we reconceptualize critical issues?

Rosalind Petchesky (1985) argued that many reproductive health issues such as contraception, abortion, and sterilization need to be viewed differently. They should not be seen simply as medical, moral, or individual rights issues as is often argued. She proposed that we move toward embedding these issues into a broad, socially based health model that includes all aspects of life conditions as well as services that promote or impede health. This definition would reflect the WHO (1947) definition of health as, "a state of complete physical, mental, and social well-being and not merely the absence of infirmity" (p. 1). Let us consider how this approach would shape our reasoning about certain birth issues.

Surely, within the WHO definition, coercing women to accept unwanted services in the name of responsibilities engendered by a health rights model would be inappropriate. Expending resources to make primary care available to all pregnant women and expanding maternity leaves and providing supplemental food to pregnant and lactating women and their young children surely would be appropriate.

In sum, the way we define health itself is a core issue and shapes even what we view as the important social and ethical issues in birth. Our research priorities also might be subjected to greater scrutiny within a health model. Given the size of our research enterprise, one would hope that the results of research, when done well, would influence or direct clinical practice. Currently, we elevate research to an exalted status, but simultaneously ignore its implications for clinical practice when it contradicts other "system needs." What is the point of research if it fails to shape what we do?

The social and economic consequences of supporting unjustifiable medical tinkering and failing to provide a "floor of equity" for birth are so enormous that the pattern must be changed. A first step is reconceptualizing the nature of health for pregnant women and their families in a manner that promotes community and social stability rather than purely individual self-interest.

ACKNOWLEDGMENTS

The author wishes to thank Diane Depken for valuable research assistance in preparing this article. Janice Cranmer also made significant contributions in locating literature.

REFERENCES

American College of Obstetricians & Gynecologists (1985). *Professional liability insurance and its effect: Report of a survey of ACOG's membership.* Prepared by Needham, Porter, Novelli, Washington, DC.

Annas, G. J. (1982). Forced cesareans: The unkindest cut of all. *Hastings Center Report, 12*(3), 16-17.

Annas, G. J. (1986). Pregnant women as fetal containers. *Hastings Center Report, 16*(6), 13-14.

Avery, M. D., & Burket, B. A. (1986). Effects of perineal massage on the incidence of episiotomy and perineal laceration in a nurse-midwifery service. *Journal of Nurse-Midwifery, 31*(3), 128-134.

Banta, H. D., & Behney, C. J. (1981). Policy formation and technology assessment. *Milbank Memorial Fund Quarterly, Health and Society, 59,* 445-479.

Banta, H. D., Behney, C. J., & Willems, J. S. (1981). *Toward rational technology in medicine.* New York: Springer.

Banta, H. D., & Thacker, S. B. (1979). *Cost and benefits of electronic fetal monitoring* (DHEW Publication No. 79-3245). Hyattsville, MD: National Center for Health Services Research, DHEW.

Beauchamp, D. E. (1988). *The health of the republic: Epidemics, medicine, and moralism as challenges to democracy.* Philadelphia: Temple University Press.

Bell, S. E. (1986). A new model of medical technology development: A case study of DES. *Research in the Sociology of Health Care, 4,* 1-32.

Brown, S. (1988). Preventing low birthweight. In H. Wallace, G. Ryan, Jr., & A. Oglesby (Eds.), *Maternal and child health practices* (3rd ed., pp. 307-324). Oakland, CA: Third Party Publishing.

Butler, L. (1989, October 3). In cutting infant deaths, simple things mean a lot, Sullivan says. *Tennessean,* Nashville. (Reprinted from *CDF in the News,* July 1989-December 1989, p. 7)

Campbell, R., & Macfarlane, A. (1986). Place of delivery: A review. *British Journal of Obstetrics and Gynecology, 93,* 675-683.

Cartwright, A. (1979). *The dignity of labour? A study of childbearing and induction.* London: Tavistock.

Chalmers, I. (1979, November). The epidemiology of perinatal practice. *Journal of Maternal and Child Health,* pp. 435-436.

Collins, J., & David, R. (1990). The differential effect of traditional risk factors on infant birthweight among Blacks and Whites in Chicago. *American Journal of Public Health, 80*(6), 679-681.

Eakins, P. S. (Ed.). (1986). *The American way of birth.* Philadelphia: Temple University Press.

Fraser, C. M. (1983). Selected perinatal procedures: Scientific basis for use and psycho-social effects. *Acta Obstetrica et Gynecologica Scandinavica* (Suppl. 117), 1-39.

Gallagher, J. (1987a, May). *Fetus as patient.* Paper presented at the Rutgers University Forum on Reproductive Laws for the 1980s, New York.

Gallagher, J. (1987b). Prenatal invasions & interventions: What's wrong with fetal rights. *Harvard Women's Law Journal, 10,* 9-58.

Guillemin, J. (1981). Babies by cesarean: Who chooses, who controls? *Hastings Center Report, 11*(3), 15-17.

Harrison, R. F., Brennan, M., North, P. M., Reed, J. V., & Wickham, E. A. (1984). Is routine episiotomy necessary? *British Medical Journal, 288,* 1971-1975.

Haverkamp, D. H., & Orleans, M. (1982). An assessment of electronic fetal monitoring. *Women and Health, 7,* 115-134.

Hines, M. W., Bergeisen, G. H., & Allen, D. T. (1985). Neonatal outcome in planned out-of-hospital births in Kentucky. *Journal of the American Medical Association, 253,* 1578-1582.

Hoff, G. A., & Schneiderman, L. J. (1985). Having babies at home: Is it safe? *Hastings Center Report, 15*(6), 19-27.

Hubbard, R. (1982). Personal courage is not enough: Some hazards of childbearing in the

1980's. In R. Arditti, R. D. Klein, & S. Minden (Eds.), *Test-tube women: What future for motherhood?* (pp. 331–355). Boston: Pandora.

Hugh, D., Johnson, K., Rosenbaum, S., & Butler, E. (1987). *The health of America's children: Maternal and child health data book.* Washington, DC: Children's Defense Fund.

Hutson, J. M., & Petrie, R. H. (1986). Possible limitations of fetal monitoring. *Clinical Obstetrics and Gynecology, 29*(1), 104–113.

Institute of Medicine Committee to Study the Prevention of Low Birthweight. (1985). *Preventing low birthweight.* Washington, DC: National Academy Press.

Janowitz, B., Nakamura, M. S., Lins, F. E., Brown, M. L., & Clopton, D. (1982). Cesarean section in Brazil. *Social Science & Medicine, 16,* 19–25.

Joyce, T. (1990). The dramatic increase in the rate of low birthweight in New York City: An aggregate time-series analysis. *American Journal of Public Health, 80*(6), 679–681.

Kotelchuck, M. (1984). Response to David Rush's comments. *American Journal of Public Health, 74*(10), 1146–1148.

Kotelchuck, M., Schwartz, J., Anderka, M., & Finison, K. (1984). WIC participation and pregnancy outcomes: Massachusetts statewide evaluation project. *American Journal of Public Health, 74*(10), 1086–1092.

Mackenzie, T. B., & Nagel, T. C. (1986). When a pregnant woman endangers her fetus. *Hastings Center Report, 16*(1), 24–25.

Marieskind, H. I. (1979). *An evaluation of cesarean section in the United States.* Washington, DC: U.S. Department of Health, Education & Welfare.

Marieskind, H. I. (1982). Cesarean section. *Women and Health, 7*(3, 4), 179–198.

Marquis, D. (1983). Leaving therapy to chance. *The Hastings Center Report, 13*(4), 40–47.

McKinlay, J. (1981). From "promising report" to "standard procedure": Seven stages in the career of a medical innovation. *Milbank Memorial Fund Quarterly, Health and Society, 59*(3), 374–409.

Mercer, R. T. (1977). *Nursing care for parents at risk.* Thorofare, NJ: Charles Slack.

Mullen, F. M., & Jacoby, I. (1985). The town meeting for technology. *Journal of the American Medical Association, 254,* 1068–1089.

National Center for Health Services Research & Health Care Technology Assessment. (1989). *Research Activities, October*(122), 2.

National Center for Health Statistics. (1987). Advance report of final mortality statistics, 1985. *Mortality Vital Statistics Report, 36* (Suppl. 5), 1–47.

Nelson, L. J. (1987, May/June). Challenging obstetrics as usual: The Cesarean Prevention Movement. *National Women's Health Network News,* p. 3.

O'Reilly, W. B., Eakins, P. S., Gilfax, M. G., & Richwald, G. A. (1986). Childbirth and the malpractice insurance industry. In P. Eakins (Ed.), *The American way of birth* (pp. 196–217). Philadelphia: Temple University Press.

Perry, S., & Kalberer, J. T. (1980). The NIH consensus development program and the assessment of health care technologies. *New England Journal of Medicine, 303,* 169–172.

Petchesky, R. (1985). Abortion in the 1980's: Feminist morality and women's health. In E. Lewin & V. Oleson (Eds.), *Women, health and healing* (pp. 139–173). New York: Tavistock Publications.

Placek, P. J., Taffel, S. M., & Liss, T. (1987). Trends in the United States cesarean section rate and reasons for the 1980–85 rise. *American Journal of Public Health 77*(8), 955–959.

Reading, A. E., Stedmere, C. M., Cox, D. N. et al. (1982). How women view episiotomy pain. *British Medical Journal, 284,* 243–246.

Rooks, J., Weatherby, N., Ernst, E., Stapleton, S., Rosen, D., & Rosenfield, A. (1990). Outcomes of care in birth centers: The national birth center study. *New England Journal of Medicine, 321*(26), 1804–1811.

Rothman, B. K. (1985). The products of conception: The social context of reproductive choices. *Journal of Medical Ethics, 11*(4), 188–195.

Rothman, B. K. (1986). When a pregnant woman endangers her fetus; commentary. *Hastings Center Report, 16*(1), 24–25.

Rush, D. (1984). Some comments on the Massachusetts WIC evaluation. *American Journal of Public Health, 74,* 1145–1146.

Ruzek, S. B. (1978). *The women's health movement. Feminist alternatives to medical control.* New York: Praeger.

Ruzek, S. B. (1980). Ethical issues in childbirth technologies. In H. Holmes, B. Hoskins, & M. Gross (Eds.), *Birth control and controlling birth: Women centered perspectives* (pp. 197–201). Clifton, NJ: Humana.

Ruzek, S. B. (1983). How critically do we examine obstetrical technologies? *Mobius, 3*(3), 91–96.

Schramm, W. F. (1985). WIC prenatal participation and its relationship to newborn Medicaid costs in Missouri: A cost/benefit analysis. *American Journal of Public Health, 75*(8), 851–857.

Showstack, J. A., Budetti, P. P., & Minkler, D. (1984). Factors associated with birthweight: An exploration of the roles of prenatal care and length of gestation. *American Journal of Public Health, 74,* 1003–1008.

Shy, K., Luthy, D. A., Bennett, F., Whitfield, M., Larson, E. B., van Belle, G., Hughes, J. P., Wilson, J. A., & Stenchever, M. A. (1990). Effects of electronic fetal-heart-rate monitoring, as compared with periodic auscultation, on the neurologic development of premature infants. *New England Journal of Medicine, 322*(9), 588–593.

Stafford, R. (1990a). Cesarean section use and source of payment: An analysis of California hospital discharge abstracts. *American Journal of Public Health, 80*(3), 313–315.

Stafford, R. (1990b). Alternative strategies for controlling rising cesarean section rates. *Journal of the American Medical Association, 263*(5), 683–687.

Stockbauer, J. W. (1987). WIC prenatal participation and its relation to pregnancy outcomes in Missouri: A second look. *American Journal of Public Health, 77,* 813–818.

Summey, P. S. (1986). Cesarean birth. In P. Eakins (Ed.), *The American way of birth* (pp. 175–195). Philadelphia: Temple University Press.

Tew, M. (1985). Place of birth and perinatal mortality. *Journal of the Royal College of General Practitioners, 35,* 390–394.

Thacker, S. B., & Banta, H. D. (1982). Benefits and risks of episiotomy. *Women and Health, 7,* 161–178.

U.S. Department of Health & Human Services. (1990). *Promoting health/preventing disease: Year 2000 objectives for the nation.* Washington, DC: U.S. Government Printing Office.

Waitzkin, H. (1979). A Marxian interpretation of the growth and development of coronary care technology. *American Journal of Public Health, 69,* 1260–1268.

Wallace, H. M. (1988). Infant mortality. In H. M. Wallace (Ed.), *Maternal and child health practices* (3rd ed., pp. 411–426). Oakland, CA: Third Party Publishing.

World Health Organization. (1947). Constitution of the World Health Organization. *Chronicle of WHO, 1*(1).

Yankauer, A. (1984). Science and social policy. *American Journal of Public Health, 74*(10), 1148.

Yankauer, A. (1990). What infant mortality tells us. *American Journal of Public Health, 80*(6), 653–654.

Young, D. (Ed.). (1982). Obstetrical intervention and technology in the 1980s. *Women and Health, 7*(3, 4).

7

Women and Advances in Medical Technologies: The Legal Issues

Ellen Wright Clayton
Vanderbilt University

In recent decades, we have learned more about reproduction—about how to procreate in the face of infertility and about what is happening to the unborn child during gestation. This new knowledge has led to increased scrutiny of women's decisions regarding procreation and has given rise to a host of legal issues. On the one hand, we ask whether there exists a right to procreate. In the past, the question was whether the state could prevent or even discourage fertile individuals from having children. The answer to both these questions was—and still is—a limited yes. Today, we also are being asked to consider whether people who are infertile either involuntarily or as a result of choice of lifestyle have a right, under certain circumstances, to technologies that would enable them to have children with whom they are connected genetically.

On the other hand, there has been increasing scrutiny of women's decisions regarding conception and their behavior during pregnancy and at the time of delivery. To some extent, this is hardly surprising in light of law's and medicine's traditional lack of respect for decisions made by patients and in light of the fact that some individual choices have always been overridden for the benefit of others. Two new forces have emerged that have radically transformed the role of women in reproduction. The first, and less important, is the fact that procreation increasingly is viewed as a medical/health issue and hence as an area in which physicians appropriately make decisions. The second, and more powerful, is the increasing tendency to view the fetus as having interests separate from those of the pregnant woman. These two notions have radically changed public discussion about abortion, about behavior of women during pregnancy both in their private actions and in their ability to participate in the workplace, and about new reproductive technologies. In all instances, albeit to different degrees, the trend has been toward decreasing women's freedom of choice.

Women face interference with their decisions about procreation from numerous sources, ranging from physicians to the state and to third parties, such as employers. With so many different issues and actors, it is hardly surprising that the evolving rules and approaches are often inconsistent with each other. The purpose of this chapter is to look at these issues in the hope of beginning to develop a more unified, consistent approach.

Throughout this discussion, we focus on three aspects of the law. The first is the presence of immunity rights, that is, the extent to which the law bars the state, doctors, or other third parties from intervening in individuals' choices. The second is the definition of entitlement rights, that is, the extent to which the law forces the state or doctors to enable individuals to act upon their choices. The third is when the law permits individuals' desires to be overridden. In thinking about these three aspects of the law, we must consider also whether the law will enforce its rules proactively, that is, by ordering or enjoining a person to act in a certain way, or retroactively, that is, by imposing civil or criminal liability after a person has not acted in accordance with what the law requires. As a general rule, forcing a person to do what she does not want to do is more intrusive and hence more extraordinary under the law.

WHO CAN PROCREATE?

At the threshold, we must ask whether there is any right to procreate at all, and if so, how far it extends (Binion, 1988). Ofttimes, this question is asked in terms of whether decisions regarding childbearing are protected under a constitutional right to privacy that excludes intervention by the state. Some commentators argue strenuously that there clearly is a constitutional right to procreate (Robertson, 1983, 1988). But in contrast to the Supreme Court's extensive elaboration of the constitutional basis of the right not to procreate (*Carey v. Population Servs. Int'l.,* 1977; *Eisenstadt v. Baird,* 1972; *Griswold v. Connecticut,* 1965; *Roe v. Wade,* 1973; *Webster v. Reproductive Health Servs.,* 1989), the Court in fact has said relatively little about the right to bear children. Forty-five years ago, the Supreme Court did characterize procreation as "one of the basic civil rights of man" in *Skinner v. Oklahoma* (1942), in which it struck down on the grounds of impermissible discrimination a statute requiring sterilization of certain criminals. But it has never repudiated its earlier opinion in *Buck v. Bell* (1927) in which the Supreme Court upheld the eugenic sterilization of an allegedly retarded woman. Indeed, *Buck* was cited with approval in *Roe v. Wade* (1973) for the proposition that individuals do not have an unlimited right to do as they wish with their bodies. Moreover, several states even today permit the unconsented sterilization of certain retarded people (In re *Matter of Moe,* 1982; *Sterilization of Moore,* 1976).

To the extent that *Skinner* (1942) defined a right to procreate, it dealt only with the power of the state to impair irrevocably a person's ability to have children. To be sure, other cases have mentioned in passing a right to make decisions to have children as support for other important freedoms, such as the right to marry (*Zablocki v. Redhail,* 1978) and the right to contraception (*Eisenstadt v. Baird,* 1972). But none of these cases says anything about the permissibility of erecting lesser barriers to childbearing. Any suggestion that the state might have an affirmative duty to promote procreation is cast in serious doubt by the Supreme Court's repeated statements that the state has no constitutional obligation either to fund pregnancy or to avoid penalizing families who choose to have large numbers of children so long as it does not discriminate inappropriately in the funding it does provide (*Dandridge v. Williams,* 1963; *Maher v. Roe,* 1977).

Until now, there has been relatively little need to analyze the right to procreate because until recently there has been little that the state could do (short of sterilization or financial incentives) either to ban or to promote childbearing. The advances in medical technology that allow us to ensure procreation in the face of infertility mean that we now must think seriously about the scope of the right to procreate. In particular, we must ask to what extent are women entitled to the aid of medicine and of the state in furtherance of their desire to procreate.

The first problem confronted by women who seek to use the new reproductive technologies is often economic. Artificial insemination (AI) is relatively inexpensive, but in vitro fertilization (IVF), the next most commonly used technology, is quite expensive, costing thousands of dollars per round and often requiring more than one round. Initially, this cost limited IVF to the relatively well-to-do because these expenses were paid for out of pocket. Increasingly, however, insurance companies are paying for such treatments for infertility. The growing role of third-party payment in this area merits a closer look. On the one hand, insurance companies are largely free to define the scope of their policies' coverage, and in many instances, these companies specifically have excluded payment for IVF. On the other, courts increasingly are accepting insureds' arguments that infertility is a health or medical problem and that IVF is no longer experimental and are, therefore, requiring insurers who have not made specific exclusions to pay for such treatments (*Reilly v. Blue Cross and Blue Shield of Wisconsin,* 1988).

The main problems with access exist not for middle-class people who may or may not have insurance but for poor women and women who live in nontraditional relationships. For poor women, who have a higher prevalence of infertility than do upper middle-class women (Nsiah-Jefferson, 1989), the problem often simply is one of money. Whatever may be happening in the main insurance market, there has been no move by the states or Congress to provide the new reproductive technologies to the infertile poor who might benefit from them. Moreover, physicians who provide infertility treatment to poor women occasionally have been punished for so doing. In one instance, a doctor in Wisconsin almost lost his license for providing AI to a woman on Medicaid (Gallagher, 1989).

Even more pervasive is the fact that most physicians are unwilling to provide even such basic infertility treatments as AI to women who are poor or unmarried. These doctors act as gatekeepers, as moral arbiters who decide which women are fit to be parents. Their role in allocation, in many instances, has been promoted by statute. A few states have simply declared artificial insemination performed without the aid of a physician illegal (Ga. Code Ann., 1990; Idaho Code, 1990a; Ore. Rev. Stat., 1990a). More commonly, the states allow only those women who use physicians to avail themselves of statutory protections that prevent the semen donor from seeking parental rights so that women who choose to become pregnant outside the health-care system do so at their own risk. Thus, in *Jhordan C. v. Mary K.* (1986), the court upheld the semen donor's request for visitation with the child born to a lesbian mother, saying that the mother could have prevented his access to her son if a physician had obtained the sperm as provided by statute. In the court's discussion, there was no suggestion of why the mother chose to self-inseminate. If, however, she had done so because physicians had refused to provide her with AI, the constitutional questions about the scope of the right to procreate and the permissibility of enshrining physicians as moral gatekeepers would have been posed more clearly.

One can only wonder why so many legislatures gave doctors power over the use of even simple techniques to overcome infertility. By far the most likely reason is that the legislators simply thought of infertility as a medical problem that "naturally" should be cared for by physicians. But this does not explain why doctors should be entitled to decide who receives AI or IVF. It is not enough to say that physicians will act to protect the welfare of children who are born by these technologies. To begin with, the cases forbidding claims for wrongful life show that we hesitate to say that any child, whether born to single, poor, or virtually any other type of parents, would have been better off not having been born (*Becker v. Schwartz,* 1978; *Nelson v. Krusen,* 1984; *Speck v. Finegold,* 1981; *Zepeda v. Zepeda,* 1963). Moreover, allowing doctors to try to ensure that children are born only to stable heterosexual couples fails to recognize that many children in our society live in settings that do not comply with these norms. Most people can become parents for any reason or for no reason at all. Even adoption agencies, which until recently accepted only people living in traditional marital relationships as potential adoptive parents, increasingly have permitted single and homosexual people to adopt. It is fundamentally unfair to hold the one sixth of all women in this country who are infertile to radically different and higher standards before they can become parents. Finally, even were it appropriate to require women who use the new reproductive technologies to meet some minimal standards of parenting, there is no reason to think that the medical profession is particularly qualified to determine which women pass the test.

Even were we able to formulate appropriate criteria for deciding who should receive AI or other technologies and to designate people or agencies able to apply these standards, we must still ask what other screening should be done. It is reasonable to suggest that potential donors be screened for infectious diseases such as AIDS to protect both the prospective mother and the child-to-be. Genetic screening of potential donors is also desirable so that recipients can make informed decisions regarding procreation. Physicians may well be liable if they fail to provide prospective parents with appropriate information about genetic risk ("Father and mother know best," 1978; *Howard v. Lecher,* 1977; *Phillips v. United States,* 1981). What is less clear is whether genetic screening can be required in order to exclude certain people as potential donors on the ground that they present too great a risk to the public health. Although several states have enacted laws providing that men who have a "disease or defect known by [them] to be transmissible by genes" may not be donors (Idaho Code, 1990b; Ore. Rev. Stat., 1990b), such statutes are difficult to reconcile with the distrust of eugenics demonstrated in the cases that ban entirely (In re *Eberhardy,* 1981) or limit eugenic sterilization to instances in which avoiding procreation is in the best interests of the person to be sterilized (*Matter of A. W.,* 1981; *Matter of Moe,* 1982).

INTERVENTION BY OTHERS ON BEHALF OF THE FETUS

As the aforementioned cases begin to demonstrate, limits on procreation sometimes are justified on the basis that they benefit the fetus. This basis for intervention runs head on into the prospective parent's freedom of choice. But before we turn to an analysis of current efforts to limit women's procreative decision making for the sake of the fetus, it is useful to consider briefly the way the law looks at patients in general in order to realize that patients' autonomy traditionally has received relatively little respect.

The Limited Growth of Patient Autonomy
in the Face of Medical Technology

The law often states that patients should be allowed to make their own health-care decisions. It often pays homage to patients' rights to "thorough-going self-determination" (*Schloendorff v. Society of New York Hosp.,* 1914). And the law in the last 20 to 30 years has made major strides toward protecting patients' autonomy, through creating rights to informed consent and to refuse life-sustaining therapy. But the rights actually ensured by the law are limited. For example, when a patient claims that she was injured because she was treated without her informed consent (Katz, 1984), she can recover damages only if the information that she did not get was information that a reasonable doctor would tell (Ark. Stat. Ann., 1990) or that a reasonable patient would want (*Canterbury v. Spence,* 1972; *Cobbs v. Grant,* 1972) and that a reasonable patient would have changed her mind had she gotten the omitted information. There is no room for patients whose beliefs are outside the norm here. And note that the only option the law of informed consent protects is the decision to receive or to reject proffered treatment. There is never any suggestion that a patient has the right to get a therapy that her physician does not want to provide. Her only option is to look for a doctor who will do as she wishes. Even that option is limited by the fact that patients do not have rights to obtain (*Custody of a Minor,* 1979; *United States v. Rutherford,* 1979) and physicians are not permitted to provide unconventional therapies that fall outside the confines of medical practice as defined by the medical profession and agencies of the government such as state licensing boards and the Food and Drug Administration (FDA; *People v. Privitera,* 1979). Yet it is important to note that what constitutes appropriate medical care is not solely a matter of scientifically proven efficacy, but rather reflects a host of external, societal pressures that change over time. We see then that the law has a limited commitment to enabling patients to proceed by their own lights.

Patients' choices are limited in another important way as well. They may be forced to undergo all sorts of invasions of their privacy and bodily integrity if those intrusions are necessary to avoid harm to others. For instance, individuals may be vaccinated, quarantined, and reported to the state, all in the name of public health (Cal. Health & Safety Code, 1990; Ill. Ann. Stat., 1990). And the fear of contagion is not the only permissible reason for state intervention. The state can commit a mentally ill person who presents a risk of serious danger to others (Ind. Code Ann., 1990; Wis. Stat. Ann., 1990c). A controversial series of cases have held that the state can even treat a mother over her religious objection if her death would leave minor children (*Application of the Pres. & Directors of Georgetown College, Inc.,* 1964; In re *Winthrop University Hospital,* 1985).

Thus, the law clearly is not devoted wholeheartedly to the protection of individuals' decisions. But, as this last example suggests, women are not just self contained patients whose choices are subject to the law's usual ambivalence toward protecting patients' autonomy. Women's capacity to procreate raises special legal problems. One set of issues turns on the woman's personal interest in decisions about whether or not to procreate, choices for which, we have seen, the law provides only limited constitutional and economic protection. The other set of interests are those of the fetus, whether or not the conception was intended. Thus, we must confront the questions of what, if any, claim the fetus has for legal protection against the actions of the pregnant woman and who, if anyone, is entitled to assert the fetus's claim.

Abortion

Although the cases addressing abortion raise a host of issues, two are particularly relevant for this discussion. The first is when abortion may be forbidden for the benefit of the fetus. In elaborating its trimester analysis, the Supreme Court in *Roe v. Wade* (1973) declared that the state's interest in the fetus became compelling — sufficiently great to justify regulation to protect the fetus — only after viability. Indeed, until recently, there was evidence that the state's interest was not particularly strong even after viability. For example, the Supreme Court invalidated two statutes that required physicians to use techniques that would permit survival of the fetus in postviability abortions where the technique would not impose any "significantly greater medical risk" on the woman's health. The Court said that the states may not force physicians to impose any greater risk on the woman's health in order to save the fetus's life (*Colautti v. Franklin,* 1979; *Planned Parenthood Ass'n v. Ashcroft,* 1983; *Thornburgh v. American College of Obstetrics and Gynecology,* 1986). Yet if it became necessary for the benefit of the woman to terminate pregnancy late in third trimester, when the fetus would have a good chance of extrauterine survival, one can ask why a serious effort should not be made to deliver rather than to abort the fetus even if the pregnant woman were thereby exposed to some slightly increased risk. Thus, it was hard to characterize the state's interest in survival of the viable fetus as compelling.

Recently, however, the Supreme Court's view of when regulation for the benefit of the fetus is permissible seems to be changing. In *Webster v. Reproductive Health Services* (1989), the Court upheld a Missouri statute that, among other things, attempted to regulate the way that physicians determine viability. Along the way, however, Justices Rehnquist, White, and Kennedy made clear that they felt the state had a protectable interest in the fetus prior to viability, a position that had earlier been espoused to some extent by Justice O'Connor in *Thornburgh v. American College of Obstetrics and Gynecology* (1976), and Justice Scalia made clear his dissatisfaction with the entire framework of *Roe v. Wade* (1973). Thus, although the plurality of the Court rather surprisingly and disingenuously read the statute as merely providing guidance to the physician and as not challenging the basic notion that the state's interest became compelling only after viability, their language certainly signals a change in the wind.

The second aspect of the law of abortion relevant here is the fact that from its initial pronouncement in *Roe v. Wade* (1973), the Court has spoken about the decision to abort in the first trimester as one to be made by the woman and her physician. The Court's position that this decision is to be made by two people is striking because it stands in stark contrast to the general rhetoric embodied in the cases about informed consent, that the patient is the one who decides, and because it is justified nowhere. It is certainly clear that decisions whether or not to continue a pregnancy usually involve value judgments for which doctors have no particular claim to expertise. In addition, this formulation of two-party decision making grants physicians — and the institution of medicine — unusual power over the destiny of women. This power influences women's options and choices in many ways that have not been appreciated fully. Yet it is clear that this formulation was chosen deliberately. The Court on several occasions has struck down state legislature's efforts to prescribe what physicians must tell women who are about to undergo abortion in part because it impermissibly interferes with the decision between the woman and her doctor (*City of Akron v. Akron Center for Reproductive Health,* 1983; *Thornburgh v. American College of Obstetrics and Gynecology,* 1986).

Moreover, the physician actually has been used as a shield against state regulation of abortion. Thus, efforts by state legislatures to define viability have been struck down as impermissibly intruding on the doctor's domain (*Colautti v. Franklin,* 1979; *Planned Parenthood of Cent. Missouri v. Danforth,* 1976), although the continuing vitality of these cases, too, has been called into question by *Webster v. Reproductive Health Services* (1989). One can only ask whether physicians ought to play such an important role in drawing constitutionally significant lines (Rhoden, 1986) or whether, as some commentators have suggested recently and rather incredibly, the earlier viability cases ought to be read not as protecting women's right to choose abortion but as holding that the doctor–patient relationship is protected by a constitutional right to privacy (Annas, Glantz, & Mariner, 1990).

Thus, the law of abortion gives confused and confusing guidance. Certainly, it appears that the present Court is willing to allow the states to provide greater protection to the fetus against the pregnant woman's right to choose abortion, although the limits of this intervention are by no means clear. In addition, the Court contemplates a role for physicians' participation in women's decisions about abortion that is unparalleled elsewhere in medicine and that somehow is more important than state intervention. The question then is whether these same rules apply when looking at efforts to control the behavior of women who elect to continue their pregnancies.

Opting Out of the Health-Care System

Let us look first at efforts to remove procreation from the realm of medicine. Many women seek to deliver their children at home with the aid of lay midwives. They urge that delivery is not a medical matter at all but rather a natural process. This position is supported by the weight of history. As we have already seen in chapter 2, childbirth traditionally has been a matter that women control; medicalization is a recent historical development (Leavitt, 1986). Many women further assert that for low-risk pregnancies, delivery at home is actually safer for the child and the mother because of the doctor-created side effects of the obstetric suite ("Choice in childbirth," 1986; Wolfson, 1986).

The states, however, have not been receptive to women who wish to bear their children without the aid of medicine. They often regulate or even ban lay midwifery, if they address the subject at all (McIntosh, 1989). And the courts, in recent challenges to restrictions on midwifery, generally have upheld the statutes (*Bowland v. Municipal Ct.,* 1977; *Leggett v. Tennessee Board Nursing,* 1980; *Leigh v. Board Regis. Nursing,* 1987; *State ex rel. Missouri Board of Regis. v. Southworth,* 1986). To the extent that they address constitutionality at all, these courts look only at the scope of the right to privacy and to problems of equal protection. Notably, they do not make the only justifiable constitutional argument, that is, that the state may intervene under its police power if it believes that home delivery presents a risk of harm to the child. The medical professional also works to limit women's options for home delivery, not only by supporting statutes regulating lay and nurse midwives but also by disciplining physicians who perform home deliveries and who "back up" midwives. Limitations on midwives and physicians are not the only state-erected barriers to home deliveries; women who knowingly or even negligently deliver a high-risk pregnancy at home with resultant injury to the child could be subjected to civil and criminal liability. A reasonable resolution to this situation might be to permit home delivery with the aid of a lay midwife so long as the woman has had an evaluation to determine that her pregnancy is one at low risk (Wolfson, 1986) and so long as medical back-up is available.

Another area in which women have sought to wrest their care from the health-care system is in self-insemination (Wikler & Wikler, in press). As we saw earlier, doctors have been given power over AI and have acted as moral gatekeepers, deciding who can and cannot have access to these technologies. There is little reason to think that physicians have any particular claim to expertise or justifiable authority to make these allocation decisions, and one can even argue that some of the possibly desirable screening of potential donors need not be done by medical professionals. But whatever deference should be given to women's arguments that they should be allowed to decide how they are going to become pregnant and how their babies are going to be delivered, the law currently regards these choices as ones in which physicians appropriately are involved.

Maternal–Fetal Conflict

For all that these cases demonstrate a limited commitment to allowing women to make their own decisions regarding procreation, our new understanding of the impact of maternal behavior on fetal development, our abilities to perform prenatal diagnosis and fetal therapy, and our evolution of high-risk obstetrics threaten to affect women even more. This situation is not entirely a new one. At the turn of the century, the relief of cephalopelvic disproportion—a baby too big to be born vaginally—by craniotomy began to be replaced by cesarean section. The former technique killed the unborn child but was relatively safe for the woman, whereas the latter sometimes saved the baby but, at the time, greatly increased the risk for women. Although many forces contributed to this change, one important argument by the proponents of cesarean section was the interests of the unborn child (Leavitt, 1987). Put simply, our current knowledge gives women and physicians the power to make unborn children healthier than they otherwise would be and at the minimum to avert some foreseeable harms. The question for society, then, is to what extent will we use the law to allow physicians and others to force women at some cost or risk to themselves to act on behalf of their fetuses.

A growing number of courts are allowing physicians and the state to intervene at various points in pregnancy to protect fetuses from the actions of their mothers. In *People v. Pointer* (1984), a woman adhered for religious reasons to a macrobiotic diet for both herself and her children, to the harm of her children. The trial court, as part of its decree, enjoined the woman not to bear any more children for 5 years. The appellate court overturned this injunction as being tantamount to sterilization and impossible to enforce but suggested that she could be required to undergo periodic pregnancy testing, and if pregnant, "to follow an intensive prenatal and neonatal treatment program monitored by both the probation officer and by a supervising physician." In other cases, women have been enjoined from taking drugs and subjected to monitoring (Gallagher, 1989; Shaw, 1984) or even committed (In re *Steven S.,* 1981) or incarcerated (Keenan & Hinds,

1990) for the benefit of their unborn children. On more than one occasion, courts have said that pregnant women who are Jehovah's Witnesses may be given blood transfusions over their objection if their fetus's life otherwise would be endangered (In re *Application of Jamaica Hosp.*, 1985; *Raleigh Fitkin–Paul Mem. Hosp. v. Anderson,* 1964).

Some courts also have stated that this prenatal duty of care could be enforced by remedies imposed after delivery. Thus, in *Grodin v. Grodin* (1980), a Michigan court held that a child with darkened teeth from his mother's use of tetracycline during pregnancy could obtain damages from her if she was negligent in taking the drug. Notably, however, other courts more recently have refused to permit children to sue their mothers for injuries allegedly inflicted before birth (*Stallman v. Youngquist,* 1988). In addition, some courts have held that a woman's actions during pregnancy may be relevant in a subsequent custody dispute or effort by the state to obtain custody of the child after he or she is born (In re *Baby X,* 1980; In re *Ruiz,* 1986; In re *Smith,* 1985). Finally, and perhaps most troubling, some states recently have enacted statutes requiring the reporting of nonmedical drug use by pregnant women (Minn. Stat. Ann., 1990) and even permitting women to be prosecuted for murder or assault or other crimes if their actions kill or injure their viable fetuses (Johnsen, 1989; Keenan & Hinds, 1990; Tenn. Code Ann., 1990). A bill was even introduced in the Senate to encourage the states to criminalize drug use during pregnancy (Child Abuse During Pregnancy Prevention Act of 1989).

The courts also have enjoined women to comply with an intrapartum duty of care. In the most famous opinion, a woman was ordered to have a cesarean section over her religious objections because an alleged placenta previa threatened the lives of her and her fetus (*Jefferson v. Griffin Spaulding County Hosp.,* 1981; see also In re *Madyun,* 1986; Kolder, Gallagher, & Parsons, 1987). In addition, a woman who had had a placenta previa and was an amphetamine abuser was charged with criminal child abuse when her child died after she refused to heed her doctor's advice to refrain from drugs and sexual intercourse and to seek hospital care at the first sign of vaginal bleeding (Annas, 1987; Johnsen, 1987; Maternal Substance Abuse, 1987). The charges ultimately were dismissed on the grounds that the statute under which the charges were brought was intended primarily to ensure financial support to children (Oloroso, 1987).

Notably, the trend toward judicially ordered cesarean sections has not been entirely unrestrained. In the tragic case of In re *A. C.* (1987, 1990), the woman was 26 weeks pregnant and was imminently dying of cancer. Even though there was real doubt about whether she wanted to deliver the child, particularly in light of the problems faced by children born that prematurely, the hospital sought and was granted judicial permission to perform a cesarean section. The baby, as it turned out, was not viable, living only 2½ hours after delivery, and the woman died 2 days later. A panel of the District of Columbia Court of Appeals initially approved the trial court's actions, reasoning that in light of the woman's poor prognosis, "the trial court did not err in subordinating A. C.'s right against bodily intrusion to the interests of the unborn child and the state . . ." (In re *A. C.,* 1987). These rulings, not surprisingly, came under heavy criticism, (Clayton, 1990; Goldberg, 1989; Mother v. Fetus, 1989) and recently were reversed by the District of Columbia Court of Appeals sitting en banc (In re *A. C.,* 1990). That court ruled that:

> in virtually all cases the question of what is to be done is to be decided by the patient—the pregnant woman—on behalf of herself and her fetus. If the patient is incompetent or otherwise unable to give an informed consent to a proposed course of medical treatment, then her decision must be ascertained through the procedure known as substituted judgment.

The court then suggested that refusal could be overridden only in extraordinary circumstances.

Finally, physicians and the state are not the only parties seeking to change women's behavior during pregnancy. Increasingly, employers seek to exclude pregnant and even fertile women from the potentially toxic workplace, usually citing concern about the health of unborn children (Duncan, 1989; *Hayes v. Shelby Memorial Hospital,* 1984; *Oil, Chemical and Atomic Workers International Union v. American Cyanamid Co.,* 1984). Recently, the Seventh Circuit allowed even nonpregnant but potentially fertile women's decisions to work in battery plants to be overridden by the employer's desire to avoid the birth of children who may have been affected adversely by prenatal exposure to lead (*International Union, United Automobile, Aerospace and Agricultural Implement Workers of America v. Johnson Controls, Inc.,* 1989). Notably, the Equal Employment Opportunity Commission (1990) has expressed its disapproval of this decision, and the Supreme Court has agreed to review the case.

Ultimately, the question is whether women can be forced at some risk or cost or even bodily invasion to "rescue" their fetuses. Most people would concur that pregnant women have a moral duty to act not to injure and, to a lesser degree, to save fetuses they plan to carry to term. But does this give rise to a legally enforceable duty? The answer, except perhaps in certain narrowly circumscribed exceptions, is no. It is important to distinguish what women, as independent moral agents, may or even ought to choose to do, from what women, as a class of citizens subject to potential discrimination, may be required by law to do.

To be sure, some commentators argue that once a woman has chosen to carry her pregnancy to term, she has "a legal and moral duty to bring the child into the world as healthy as is reasonably possible" (Robertson, 1983, p. 438). Robertson (1983) suggested in the past that women be required "to avoid work, recreation, and medical care choices that are hazardous to the fetus" (p. 450), to allow established methods of fetal therapy, and even to "undergo prenatal screening when there is reason to believe that this screening may identify congenital defects correctable with available therapies" (p. 450), a position from which he has since partially retreated (Robertson & Schulman, 1987). Margery Shaw (1984) went even further than Robertson's initial position and asserted that women who do not abort fetuses with serious defects may be liable to these children for damages (see also, Feinberg, 1985). Under this line of reasoning, it could be asserted that prospective parents have a duty not to work in mutagenic workplaces even before conception in order to avert harm to their yet-to-be-conceived children.

On the other hand, a growing number of commentators in law (Gallagher, 1989; Johnsen, 1987, 1989; "Legal Rights and Issues," 1986) and medicine (American College of Obstetrics & Gynecology, 1987) are arguing against forced intervention. George Annas (1986, 1987), among others, argued vehemently that enforcement would relegate women to the position of "fetal containers" and would elevate medical advice to the force of law. Others argued that the Constitution does not permit this degree of intrusion into decisions regarding childbearing and that permitting intervention "reinforces the tradition of disadvantaging women on the basis of their reproductive capacity" ("Creation of fetal rights," 1986; Dougherty, 1985, p. 116; Johnsen, 1986, 1989). More recently, some commentators also have made the practical observation that the threat of forced intervention may well deter some high-risk women from seeking prenatal care, a result that clearly could act only to the detriment of the unborn (Gallagher, 1989; Johnsen, 1989; Nelson & Milliken, 1990).

Another problem with forced intervention is that, in general, the law has been slow to impose liability upon one who fails to rescue, even when that individual previously caused the harm that befell the victim. This reluctance is especially great when the act of rescue presents a risk of harm to the rescuer. But one could argue that the general law of rescue is not applicable because usually it involves strangers. Perhaps we could obtain more guidance from the obligations toward children that the law is willing to impose upon parents. Even that is not too helpful because the state is loathe to intrude into the family to enforce such duties. For instance, child abuse statutes penalize only actions that cause serious harm to the child (Wis. Stat. Ann., 1990a). Even the concept of neglect embodies only a notion of parental expenditure of time and financial resources for the children's benefit (Wis. Stat. Ann., 1990b). There is no suggestion that parents can be required by law to undergo bodily invasion, such as by donating bone marrow to their children, however desirable morally it might be for them to do so. Yet this is precisely the type of intervention that many of the fetal therapy cases would impose upon pregnant women. Thus, there is a significant inconsistency between our society's views of the sanctity of the family as embodied in laws on child abuse and the approach taken by the proponents of forced fetal therapy.

Indeed, one can argue seriously that those who favor forced intervention are more concerned about unborn children than about the children among us and that, therefore, their real agenda is to control and punish women during pregnancy ("The fetal rights controversy," 1989). The last decade has seen major cutbacks in access to prenatal care that we know will benefit unborn children; moreover, drug-abusing pregnant women are excluded routinely from receiving care at the too few drug treatment centers currently available (Gallagher, 1989). In addition, almost every reported case of forced intrusion involves women who are relatively powerless in society— poor women, women addicted to drugs, women of color (Kolder, Gallagher, & Parsons, 1987).

To avoid this anomalous state of affairs and in recognition of the necessary intrusion of forced intervention, women should be free to make their own decisions regarding their behavior during pregnancy. The highest standard to which a pregnant woman ought to be held, if there is ever to be any intrusion on behalf of the fetus, is that applied to parents in the care of their children (Mathieu, 1985). If courts are ever to issue injunctions requiring women to act on behalf of their fetuses, they should do so only when the following conditions are met:

1. The injury to the fetus if the therapy is not undergone or the activity not foregone must be life or seriously health threatening.
2. The intervention, whether giving treatment or limiting activity, must be one of proven efficacy that will avert most or all of the harm that otherwise would befall the fetus. Halfway technologies will not suffice.
3. The intervention or forbearance of activities does not present a significant risk of harm to the woman.
4. In weighing the risks and benefits, differences in values and culture must be considered; these are not merely medical decisions.
5. The woman must have been given a realistic opportunity to avert the harm and failed to do so.
6. Society and others, such as employers, who seek to intervene must have also tried to eliminate potential sources of harm to the fetus, such as toxins in the workplace and lack of accessible prenatal care.
7. There are no less intrusive alternatives available.

Admittedly, these criteria are virtually impossible to fulfill, but they make clear that decisions made by women during pregnancy ought to be overridden, if ever, only in the most extraordinary circumstances. But as the cases and statutes discussed earlier clearly demonstrate, the recent trend has been away from protecting women from intervention by others and toward promoting the interest of the unborn child.

The New Reproductive Technologies

The final area in which debate about the status of the fetus and the rights of women has emerged is in the area of new reproductive technology. We already have had a small glimpse of this trend in the discussion of the propriety of doctors acting as moral gatekeepers in the allocation of AI, particularly in light of the widespread practice of discriminating against women who are poor or living in nontraditional relationships on the ground that they would not be good enough parents.

These issues, however, are raised much more clearly in the context of IVF. The moral and legal status of the fetus and embryo has been a concern since the earliest days of this technology due primarily to the fact that the embryo exists for at least a few days outside anyone's body (Hull, 1990; Lorber, 1988; Robertson, 1990). This extrauterine existence means that the embryo is not so obviously subject to a woman's right to control her own procreation. As a result, for example, Illinois enacted a law in the early 1980s that gave custody of embryos created by IVF to the physicians who performed the fertilization. This statute was challenged by fertility clinics who feared that they would be prosecuted if any of the embryos were destroyed and by prospective parents who argued that they could not receive IVF because of the deterrent effect of the statute (*Smith v. Hartigan*, 1983). The case was dismissed after prosecutors argued that they had no intention of bringing charges under the statute, and the law subsequently was repealed. A few states, however, have enacted laws requiring that all embryos created by IVF be implanted (La. Rev. Stat. Ann., 1990), apparently on the ground that each embryo had an independent right to life.

In no case, however, has the status of the embryo been presented more clearly and confused more completely than in the trial court's opinion in *Davis v. Davis* (1989). In that case, the couple had attempted IVF on several occasions. On the last round, nine embryos were created; two were unsuccessfully implanted and the remaining seven were frozen. The couple was not asked at that time what they wished to do with the frozen embryos in the event that anything happened. Before any further efforts at implantation could occur, the husband filed for divorce, in which the only substantial issue was the disposition of the frozen embryos. The wife, Mary

Sue Davis, wanted them herself, arguing that they were children and that she wanted to bear them. The husband, Junior Davis, did not want them to be implanted, arguing that they were property and that he did not want to become a father against his will. The trial court ruled in the first opinion to do so that life begins at conception. Holding (incorrectly as it later developed) that there was no countervening constitutional law or Tennessee public policy, the court then ruled that the embryos were morally and legally equivalent to children and that their best interest required that they be implanted in the wife.

Although the trial court's decision appeared to give Mary Sue Davis what she asked for, its effect was actually quite different. What she sought was the right to make her own decisions about procreation over the objections of her estranged husband. What the court did instead was to base its decision solely on the frozen embryos's status as "children" and their potential for life. Thus, the court, far from protecting her right to choose, transformed Ms. Davis into a "uterine hostess" (Atwood, 1986). Under the logic of his decision, were it to be followed, all embryos created by IVF would have to be implanted in the egg donor, even if this meant that Mary Sue Davis had to bear seven children, or in some other willing recipient, if one could be found. Such an effect could only chill the use of IVF. Moreover, holding that life begins at conception certainly brings into question all efforts by women to control their procreation and their behavior during pregnancy.

Fortunately, however, the trial court's ruling was overturned by the Tennessee Court of Appeals (*Davis v. Davis,* 1990). Looking first directly at the procreative liberty of the prospective parents and implicitly at the disagreement between Mary Sue and Junior Davis, the appellate court stated that the husband had a "constitutionally protected right not to beget a child where no pregnancy has taken place" (p. 4). In so ruling, the court realized that allowing the husband to have a voice in the disposition of frozen embryos is appropriate even though it is not acceptable to permit him to order or to veto the abortion of an ongoing pregnancy. More importantly, the court then reasoned that the interests of the prospective parents superseded those of the embryos, saying that because Tennessee law does not provide the full protection of the law even to viable fetuses, it certainly could not elevate the frozen embryos to a status above that of all the other parties.

This sampling of the range of judicial and legislative responses to IVF demonstrates tremendous tensions—between sperm and egg donors and between prospective parents and the ever more stridently asserted claims on behalf of fetuses and embryos and the children that they may become—tensions that arise in surrogacy and AI as well. This debate, to be sure, has the salutory effect of focusing our attention on what it means to have children and of making it clear that these are not decisions to be entered lightly. But until our society develops consistently greater regard for children, chilling these technologies particularly for the sake of the children who would be born by them, is not the answer.

CONCLUSION

The advances in medicine have had a dramatic effect on the lives of women. They help us increasingly to live and to bear children when we otherwise would not have been able to do so, and they help us to know the ways in which our actions and the actions of others affect the health of ourselves and our children. This power, however, is bought only at the cost of the technological imperative, at the suggestion that in some situations we ought to confer control of our bodies upon the state and upon physicians for the benefit of our continued bodily existence and of our children. We are confronted with arguments that the "doctor knows best" when it comes to medical therapy for ourselves and for our unborn children and to matters of procreation.

Two themes emerge from this overview of legal issues ranging from informed consent to procreation, fetal therapy, and new reproductive technologies. The first is that physicians traditionally have imposed a distinct set of values on patients in general and women in particular. This is evidenced in many ways, including by the deeply held beliefs that patients should have at best a minor role in health-care decisions and by the practice of helping only married persons to reproduce. The states have permitted and even encouraged physicians to act as moral gatekeepers. In feminist terms, the deference to physicians reflects and reproduces the male hierarchy. Moreover, this power, by being placed in the hands of physicians, has until now escaped much of the scrutiny that would have been brought to bear had these questions been raised in the political process. Thus, we must look carefully at the ways in which the medicine and the laws governing its practice affect women with the clear view that past practice has disadvantaged women.

The other major theme is that advances in medicine have brought the interests of the unborn more clearly into focus. There is great pressure to force women to act on behalf of their fetuses. We must recognize, however, that the state intrudes gingerly into parents' decisions about the health care of their already born children. Although we need to examine whether the state ought to do more to ensure the welfare of children, we must resist the temptation to intervene more deeply for the benefit of the unborn than we do for the children already among us. Otherwise we will recapitulate the inconsistency of our society's present stance toward defective newborns —

we spare no expense to save all but the most impaired, but once they "graduate" from the special care nursery, we limit the resources needed for their care and rehabilitation. For newborns with defects, society's view is "out of the nursery, out of mind." For the unborn, we seem to be moving toward a position that is doubly inconsistent—we protect children more before birth than after, and we enjoin women to act on behalf of their unborn at that same time that we withdraw the economic support that would enable women to seek adequate prenatal care and diet.

I do not base my suggestion that the state should hesitate to intrude upon women's bodies on behalf of the unborn on the notion that parents will do what is best for the child. They often may know what is best, but the epidemic of child abuse in this country attests to the fact that children are not always well served by their parents' actions. Even people who act out of religious beliefs may act to their children's physical detriment. Instead, I base my argument on the grounds that society must act consistently in its protection of children, both born and unborn, and that women's bodies and privacy ought not to be entered lightly.

In conclusion, women do have a moral duty to act on behalf of fetuses they intend to carry to term. For the rest, women must be free to use or reject medical technology. The state's intervention, far from attempting to limit women's choices against their will, should be addressed to providing women with the resources they need to act on behalf of themselves and their unborn children.

REFERENCES

In re A. C., 533 A.2d 611 (D.C. Ct. App. 1987), *vacated,* 573 A.2d 1235 (D.C. Ct. App. 1990) (en banc).

In re A. C., 573 A.2d 1235 (D.C. Ct. App. 1990) (en banc).

American College of Obstetrics & Gynecology (ACOG). (1987, October). *Patient choice: Maternal-fetal conflict.* (Ethics Committee Opinion No. 55).

Annas, G. J. (1986, December). Pregnant women as fetal containers. *Hastings Center Report, 16,* 13–14.

Annas, G. J. (1987). Protecting the liberty of pregnant patients. *New England Journal of Medicine, 316,* 1213–1215.

Annas, G. J., Glantz, L. H., & Mariner, W. K. (1990). The right of privacy protects the doctor–patient relationship. *Journal of the American Medical Association, 263,* 858–861.

In re Application of Jamica Hospital, 128 Misc.2d 1006, 491 N.Y.S.2d 898 (Sup. Ct. 1985).

Application of the President and Directors of Georgetown College, Inc., 331 F.2d 1000 (D.C. Cir.), *cert. denied,* 371 U.S. 978 (1964).

Ark. Stat. Ann. § 34-2614(B) (1) (1990).

Atwood, M. (1986). *The handmaid's tale.* New York: Fawcett Crest.

In re Baby X, 97 Mich. App. 111, 293 N.W.2d 736 (1980).

Becker v. Schwartz, 46 N.Y.2d 401, 386 N.E.2d 807, 413 N.Y.S.2d 895 (1978).

Binion, G. (1988). Reproductive freedom and the Constitution: The limits on choice. *Berkeley Women's Law Journal, 4,* 12–41.

Bowland v. Municipal Ct., 556 P.2d 1081, 135 Cal. Rptr. 630 (Cal. 1977) (en banc).

Buck v. Bell, 274 U.S. 200 (1927).

Cal. Health & Safety Code § 3380 (West 1990).

Canterbury v. Spence, 464 F.2d 772 (D.C. Clr.), cert. denied, 409 U.S. 1064 (1972).

Carey v. Population Servs. International, 431 U.S. 684 (1977).

Child Abuse During Pregnancy Prevention Act of 1989, S. 1444, 101st Cong., 1st Sess. (1989).

Choice in childbirth: Parents, lay midwives, and statutory regulation. (1986) St. Louis University Law Journal, 30, 985–1029.

City of Akron v. Akron Center for Reproductive Health, 462 U.S. 416 (1983).

Clayton, E. W. (1990). The legal status of the fetus: Reflections on the duties of pregnant women and of society. In R. Bellisario & G. J. Mizejewski (Eds.), Transplacental disorders: Perinatal detection, treatment, and management (including pediatric AIDS) (pp. 243–253). New York: Alan R. Liss.

Cobbs v. Grant, 8 Cal.3d 229, 501 P.2d 1, 104 Cal. Rptr. 505 (1972).

Colautti v. Franklin, 439 U.S. 379, 394 (1979).

The creation of fetal rights: Conflicts with women's constitutional rights to liberty, privacy, and equal protection. (1986) Yale Law Journal, 95, 599–625.

Custody of a Minor, 378 Mass. 712, 393 N.E.2d 379 (1979).

Dandridge v. Williams, 397 U.S. 471 (1970).

Davis v. Davis, 15 F.L.R. 2097 (Tenn. Cir. Ct. 1989), rev'd, No. 180 (Tenn. Ct. App., Sept. 13, 1990), cert. granted.

Davis v. Davis, No. 180 (Tenn. Ct. App., Sept. 13, 1990), cert. granted.

Dougherty, C. J. (1985). The right to begin life with sound body and mind: Fetal patients and conflicts with their mothers. University of Detroit Law Review, 63, 89–117.

Duncan, A. D. (1989). Fetal protection and the exclusion of women from the toxic workplace. North Carolina Central Law Journal, 18, 67–86.

In re Eberhardy, 102 Wis.2d 539, 307 N.W.2d 881 (1981).

EEOC Withholds Approval of Broad Fetal Protection Plans, 58 U.S.L.W. 2461 (1990).

Eisenstadt v. Baird, 405 U.S. 438 (1972).

Father and mother know best: Determining the liability of physicians for inadequate genetic counseling. (1978). Yale Law Journal, 87, 1488–1515.

Feinberg, J. (1985). Comment: Wrongful conception and the right not to be harmed. Harvard Journal of Law and Public Policy, 8, 57–77.

The fetal rights controversy: A resurfacing of sex discrimination in the guise of fetal protection. (1989). University of Missouri at Kansas City Law Review, 57, 261–288.

Ga. Code Ann. § 43-34-42(a) (1990).

Gallagher, J. (1989). Fetus as patient. In S. Cohen & N. Taub (Eds.), Reproductive laws for the 1990s (pp. 185–235). Clifton, NJ: Humana.

Goldberg, S. (1989). Medical choices during pregnancy: Whose decision is it anyway? Rutgers Law Review, 41, 591–623.

Griswold v. Connecticut, 381 U.S. 479 (1965).

Grodin v. Grodin, 102 Mich. App. 396, 301 N.W.2d 869 (1980).

Hayes v. Shelby Memorial Hospital, 726 F.2d 1543 (11th Cir. 1984).

Howard v. Lecher, 42 N.Y.2d 109, 366 N.E.2d 64, 397 N.Y.S. 363 (1977).

Hull, R. T. (Ed.). (1990). Ethical issues in the new reproductive technologies. Belmont, CA: Wadsworth.

Idaho Code § 39-5402 (1990a).

Idaho Code § 39-5404(1) (1990b).

Ill. Ann. Stat. ch. 111-1/2 § 22 (Smith-Hurd 1990).

Ind. Code Ann. § 16-14.91.1-10 (West 1990).

International Union, United Automobile, Aerospace and Agricultural Implement Workers of America v. Johnson Controls, Inc., 886 F.2d 871 (7th Cir. 1989) (en banc), cert. granted,

58 U.S.L.W. 3614 (1990).

Jefferson v. Griffin Spaulding County Hosp., 247 Ga. 86, 274 S.E.2d 457 (1981).

Jhordan C. v. Mary K., 179 Cal. App.3d 386, 224 Cal. Rptr. 530 (1986).

Johnsen, D. (1987, August). A new threat to pregnant women's autonomy. *Hastings Center Report, 17,*33–40.

Johnsen, D. (1989). From driving to drugs: Governmental regulation of pregnant women's lives after *Webster. University of Pennsylvania Law Review, 138,* 179–215.

Katz, J. (1984). *The silent world of doctor and patient.* New York: Free Press.

Keenan, M. R., & Hinds, J. (1990, January 21). Drugs in the womb: Punishing the mom prompts debate over maternal vs. fetal rights. *Nashville Tennessean,* p. E-3.

Kolder, V., Gallagher, J., & Parsons, M. T. (1987). Court-ordered obstetrical interventions. *New England Journal of Medicine, 316,* 1192–1196.

La. Rev. Stat. Ann. § 9:121–133 (West 1990).

Leavitt, J. W. (1986). *Brought to bed: Childbearing in America 1750–1950.* New York: Oxford University Press.

Leavitt, J. W. (1987). The growth of medical authority: Technology and morals in turn-of-the century obstetrics. *Medical Anthropology Quarterly, 1,* 230–255.

Legal rights and issues surrounding conception, pregnancy, and birth. [Special Project]. (1986). *Vanderbilt Law Review, 39,* 597–850.

Leggett v. Tennessee Board Nursing, 612 S.W.2d 476 (Tenn. Ct. App. 1980), *cert. denied, id.*

Leigh v. Board Regis. Nursing, 399 Mass. 558, 506 N.E.2d 91 (1987).

Lorber, J. (1988). In vitro fertilization and gender politics. In E. H. Baruch, A. F. D'Adamo, Jr., & C. J. Seager (Eds.), *Embryos, ethics, and women's rights: Exploring the new reproductive technologies* (pp. 117–133). New York: Harrington Park.

In re Madyun, Daily Wash. L. Rptr. 2233 (D.C. Super. Ct. July 26, 1986).

Maher v. Roe, 432 U.S. 468 (1977).

Maternal substance abuse: The need to provide legal protection for the fetus. (1987). *Southern California Law Review, 60,* 1209–1238.

Mathieu, D. (1985). Respecting liberty and preventing harm: Limits of state intervention in prenatal choice. *Harvard Journal of Law and Public Policy, 8,* 19–55.

Matter of A. W., 637 P.2d 366 (Colo. 1981).

Matter of Moe, 385 Mass. 555, 432 N.E. 2d 712 (1982).

McIntosh, K. E. (1989). Regulation of midwives as home birth attendants. *Boston College Law Review, 30,* 477–522.

Minn. Stat. Ann. § 626.5561 (West 1990).

Mother v. fetus — The case of "do or die": *In re* A.C. (1989). *Journal of Contemporary Health Law and Policy, 5,* 319–337.

Nelson v. Krusen, 678 S.W.2d 918 (Tex. 1984).

Nelson, L. J., & Milliken, N. (1990). Compelled medical treatment of pregnant women. In R. T. Hull (Ed.), *Ethical issues in the new reproductive technologies* (pp. 224–240). Belmont, CA: Wadsworth.

Nsiah-Jefferson, L. (1989). Reproductive laws, women of color, and low income women. In S. Cohen & N. Taub (Eds.), *Reproductive laws for the 1990s* (pp. 23–67). Clifton, NJ: Humana.

Oil, Chemical and Atomic Workers International Union v. American Cyanamid Co., 741 F.2d 444 (D.C.Cir. 1984).

Oloroso, A. (1987, March 13). California judge dismisses charges in fetal neglect case. *American Medical News* 12.

Ore. Rev. Stat. § 677.360 (1990a).

Ore. Rev. Stat. § 677.370(1) (1990b).

People v. Pointer, 151 Cal. App.3d 1128, 199 Cal. Rptr. 357 (1984).

People v. Privitera, 23 Cal. 3d 697, 591 P.2d 919, 153 Cal. Rptr. 431 (1979) (en banc).

Phillips v. United States, 566 F.Supp. 1 (D.C.S.C. 1981).

Planned Parenthood Association v. Ashcroft, 462 U.S. 476 (1983).

Planned Parenthood of Cent. Missouri v. Danforth, 428 U.S. 52 (1976).

Raleigh Fitkin-Paul Memorial Hospital v. Anderson, 42 N.J. 421, 210 A.2d 537 (per curiam), cert. denied, 377 U.S. 985 (1964).

Reilly v. Blue Cross & Blue Shield of Wisconsin, 846 F.2d 416 (7th Cir.), cert. denied, 109 S.Ct. 145 (1988).

Rhoden, N. K. (1986). Trimesters and technology: Revamping Roe v. Wade. Yale Law Journal, 95, 639-697.

Robertson, J. A. (1983). Procreative liberty and the control of conception, pregnancy, and childbirth. Virginia Law Review, 69, 405-464.

Robertson, J. A. (1988). Procreative liberty, embryos, and collaborative reproduction: A legal perspective. In E. H. Baruch, A. F. D'Adamo, Jr., & C. J. Seager (Eds.), Embryos, ethics, and women's rights: Exploring the new reproductive technologies (pp. 179-194). New York: Harrington Park.

Robertson, J. A. (1990). In the beginning: The legal status of early embryos. Virginia Law Review, 76, 437-517.

Robertson, J. A., & Schulman, J. D. (1987, August-September). Pregnancy and prenatal harm to offspring: The case of mothers with PKU. Hastings Center Report, 23, 23-24.

Roe v. Wade, 410 U.S. 113 (1973).

In re Ruiz, 27 Ohio Misc.2d 31, 500 N.E.2d 935 (1986).

Schloendorff v. Society of New York Hosp., 211 N.Y. 125, 105 N.E.2d 92 (1914).

Shaw, M. W. (1984). Conditional prospective rights of the fetus. Journal of Legal Medicine, 5, 63-116.

Skinner v. Oklahoma, 316 U.S. 535, 541 (1942).

In re Smith, 128 Misc.2d 976, 492 N.Y.S.2d 331 (Fam. Ct. 1985).

Smith v. Hartigan, 556 F.Supp. 157 (N.D.Ill. 1983).

Speck v. Finegold, 497 Pa. 77, 439 A.2d 110 (1981).

Stallman v. Youngquist, 125 Ill.2d 267, 531 N.E.2d 355 (1988).

State ex rel. Missouri State Board of Regis. v. Southworth, 704 S.W.2d 219 (Mo. 1986) (en banc).

In re Sterilization of Moore, 289 N.C. 95, 221 S.E.2d 307 (1976).

In re Steven S., 126 Cal. App.3d 23, 178 Cal. Rptr. 525 (1981).

Tenn. Code Ann. §§ 39-13-107 & 39-13-210 (1990).

Thornburgh v. American College of Obstetrics and Gynecology, 476 U.S. 747 (1986).

United States v. Rutherford, 442 U.S. 544 (1979).

Webster v. Reproductive Health Services, 109 S.Ct. 3040 (1989).

Wikler, D., & Wikler, N. (in press). Turkey baster babies: Artificial insemination, single women, and social policy. Milbank Memorial Fund Quarterly.

In re Winthrop University Hospital, 128 Misc.2d 804, 490 N.Y.S.2d 996 (Sup. Ct. 1985).

Wis. Stat. Ann. § 48.981, 940.201 (West 1990a).

Wis. Stat. Ann. § 48.981(1)(d) (West 1990b) (neglect).

Wis. Stat. Ann. § 51.20 (West 1990c).

Wolfson, C. (1986). Midwives and home birth: Social, medical, and legal perspectives. The Hastings Law Journal, 37, 909-976.

Zablocki v. Redhail, 434 U.S. 374 (1978).

Zepeda v. Zepeda, 41 Ill. App.2d 240, 190 N.E.2d 849 (1963), cert. denied, 379 U.S. 945 (1964).

Psychological Issues in New Reproductive Technologies: Pregnancy-Inducing Technology and Diagnostic Screening

Nancy E. Adler
Susan Keyes
Patricia Robertson
University of California, San Francisco

New reproductive technologies[1] provide women and couples[2] with more options during pregnancy than their parents could have imagined. These choices can provide more assurance of the birth of a healthy infant but entail psychological hazards that arise from the fact that use of these technologies involves considerable uncertainty. Although technological intervention may increase the chances of a favorable outcome, their effectiveness is not assured and adverse outcomes can occur. Decisions regarding whether or not to undergo a given procedure are likely to involve uncertainty, and potential conflicts of values and risks. Relatively little attention has been paid to the psychological issues associated with the new technologies, including how decisions to use them (or not) are made and how their application impacts psychological functioning and distress.

This chapter examines two new reproductive technologies that are posing difficult choices: technological induction of pregnancy and diagnostic genetic testing. Although these involve different experiences and pose different challenges to the woman, they present a number of common themes. One is the difficulty of assuring accurate perception of the probabilities of positive or negative outcomes. Second is the impact of how the technology is used and the role of the medical personnel. Third is the

---

[1]Portions of this chapter dealing with prenatal diagnostic screening are taken from Adler, Keyes, and Robertson (1990).

[2]Throughout the rest of the chapter, we discuss the implications of these technologies for the woman. Most studies have studied only the woman; those that have examined effects on the male partner are noted when available. For convenience we refer to "the woman" and "she," but realize that many of the same issues arise for the man.

stress caused by the necessity of waiting for results of the interventions. Fourth is how the meaning of the pregnancy for the woman affects her response. A final theme is the substantial individual variability in how women experience the technologies.

TECHNOLOGIES TO INDUCE PREGNANCY

Perhaps the most dramatic of the new technologies are those used to induce pregnancy. Thatcher and De Cherney, in chapter 3, describe the biological and medical implications of the new pregnancy-inducing technologies, particularly in vitro fertilization (IVF) and gamete intra-fallopian tube transfer (GIFT). Because GIFT is a relatively recent development, most of the research currently available involves IVF patients.

Decision to Attempt Pregnancy Induction and Expectations of Success

The existence of pregnancy-inducing technologies can create a dilemma for infertile women. The technologies provide hope for those who have tried other infertility treatments and have failed to conceive, but they offer a relatively low probability of success. In addition, they are costly and often not covered by medical insurance, making them financially inaccessible to many women. Because of these considerations, a woman may choose not to avail herself of the technology, but the decision may be painful. Reading and Kerin (1989) noted that the potential availability of the technology can undermine a woman's adjustment to her infertility: "In the past a patient might have felt that she had left no avenue unexplored, [but] that is no longer the case. It is now difficult to disclaim the possibility that one last try may be beneficial" (p. 865). The impact of the new reproductive technologies on women who do not or cannot avail themselves of it has not been examined empirically. Rather, research has focused on the psychological characteristics of women enrolling in IVF programs and on their psychological responses to treatment.

In considering how a woman may respond to IVF or GIFT, one must realize that she is likely to enter treatment in an already vulnerable emotional state. Women obtaining IVF have had an average of 6.4 years' experience of infertility, including at least 2 years of infertility evaluation and treatment (Greenfield & Haseltine, 1986). The experience of infertility is stressful itself and associated with feelings of diminished self-worth, isolation from others who have children, and loss of control (see Stanton & Dunkel-Schetter, in press). The pregnancy-inducing technologies offer new hope after what may have been years of frustration and women may not be realistic about their chances of actually having a baby through their application.

Women choosing to undergo IVF or GIFT are likely to overestimate the chances of success. Given the physical, financial, and emotional demands of treatment, potential users may need to bolster a decision to risk trying it. Despite the fact that the rates of pregnancy are around 20% for any given attempt and that the live birth rate is generally lower than 15% (see chapter 3), the clinical experience reported by Stewart and Glazer (1986) is that "almost every couple beginning IVF expects to achieve a successful pregnancy" (p. 104). Concern has been voiced about how the odds of success are presented to women. Reading and Kerin (1989) noted that rates can be expressed in various ways and cite a resolution passed by a congressional committee urging use of the "take home baby" rate as the standard to be given infertile couples considering pregnancy induction.

Several researchers have obtained subjective estimates of success from the procedure from women or couples waiting to enter IVF programs. These studies consistently find an overestimation of the chances of pregnancy (Callan & Hennessey, 1988; Daniels, 1990; Holmes & Tymstra, 1987; Reading & Kerin, 1989). In a study of patients at a clinic in the Netherlands at which 15% of attempts were successful, and 38% of women were successful in three attempts, women estimated a mean 51% success rate for themselves after three attempts. In addition, they overestimated the total number of "test-tube" babies that had been born in the Netherlands up to that time (Zoeten, Tymstra, & Alberda, 1987).

Individuals vary widely in their expectations of success. Among 66 couples awaiting IVF in a program in New Zealand, estimates of eventual success ranged from 10% to 80%. In a sample of British IVF patients studied by Johnston, Shaw, and Bird (1987), estimates of success given by patients ranged from less than 10% to over 90%.

Operation of the "availability" heuristic may contribute to overestimating the likelihood of success (Johnston et al., 1987). According to Tversky and Kahneman (1973), individuals' estimates of the likelihood that a given outcome will occur will be affected by the ease with which they can think of concrete examples of the instance. Vivid or concrete examples of a particular outcome will increase the perceived likelihood that the outcome will occur. With regard to IVF and GIFT, available images are generally of successful outcomes. News reports, particularly when IVF was first introduced, pictured successful couples (Johnston et al., 1987). Births of test-tube babies were reported on television and pictures appeared in newspapers. There were no comparable images of couples who failed to conceive using the technology. Because the number of women who have had

IVF or GIFT is still quite small, women are unlikely to have personal acquaintances who have undergone the procedure. Thus, their estimates are likely to be swayed by those impersonal but dramatic instances.

The staff of clinics may contribute unwittingly to overestimates of success. Greenfield and Haseltine (1986) observed pressures on IVF staff to be positive and upbeat about the chances of success: "Every success is documented by a picture of the baby on the wall of the office where patients are seen. Frequently pictures of the staff with white coats proudly holding a child are displayed" (p. 125). These pictures provide concrete instances of success. Again, there are no comparable pictures of women who have not been able to conceive. Women can visualize themselves more easily in a picture showing successful treatment than failed. Even though they may be given statistics showing that success is less likely to occur than failure, statistical figures may seem abstract compared to the concrete image of oneself holding a baby in a picture on the clinic wall.

Although there is no research documenting this in relation to pregnancy induction, other studies have shown that the way in which success and failure rates are presented or "framed" can influence subjective responses. When presented with a 15% or 20% success rate, women may develop a stronger subjective sense that they will succeed than if they are told that there is an 80% or 85% failure rate, even though the objective information is the same. Given a focus on success, it is likely that discussions with potential patients more often present success rates than failure rates. To offset other pressures toward overestimation of the chances of success, framing the likelihoods in terms of failure rates may be preferable.

In addition to overestimating the chances of success, women also appear to underestimate how negatively they will respond to failed treatment. Mahlstedt, MacDuff, and Bernstein (1987) found that 56% of women intended to repeat treatment if the initial attempt at IVF failed. However, following a failed treatment only 37% actually attempted a subsequent treatment cycle.

Psychological Responses to Treatment

Psychological responses to pregnancy-inducing technologies involve both responses to treatment and to its outcome, particularly failed treatment. However, even successful treatment can create later difficulties; because the technology involves implantation of several embryos, it is not uncommon for women to have a multiple pregnancy, with all the complications that are associated with such pregnancies.

Patients report IVF treatment to be extremely stressful (Freeman et al., 1987). Women frequently refer to the emotional "roller coaster" they experience during the treatment cycle (Stewart & Glazer, 1986). In several descriptive studies in which women were asked to identify the most stressful aspects of the procedure, the waiting time between embryo transfer and confirmation (or disconfirmation) of pregnancy 2 weeks later was mentioned most commonly (Milne, 1987; Stewart & Glazer, 1986). Also frequently mentioned was the sense of loss of control during IVF (Campbell, Dunkel-Schetter, & Peplau, in press).

Although the procedures involved in IVF are inherently stressful, their impact on the woman may be affected strongly by the way it is handled by the medical personnel. Milne (1987) asked 28 couples who had completed at least one treatment cycle at an IVF clinic in Canada to identify both positive and negative aspects of their experience. The most commonly cited positive and negative aspects both concerned interactions with health-care personnel. Interactions with specific providers who were part of the IVF team were reported to be helpful and supportive by over half the 28 couples interviewed. At the same time, a similar percentage identified the routinization and impersonality of treatment as the most negative aspect. Among 94 IVF patients' studies by Mahlstedt et al. (1987), the insensitivity of members of the IVF team to their emotional vulnerability was cited as one of the stresses of their experience.

The most negative responses are likely to be found following failed treatment. Research following up on failed treatment is difficult to do. Women who have had unsuccessful treatment may or may not have resolved their feelings about their infertility or the unsuccessful IVF treatment and may be unwilling to participate in research focusing on IVF. Rates of attrition in studies of IVF patients who have been treated unsuccessfully tend to be high. For example, Mahlstedt et al. (1987) distributed 246 questionnaires to patients entering three IVF programs. Patients were requested to return the forms by mail at the end of the treatment cycle or when they knew of their pregnancy status. Of the 246 questionnaires distributed, only 94 were returned. In contrast, all 49 women who had conceived successfully through IVF or GIFT and who were recruited for a research study by Reading, Chang, and Kerin (1989) agreed to participate. Although the rates of participation may be due in part to differences in recruitment procedures, the high attrition in the Mahlstedt et al. (1987) study seems likely to reflect negative feelings about the experience and/or a desire to go on with one's life without reflecting on the IVF experience. Negative feelings about IVF may thus be underestimated in follow-up studies of patients who have experienced an unsuccessful IVF attempt.

Responses to IVF treatment and its failure are linked to the psychological vulnerabilities of the woman, her feelings regarding childbearing and infertility, and her prior experience of infertility. Several studies have examined the psychological characteristics of women undergoing IVF. In general, these studies have shown the women to be within normal bounds on measures of psychological functioning. For example, Freeman et al. (1987) examined anxiety, depression, self-esteem, and marital adjustment among women who had enrolled in an IVF program, comparing 82 women who had been unsuccessfully treated by IVF, 37 who had withdrawn from the program without receiving treatment, and 37 who had conceived after IVF. On all measures the mean scores for women in all three groups were in the normal range, although women who had experienced unsuccessful treatment scored higher on depression than did either of the other two groups. Fagen et al. (1986) conducted a psychological assessment of both members of 45 couples enrolling in an IVF program. Of the total sample, 14.4% were given a psychiatric diagnosis apart from a diagnosis involving psychosexual dysfunction. In addition, 15.5% had a psychosexual dysfunction. These figures are not significantly higher than estimates in the general population.

A few studies, however, have reported higher rates of psychopathology among IVF patients than would be expected on a population basis, particularly among individuals who have had unsuccessful treatment. Baram et al. (1988) found a depressive reaction in 66% of the women and 49% of the men after unsuccessful treatment with IVF. Garner, Arnold, and Gray (1984) reported that 38% of women studied experienced a mood disturbance prior to undergoing IVF and that this increased significantly to 64% after an unsuccessful attempt; comparable figures among the men were 26% prior to IVF and 46% after unsuccessful treatment. In a study of 38 women receiving IVF treatment or waiting for treatment, Campbell et al. (in press) found depression scores on the Center for Epidemiologic Studies Depression Scale (CES-D) to be higher than those obtained in community samples, but lower than normative scores for psychiatric patients.

There are not enough well-designed studies with adequate sample sizes to provide conclusive evidence regarding the psychological effects of IVF. Studies have been based on small numbers who represent a self-selected subsample of the broader population of women who experience IVF and have not included long-term follow-up. However, some trends have appeared with sufficient consistency across studies that one may place some faith in them. In general, patients coming into treatment for infertility do not appear to be unusually maladjusted. They are likely to be experiencing emotional distress, but within normal (i.e., nonpathological) limits. Hearn, Yuzpe, Brown, and Casper (1987) studied 300 couples admitted to an IVF program and found low levels of psychopathology. They noted that most couples entering IVF programs will have normal personality functioning. Thus, rather than focus on psychopathology, these authors suggested that it will be most useful to concentrate on personality styles and efforts made at coping with the stresses involved.

Although psychopathology may not be common, women are experience emotional distress. Even though functioning within normal ranges on standard measures of psychopathology, women may desire psychological intervention (Daniluk, 1988). They may not require psychotherapy; however, they may benefit from an opportunity to discuss their fears, anxieties, and frustrations with a knowledgeable and supportive person.

As IVF and GIFT become more routine, some negative emotional effects may increase. Women may no longer feel like "special" patients who have access to the latest technology. Patients studied by Milne (1987) reported that they felt privileged to be among a small group who could use the technology. Thus, even if it failed, they may have had some residual pride in having tried the best and latest technology. They also may have been given special attention because of the newness of the technology. As care is routinized, women may receive less individualized care and, as a result, may respond more strongly to the stressful aspects of the procedures.

PRENATAL DIAGNOSTIC SCREENING

Prenatal diagnosis constitutes a cluster of procedures, all of which are designed to detect problems with the developing fetus. Diagnostic procedures differ on a number of dimensions, including timing during pregnancy, invasiveness, risk, and thoroughness and accuracy of the results. Among the less invasive procedures are ultrasound scanning, which provides visual evidence of structural defects, and alpha fetal protein (AFP) testing of the maternal serum, which can screen for neural tube defects and some chromosomal abnormalities. Amniocentesis and chorionic villus sampling (CVS) are more invasive than ultrasound and AFP but provide more information.

The availability of prenatal diagnosis raises complex questions for pregnant women. Stresses can arise either from the procedure itself or from the information the test reveals about the fetus. Women must decide if they wish to have a diagnostic procedure performed and, if so, which one. Beyond this, if they receive abnormal results, they must decide what to do. Because of their potentially greater impact on women, in this chapter we discuss amniocentesis and CVS.

Amniocentesis

Amniocentesis generally is performed at around 16 weeks of gestation, although the possibility of using it earlier in pregnancy (around 13 to 14 weeks) is being studied. The procedure involves the withdrawal of approximately 2 tbsp. of the amniotic fluid surrounding the fetus through a needle inserted through the maternal abdomen and into the uterus. Frequently this procedure is done with the guidance of a simultaneous ultrasound to direct the correct placement of the needle.

Decision to Undergo Amniocentesis.   Amniocentesis is an elective procedure for which the most common indication is advanced maternal age. At 35 years of age, the risks for chromosomal abnormalities (including Down's syndrome) reach .56%, exceeding the risk of miscarriage from the procedure, which is about .5%. Before 35 years of age, there is still a risk of chromosomal abnormalities, but in the absence of other risk factors it is less than the risk of complications from the procedure. The threshold for recommending amniocentesis on a population basis is age 35 years in the United States; in other countries it is sometimes higher. Women also will be referred for amniocentesis on the basis of a family history of genetic diseases (e.g., hemophilia and sickle cell anemia) or an individual history of previously having an affected child.

The extent to which women who are eligible for diagnostic testing use the technology has increased over time, but utilization rates vary by area (Baird, Sadovnick, & McGillivray, 1985; Hook & Schreinemachers, 1983). Statistics from urban areas in Sweden indicate that amniocentesis and/or CVS are widely accepted, with only about 15% of all women over age 37 years declining prenatal diagnosis (Sjögren & Uddenberg, 1988). Earlier studies in the United States found lower rates of utilization. A survey in the state of Georgia (Sokal, Byrd, Chen, Goldberg, & Oakley, 1980) reported usage rates that varied by region and ranged from 9% to 35% of all women over 40 years of age. Usage rates from a national U.S. sample (Adams et al., 1981) ranged from 6% to 28% depending on the region sampled. Both studies found that amniocentesis use was lowest among rural and/or minority women. In a somewhat later study, Hook and Schreinemachers (1983) reported that, in New York state, 35.3% of women over age 35 years were utilizing amniocentesis.

Rates of utilization do not necessarily reflect objective risk status. For example, Adams et al. (1981) found only a one-fold increase in usage of amniocentesis for women 40 years of age and older compared to those under 40 years of age, despite the fact that those over age 40 years have a five-fold risk for bearing genetically impaired fetuses. As amniocentesis has become safer and more routine, utilization has increased. Hunter, Thompson, and Speevak (1987) found steadily increasing use of amniocentesis in eastern Ontario, Canada since 1975. Less than 2% of women over age 35 years had amniocentesis up through 1975 at which point utilization increased every year, reaching just over 50% in 1985. Rates reported earlier from the United States are also likely to have increased but probably do not approach the rates from Scandinavia (Mikkelsen, Fischer, Hansen, Pilga-ard, & Nielsen, 1983; Sjogren & Uddenberg, 1988).

A number of factors may influence the likelihood that a woman over 35 years of age will undergo amniocentesis. Some arise from structural barriers in the health system. For example, in Sweden nearly all pregnant women attend state-run antenatal clinics, and in some areas prenatal diagnosis is routinely discussed and offered to at-risk groups (Sjogren & Uddenberg, 1988). In the United States, where utilization rates appear to be lower, poor women have more limited access to prenatal care and there may be practical and financial barriers to the use of amniocentesis.

Even when amniocentesis is available, some women choose not to use it. Although population statistics indicate that benefits outweigh risks at age 35 years, an individual's evaluation of benefits and risks may differ. In data from Canada from 1983 to 1985, Hunter et al. (1987) estimated that 70% of pregnant women over age 35 years in the relevant catchment area had contact with the centralized clinic. Of these women, almost 20% either refused counseling or declined to have the procedure after having been counseled.

On the benefit side, women may place quite different values on the knowledge gained from amniocentesis (see chapter 9). A study by Elkins, Stovall, Wilroy, and Dacus (1986) demonstrated this variability. The researchers followed 100 women who had had a prior Down's syndrome child. Of these women, 40 became pregnant again and had the option of receiving genetic counseling. Of the 40, half decided to have the procedure. Of the 20 women who declined amniocentesis, 14 said that they would not abort their pregnancy under any circumstance and saw no reason to have the test. The remaining 6 indicated that they feared the risks to the fetus posed by the procedure more than they feared the risks of having another Down's child. Of the 20 who did have the procedure, half indicated that they would terminate if the results were positive, and the other half reported that they had the procedure to prepare for the arrival of a Down's syndrome baby if so diagnosed.

Women who view genetic defects more negatively are more likely to undergo amniocentesis than are those who are less distressed by the possibility of having an affected child. In a sample of 202 American women accepting and 50 women rejecting amniocentesis after genetic counseling, Ekwo, Kim, and Gosselink (1987) found that women who accepted amniocentesis were more likely to feel they would be unable to cope with the consequences of a child with a genetic defect, especially one leading to prolonged illness or mental retardation, than were women who rejected the procedure.

Just as women vary in their evaluation of the benefits of amniocentesis, they differ in their estimation of the risks involved. Among women who gave a reason for declining amniocentesis in the Canadian sample studied by Hunter et al. (1987), the most frequent reason was concern about the risks of the procedure. Marteau et al. (1989) found that English women accepting amniocentesis were less concerned about the possibility of a miscarriage and less adverse to the idea of pregnancy termination than were women who elected not to have amniocentesis.

In contrast to women undergoing IVF who overestimate the chances of success, women undergoing amniocentesis appear to overestimate failure, both in terms of perceived probabilities of a complication with the procedure and the chances that the test will reveal a problem with the fetus (Adler, Keyes, Kegeles, & Golbus, 1990). The "availability heuristic" (Tversky & Kahneman, 1973), which appears to increase optimism about the success of IVF and GIFT, may heighten concern about risks of amniocentesis. Women referred for amniocentesis for advanced maternal age are likely to have friends who have had the procedure. The dramatic instances are not of routine procedures that yield negative results, but of procedures involving complications such as the need for multiple taps or a subsequent miscarriage. The concrete instance of a friend or acquaintance who experienced a problem with amniocentesis will color a woman's judgment of the population odds, even though the experience of one other person has no real implications for the woman herself. Similarly, discussion of the procedure will tend to be framed in terms of the risks. Although the percentages are small, the discussion of a 1% risk may make the potential seem greater to the woman than would discussion of a 99% chance of no complications.

The Experience of Amniocentesis.   Descriptive studies of women's reactions to amniocentesis generally have found that retrospectively it is viewed positively. The vast majority of women indicate they would have an amniocentesis for a subsequent pregnancy (Chervin, Farnsworth, Freedman, Duncan, & Shapiro, 1977; Finley, Varner, Vinson, & Finley, 1977). This does not imply an absence of stress, however. Women have expressed concerns over specific aspects of the procedure, such as worry over the results, the possibility that a decision might need to be made about terminating or continuing the pregnancy, and possible risks inherent in the procedure such as injury to the fetus, increased possibility of miscarriage, and so forth. In some studies 30% to 50% of women expressed concern about pain during the procedure. Typically 2 to 4 weeks are required before results of the tests are known and, as with IVF, the most consistent distress was voiced about the need to wait for results (see Chervin et al., 1977; Dixson et al., 1981; Evers-Kiebooms, Swerts, & Van Den Berghe, 1988; Finley et al., 1977).

The indication for genetic testing is likely to affect a woman's reaction to undergoing amniocentesis. Women who know they are at higher risk are apt to be more anxious about the procedure. Beeson and Golbus (1979) examined ratings of anxiety by both members of couples in which the wife was undergoing amniocentesis, comparing those couples who had a previous child affected by a chromosomal abnormality with those who did not have such a history. For both sets of couples there were two peaks of anxiety: one before the procedure and another just prior to receiving the results. However, couples with a previously affected child showed more anxiety at both of these times, reaching statistical significance only at the first peak.[3] Evers-Kiebooms et al. (1988) also reported higher anxiety levels for women in Belgium referred for amniocentesis because they had a previous child with Down's syndrome or a neural tube defect as compared with women referred because of maternal age. Women with a prior Down's syndrome child were more likely to report anxiety about waiting for test results, and women with a prior child with a neural tube defect were less likely to be reassured by the test results.

Although the anticipation of amniocentesis and its results may increase anxiety, receipt of results indicating no abnormalities should, and apparently does, reduce anxiety. A decline in anxiety levels following amniocentesis was reported by Fava et al. (1982) in an Italian sample. When compared with a group of normal pregnant women roughly matched for socioeconomic status (SES) and gestational age but not having amniocentesis, the amniocentesis group expressed significantly more hostility and less well-being than did the control group prior to the amniocentesis (at 8 to 12 weeks gestation). For both groups there was a significant decline in negative mood state over the course of pregnancy, with no significant differences between the two groups in mood scores by 20 to 22 weeks.

Phipps and Zinn (1986) obtained similar results with an American sample of 40 women referred for amniocentesis because of maternal age and a control group of 32 pregnant women not receiving amniocentesis but matched according to all significant demographic variables except age. Both groups showed significant variation in moods over the course of pregnancy, with amniocentesis subjects showing a marked improvement after receiving test results in comparison to controls assessed at the same time. And in a small British sample of women over 38 years of age, Marteau et al. (1989) found that women who had undergone amniocentesis were somewhat less anxious at 28 weeks gestation and significantly less anxious at 38 weeks than those who had declined amniocentesis. There are few studies examining anxiety levels of women who are at high risk of genetic defect (i.e., because of family history, prior affected child, or extremely advanced maternal age)

---

[3]Although the pattern was similar for the pregnant woman and her partner, women's anxiety levels were higher than those of men at the first peak just prior to the procedure.

but who decline amniocentesis, probably because of the difficulty of obtaining enough subjects. It is likely, however, that these women will be more anxious later in pregnancy than those women who have received reassuring results from the amniocentesis.

Although most women will obtain and be relieved by receipt of negative results from the amniocentesis, others may have residual concerns and continue to worry (Evers-Kiebooms et al., 1988).[4] Dixson et al. (1981) followed women who received genetic counseling and then either had an amniocentesis or declined. Even after the results of the amniocentesis were known, just over 20% of each group reported continued concern over possible congenital abnormalities. Similarly, in a Scandinavian sample, Tedgård, Ljung, McNeil, Tedgård, and Schwartz (1989) found that over 33% of women carriers of hemophilia continued to have significant concerns up until the time of delivery, despite obtaining negative results from an amniocentesis and a blood screening.

There is substantial individual variation in response to amniocentesis. Tedgård et al. (1989) found that half of the sample of women carriers of hemophilia reported the prenatal diagnosis procedures to be extremely distressing. The other half reported no, slight, or moderate distress and few symptoms. Evers-Kiebooms et al. (1988) reported from Belgium that women referred for amniocentesis for advanced maternal age versus for prior genetic or neural tube defects showed as much variability in response within groups as between groups.

Our own research of primigravidas referred for advanced maternal age also suggests that individual differences contribute in important ways to how amniocentesis is experienced. Prior to counseling, women participating in the study reported their feelings about anxiety in general and about specific aspects of the procedure via a series of visual analog scales running from zero (no anxiety), to 100 (extreme anxiety). Responses spanned the entire range, with some women indicating a response of "0" and others "100." Not surprisingly, women's reports of their anxiety correlated with their estimates of the likelihood they would experience complications due to the procedure and that they would obtain results indicating a problem with the fetus. A woman's past obstetrical history also related to her estimates; women who had experienced one or more previous miscarriages estimated higher probabilities for adverse outcomes than those who had not. These results parallel findings of others (Beeson & Golbus, 1979; Evers-Kiebooms et al., 1988) showing an association between risk status and reactions to amniocentesis. In the study by Beeson and Golbus, which included multiparous women, having had one or more healthy children appeared to buffer

---

[4]The actual results are unlikely to be in error; the test itself does not yield false negatives. There could be errors in the laboratory, but these instances are extremely rare.

against anxiety about the procedure. A history of previous miscarriage, spotting, and/or a previously affected child were all found to exacerbate anxiety.

As with pregnancy-inducing technologies, the experience of undergoing amniocentesis is partly a function of how the technology is handled. Some physicians are more experienced and adept than others. Mishaps also can occur. Rothman (1986) interviewed a number of women about their experiences with amniocentesis. One woman reported:

> They said a doctor was doing it — she was a doctor, but an intern. She did the test twice, and on the second try she said "Ooops — I hit something," and still didn't get any fluid. At that point I had to wait for another doctor for two to three hours, and have a third test done. One or two wouldn't have been so bad, but three was pretty hard. (p. 91)

Even in the uneventful procedure, the woman may be fearful about the potential of harm. Rothman (1986) reported on the attempt of one woman to use humor to deal with the emotional tension, only to have it denied:

> Amniocentesis itself is a very *creepy* procedure. The two specialists I had do it at the University of _____ were intensely serious, dour, and clinical. To break the tension (I was very nervous), as the doc was drawing up what seemed like a *huge* amount of amniotic fluid, I said, "Hey don't drain my kid's swimming pool!" Nothing, silence, no response. An empathic woman's presence would have been helpful. (p. 92)

Just as the availability of pregnancy-inducing technology may complicate a woman's adjustment to infertility, the existence of prenatal diagnostic tests potentially could complicate adjustment to pregnancy. Several investigators have suggested that there is a suspension of commitment to the pregnancy by women undergoing amniocentesis until the results are known (Spencer & Cox, 1988), making it a "tentative pregnancy" (Rothman, 1986). Beeson and Golbus (1979) observed a suspension of commitment among amniocentesis patients reflected both in social spheres — including not telling others about the pregnancy — and in personal domains — such as avoiding thinking about the pregnancy and, in extreme cases, having difficulty in gaining weight, taking vitamins, or quitting smoking. Similarly, Rothman noted a greater frequency of women not feeling movement until after the 18th week of pregnancy among women undergoing amniocentesis versus those who were not having the procedure. However, Dixson et al. (1981) reported contradictory findings from retrospective interviews with 53 women who had elected to have an amniocentesis and 22 women counseled about amniocentesis but declining the procedure. No significant differences between the two groups were found in timing of selecting names for the fetus/baby, or in timing or willingness to talk about the pregnancy outside of the immediate family, although this finding may reflect the small numbers and retrospective design.

Taken as a whole, studies of the impact of amniocentesis suggest that anticipation of the procedure and of the results of the tests can cause some disruptions in adjustment during the course of pregnancy. These disruptions include increased anxiety in general and about the pregnancy in particular, and some hesitancy in investing one's emotions fully in the pregnancy until results of diagnostic tests are known. The long-term consequences of these disruptions have not been determined. Once the results of diagnostic tests are known, anxiety levels generally return to normal. Although some women will experience residual anxiety, others will show more positive responses than if they had not received reassurance from the test results. Similarly, whereas women may suspend full commitment to the pregnancy prior to receipt of the results, this simply may delay the onset of "attachment" behaviors but not decrease them by the third trimester. For example, Phipps and Zinn (1986) found that amniocentesis patients in a U.S. sample showed a greater increase in fetal attachment over the course of pregnancy than did nonamniocentesis controls. However, if suspension of commitment to the pregnancy involves decreased compliance with suggested regimens (e.g., nutrition, substance use), even a delay in commitment could have adverse longer term effects. Better prospective research is needed to determine both short- and long-term effects of women's responses to the experience of amniocentesis.

Chorionic Villus Sampling (CVS)

Researchers have been developing procedures for diagnostic genetic testing earlier in pregnancy, both to diminish the distress associated with waiting until the second trimester to obtain results and to reduce the complications of second-trimester abortion if results are positive and the woman chooses to terminate. Chorionic villi sampling (CVS), which can be done as early as the 9th week of pregnancy, involves the aspiration of a small sample of tissue from the placenta, either through a catheter inserted into the cervix (transvaginally), or through a needle inserted through the abdomen. Both the transvaginal and transabdominal approaches are guided by simultaneous ultrasound. A recent multicenter collaborative study of CVS concluded that it was safe and effective, but in comparison to amniocentesis does carry a somewhat higher risk both of procedure failure and of subsequent fetal loss. The excess risk of loss of normal fetuses following CVS versus amniocentesis was estimated to be .8% (Rhoads et al., 1989). Rhoads et al. also reported that rates of procedure failure and of fetal loss varied widely from one center to another. This variability may make it difficult to inform individual women accurately of the relative risks unless each center provides its own statistics.

Because of the recency of CVS, the major focus of research has concerned its efficacy and safety (Gustavii, 1984; Kelrse, Kahal, & Gravenhorst, 1985; Ledbetter et al., 1990; Rhoads et al., 1989; Wyatt, 1985). Some studies have looked at factors affecting the acceptability of CVS and the choice of CVS versus amniocentesis (Lippman, Perry, Mandel, & Cartier, 1985; Perry, Vekemans, Lippman, Hamilton, & Fournier, 1985). Lippman and colleagues studied attitudes of women eligible for amniocentesis because of advanced maternal age. Following counseling, but prior to the procedure, women read a description of CVS and amniocentesis in five categories: comfort of the procedure, gestational age at which the procedure is performed, length of time required for results, risk of fetal loss, and method of termination should that be required/desired. Relevant aspects of each procedure were described side by side, and a graph and table were provided so that each woman could determine her own age-specific risk for bearing a Down's syndrome child. After reading these materials, women indicated which procedure they would prefer—first on the basis of each category considered independently, and then considering all categories together. Preferences also were obtained for a series of hypothetical situations where risk of fetal loss after CVS was varied from less than 1% to more than 10%.

Women in the Lippman et al. (1985) study identified timing of the procedure, time to results, risk of miscarriage, and termination method as key aspects, with from 74% to 85% of the sample noting these as important. When each category was considered in isolation, CVS was preferred in terms of timing of the procedure, length of time to obtain results, and termination method; amniocentesis was favored on the basis of risk factors. About a quarter of the women considered comfort of the procedure to be important and equal numbers preferred each procedure on the basis of comfort alone. When preferences were based on all categories, 45% of the sample preferred CVS, 50% preferred amniocentesis, and 5% stated no preference. When these overall preferences then were related to priorities of concern about the procedure, logical patterns emerged. For women who stated that the timing of the procedure was the most critical factor in making a decision, 92% preferred CVS. For women who stated that the risk of miscarriage was the most important factor, 94% preferred amniocentesis. In response to the hypothetical cases regarding risk levels, a strong preference for CVS was evidenced when risk was set at a level comparable to that of amniocentesis. If risk of miscarriage was 5% higher for CVS than for amniocentesis, however, amniocentesis was overwhelmingly the procedure of choice.

These data suggest that concerns over prenatal diagnosis revolve around consistent issues, with risk being most salient. However, individuals vary in how they evaluate and weigh different aspects of the procedure. This variability may account for variations in conflict over decisions about which prenatal diagnosis procedure to use, and in how the procedures are experienced. These data also underscore the need for good information on risks to help women make informed decisions. The fact that risk varies by clinic makes it difficult to adopt a uniform statement on risk; women need to be informed about the risks for the clinic at which they would receive treatment.

Recent studies have examined psychological reactions to CVS versus amniocentesis. Some of these studies must be evaluated with care, however. A few clinical trials of the efficacy and risks of CVS have used random assignment.[5] Women preferring amniocentesis are unlikely to have volunteered, because they could receive an amniocentesis without participating in the research and they risked not getting their preferred treatment. In contrast, because CVS was considered experimental and was difficult to obtain apart from participating in a clinical trial, women preferring CVS are more likely to have volunteered. Thus, participants in the randomized clinical trials were more likely to be women with a clear preference for CVS or with no preference. This does not pose serious problems in evaluating physical effects of the two procedures, but is problematic for evaluating psychological responses. Women undergoing CVS received a procedure they wanted whereas those undergoing amniocentesis received a procedure they probably did not want.

Spencer and Cox (1987, 1988) studied 61 women at four times during their pregnancy. The women were assigned randomly to either CVS ($n =$ 29) or amniocentesis ($n = 32$). Women in the CVS group showed significant reductions in anxiety up to 10 weeks earlier than did the amniocentesis group, who did not show reductions in anxiety until after they obtained their results. Similar findings were reported by Robinson et al. (1988). Women in the CVS group in the studies by Spencer and Cox also reported greater attachment during the second trimester than women receiving amniocentesis, and reported less procedure-related discomfort. Regardless of which procedure they had, all women in the study who considered future pregnancies indicated that CVS would be their procedure of choice (as it may have been at the outset of the study when they volunteered for the clinical trial).

Effects of Complications.   As noted earlier, the vast majority of women having either amniocentesis or CVS will experience no complications with

---

[5]In the large collaborative study of CVS, random assignment had to be dropped because of the difficulty of recruiting subjects who were willing to accept random assignment.

the procedure and will receive negative findings. Although there may be temporary elevations of anxiety and negative mood, these appear to revert to normal levels once results are known and may even contribute to lowered anxiety and worry in the third trimester. However, the situation is quite different for the small percentage of women who experience fetal loss following the procedure or receive results indicating a problem with the fetus, many of whom will terminate the pregnancy.

The most difficult situation faced by a woman is likely to be an uncertain diagnosis. The diagnostic tests may reveal an abnormality for which the implications are unclear. For some types of genetic abnormalities the prognosis is not known. Because of the recency of the diagnostic tests, there is not a sufficient history with some indicators to be able to inform the woman what the chances are that her infant will be born with or develop significant problems. The difficulty of deciding to continue or terminate the pregnancy may be exacerbated by doubts the woman will have about either option. The pain of a decision to terminate is likely to be increased by worry that the child would not have been affected seriously. Women who choose to continue the pregnancy are likely to have heightened anxiety throughout the remainder of pregnancy about the viability and health of the fetus. This concern may carry over to the early years of development. There are no studies of women who have faced this dilemma, and given the small numbers of women who experience this at any given center, such research will be difficult but important to do.

The literature on psychological responses following elective induced abortion has shown that the experience can be stressful, but does not create hazards for women's mental health (Adler et al., 1990). There is a more limited literature on responses to miscarriage, with no large-scale empirical studies. In comparison to general samples of women undergoing abortion, those who terminate following prenatal genetic testing may be at relatively greater risk of negative responses. First, they are terminating wanted pregnancies. Second, women terminating following amniocentesis will undergo a second trimester procedure, which has been associated with more negative psychological responses (Adler et al., 1990). In the few studies of women who terminated pregnancies on the basis of genetic indication (e.g., Blumberg, Golbus, & Hanson, 1975; Jones et al., 1984), psychological responses appear to be more negative than those shown by women drawn from the general population of abortion clinics.

The collaborative study of CVS and amniocentesis provides the most detailed research to date of responses to fetal loss. One hundred and twenty-one women from the study who either miscarried or terminated based on results of the procedure were assessed 1 or 2 months after the pregnancy loss and again 6 months after the loss (Black, 1989). As with studies of women following unsuccessful IVF treatment, subject attrition in this study was fairly high, around 40%. Failure to participate could reflect a number of factors, including negative feelings about the procedure and its aftermath. The largest attrition (48%) was shown by women who miscarried after CVS, and the authors noted anecdotal reports that some women did not want further contact with the CVS project after the loss because of their anger at the CVS personnel.

Compared to pregnant subjects in the study, those who had suffered a pregnancy loss showed more distress 1 to 2 months after the loss on several scales of the Profile of Mood Scale, including depression/dejection, anger/hostility, confusion/bewilderment, and total mood. Six months after the loss, they still scored significantly higher on the first two scales. There were large individual differences in responses, which were not explained by sociodemographic variables or pregnancy variables other than length of gestation at the time of loss; the greater the length of gestation the greater the mood disturbance 6 months following the loss. These findings underline the utility of performing diagnostic tests earlier in pregnancy because responses to termination will be more negative later in pregnancy.

CONCLUSION

The new reproductive technologies provide substantial benefits but also pose emotional challenges. In the case of IVF, the treatment itself can be difficult, particularly in face of substantial uncertainty about its ultimate success. For the majority of women who will not succeed, there may be a sense of failure and loss. The procedures involved in prenatal diagnostic screening, though potentially anxiety provoking, are more circumscribed; the more challenging aspect is the potential that it may lead to miscarriage or yield information regarding a problem with the fetus.

Although these experiences can be stressful, women generally appear to cope with them effectively. There is little evidence, even with adverse outcomes, that significant psychopathology results. Rather, the more common response appears to be increased negative emotion and distress within normal bounds. Such responses deserve attention and often can be ameliorated through psychological intervention. In her study of women who suffered fetal loss, Black (1989) found that women who had more support from other people who were important to her suffered less mood disturbance than those with less support. Attention from the health-care team may be of particular value for women who lack support from their own network of friends or family.

The research reported here may somewhat underestimate negative responses. Studies generally are conducted by researchers who are associated with the institutions in which care is provided. Women who feel negatively about their experience or the treatment they received may be more likely to decline participation. So, too, may women for whom the experience has been particularly painful and who wish not to focus on it. The relatively high attrition rates in some studies are problematic and suggest caution in drawing conclusions.

Given the potential stresses involved in the application of these technologies, it is critical that women understand the risks involved. Abstract probabilities often are hard for individuals to evaluate, and biases such as the availability heuristic and the effects of framing can distort perceptions. In the case of IVF, these biases seem to increase estimates of success, whereas in the use of diagnostic screening they may increase estimates of complications. In either case, distortions can increase distress. Unrealistically positive expectations could contribute to a desire to proceed with a treatment that a woman otherwise might decline, or could heighten disappointment after failure. Excessively negative expectations could engender unnecessary apprehension about the procedure or promote a decision not to avail oneself of a useful technology. Because risks may vary by clinic, each institution needs to have a clear picture of the risk for women in that setting, and not provide national figures. In addition, more attention needs to be paid to the ways in which risks and benefits are explained and understood.

There are substantial individual differences in how women respond to the experience of these technologies and to negative outcomes. Responses undoubtedly are tied to the meaning that pregnancy and childbearing have for the woman. Failure of IVF treatment involves loss of hope for bearing a biological child; responses to this failure are likely to reflect the strength of one's motivation for having a child and the meanings that biological reproduction hold for the woman. These issues, as well as the woman's psychological and social resources for dealing with stress, are apt to affect her responses. Similarly, prenatal diagnostic screening may pose challenges to values that are central to the woman's identity. A woman's view of herself and her partner may be affected by the diagnosis of a "defective" fetus. In addition, religious and ethical concerns regarding abortion may conflict with fears about having a child with significant health problems or life-threatening conditions. These meanings, along with a woman's ways of coping with stress, may influence both her anticipation of the procedure and its results and her response to obtaining a diagnosis indicating a genetic defect.

Understanding personal meanings and vulnerabilities takes both time and an ability to communicate with individuals whose perceptions may differ from one's own. In busy medical clinics, it may be difficult to accomplish this. In addition, the staff may be responding to their own feelings about the procedures and their implications. Anderson, Nero, Rodin, Diamond, and DeCherney (1989) noted the particular burden on nurse coordinators in

IVF clinics who frequently must convey the news to patients that pregnancy has not occurred, and who themselves lack control over the course of events. Stressing the positive aspects of IVF treatment to themselves and their patients may be important to maintain morale. Some smaller IVF clinics have closed because the absolute number of pregnancies observed as a result of the treatment was too small to provide sufficient meaning for the work (Greenfield & Haseltine, 1986). Similarly, staff working with diagnostic screening may find it painful to experience the anguish of parents who suffer fetal loss. They may hesitate to reach out to those who have experienced adverse outcomes.

The major focus of this chapter has been on the psychological implications of the new reproductive technologies for the women who undergo them. These technologies also may affect the male partner and those providing treatment. Little is known about these effects. They are important to consider, not only out of the concern for the individuals involved, but because their responses will have significant impact on the women who are most directly affected. For all those involved, the stakes are high: the benefits are substantial but so are the risks. Under these conditions, everyone is likely to experience stress. Attention to the psychological hazards and to ways of reducing them should be central to both clinical and research efforts on new reproductive technologies.

ACKNOWLEDGMENTS

We gratefully acknowledge the help of Dr. Bernard Lo for his helpful comments on and Anthony Schlagel for his editorial improvements in the preparation of this chapter.

Our work on this chapter was supported in part by a grant from the John D. and Catherine T. MacArthur Foundation Research Network on Determinants and Consequences of Health-Promoting and Health-Damaging Behavior.

REFERENCES

Adams, M. M., Finley, S., Hansen, H., Jahiel, R., Oakley, G. P., Sanger, W., Wells, G., & Wertelecki, W. (1981). Utilization of prenatal genetic diagnosis in women 35 years of age and older in the United States, 1977–1978. *American Journal of Obstetrics and Gynecology, 139,* 673–677.

Adler, N. E., David, H. D., Major, B. N., Roth, S. H., Russo, N. F., & Wyatt, G. E. (1990). Psychological responses after abortion. *Science, 248,* 41–44.

Adler, N. E., Keyes, S., Kegeles, S., & Golbus, M. S. (1990). Psychological responses to prenatal diagnosis: Anxiety in anticipation of amniocentesis. Unpublished manuscript.

Adler, N. E., Keyes, S., & Robertson, P. (1990). Stress of obstetrical procedures. In M. Johnston & L. Wallace (Eds.), *Stresses of medical procedures.* Oxford, England: Oxford University Press.

Anderson, S., Nero, F., Rodin, J., Diamond, M., & DeCherney, A. H. (1989). Coping patterns of in vitro fertilization nurse coordinators: Strategies for combating low outcome effectance. *Psychology and Health, 3,* 221-232.

Baird, P. A., Sadovnick, A. D., & McGillivray, B. C. (1985). Temporal changes in the utilization of amniocentesis for prenatal diagnosis by women of advanced maternal age. *Prenatal Diagnosis, 5,* 191-198.

Baram, D., Tourtelot, E., Muechler, E., & Huang, K. (1988). Psychosocial adjustment following unsuccessful in vitro fertilization. *Journal of Psychosomatic Obstetrics and Gynecology, 9,* 181-190.

Beeson, D., & Golbus, M. S. (1979). Anxiety engendered by amniocentesis. *Birth Defects: Original Article Series, XV* (5C), 191-197.

Black, R. B. (1989). A 1 and 6 month follow-up of prenatal diagnosis patients who lost pregnancies. (1989). *Prenatal Diagnosis, 9,* 795-804.

Blumberg, B., Golbus, M. S., & Hanson, K. H. (1975). The psychological sequelae of abortion performed for a genetic indication. *American Journal of Obstetrics and Gynecology, 122,* 799-808.

Callan, V. J., & Hennessey, J. F. (1988). Emotional aspects and support in in vitro fertilization and embryo transfer programs. *Journal of in Vitro Fertilization and Embryo Transfer, 5,* 290-295.

Campbell, S., Dunkel-Schetter, C., & Peplau, L. A. (in press). Perceived control and adjustment to infertility among women undergoing in vitro fertilization. In A. L. Stanton & C. A. Dunkel-Schetter (Eds.), *Psychological adjustment to infertility.* New York: Plenum.

Chervin, A., Farnsworth, P. R., Freedman, W. L., Duncan, P. A., & Shapiro, L. R. (1977). Amniocentesis for prenatal diagnosis. *New York State Journal of Medicine, August 1977,* 1406-1408.

Daniels, K. R. (1990). Psychosocial factors for couples awaiting in vitro fertilization. *Social Work in Health Care, 14,* 81-98.

Daniluk, J. C. (1988). Infertility: Intrapersonal and interpersonal impact. *Fertility and Sterility, 49,* 982-990.

Dixson, B., Richards, T. L., Reinsch, S., Edrich, V. B., Matson, M. R., & Jones, O. W. (1981). Mid-trimester amniocentesis: Subjective maternal responses. *The Journal of Reproductive Medicine, 26,* 10-16.

Ekwo, E. E., Kim, J. O., & Gosselink, C. A. (1987). Parental perceptions of the burden of genetic disease. *American Journal of Medical Genetics, 28,* 955-963.

Elkins, T. E., Stovall, T. G., Wilroy, S., & Dacus, J. V. (1986). Attitudes of mothers of children with Down Syndrome concerning amniocentesis, abortion, and prenatal genetic counseling techniques. *Obstetrics and Gynecology, 68,* 181-184.

Evers-Kiebooms, G., Swerts, A., & Van Den Berghe, H. (1988). Psychological aspects of amniocentesis: Anxiety feelings in three different risk groups. *Clinical Genetics, 33,* 196-206.

Fagen, P., Schmidt, C., Jr., Rock, J., Damewood, M., Halle, E., & Wise, T. (1986). Sexual functioning and psychologic evaluation of in vitro fertilization couples. *Fertility and Sterility, 46,* 668-672.

Fava, G. A., Kellner, R., Michelacci, L., Trombini, G., Pathak, D., Orlandi, C., & Bovicelli, L. (1982). Psychological reactions to amniocentesis: A controlled study. *American Journal of Obstetrics and Gynecology, 143,* 509-513.

Finley, S. C., Varner, P. D., Vinson, P. C., & Finley, W. H. (1977). Participants' reaction to amniocentesis and prenatal genetic studies. *Journal of the American Medical Association, 238,* 2377-2379.

Freeman, E., Rickels, K., Tausig, J., Boxer, A., Mastroianni, L. Jr., & Tureck, W. (1987). Emotional and psychosocial factors in follow-up of women after IVF-ET treatment. *Acta*

Obstet Gynecol Scand, 66, 517–521.

Garner, C. H., Arnold, E. W., & Gray, H. (1984). The psychological impact of in vitro fertilization [Abstract]. *Fertility and Sterility, 41,* 135.

Greenfield, D., & Haseltine, F. P. (1986). Candidate selection and psychosocial considerations of in-vitro fertilization procedures. *Clinical Obstetrics and Gynecology, 29,* 119–126.

Gustavii, B. (1984, March 10). Chorionic biopsy and miscarriage in first trimester. *The Lancet,* p. 562.

Hearn, M. T., Yuzpe, A. A., Brown, S. E., & Casper, R. F. (1987). Psychological characteristics of in vitro fertilization participants. *American Journal of Obstetrics and Gynecology, 156,* 269–274.

Holmes, H. B., & Tymstra, T. (1987). In vitro fertilization in the Netherlands: Experiences and opinions of Dutch women. *Journal of In Vitro Fertilization and Embryo Transfer, 4,* 116–123.

Hook, E. B., & Schreinemachers, D. M. (1983). Trends in utilization of prenatal cytogenetic diagnosis by New York State residents in 1979 and 1980. *American Journal of Public Health, 73,* 198–202.

Hunter, A. G., Thompson, D., & Speevak, M. (1987). Mid-trimester genetic amniocentesis in eastern Ontario: A review from 1970 to 1985. *Journal of Medical Genetics, 24,* 335–343.

Johnston, M., Shaw, R. W., & Bird, D. (1987). "Test-tube baby" procedures: Stress and judgements under uncertainty. *Psychology and Health, 1,* 25–38.

Jones, O. W., Penn, N. E., Shuchter, S., Stafford, C. A., Richards, T. L., Kernahan, C., Gutierrez, J., & Cherkin, P. (1984). Parental response to mid-trimester therapeutic abortion following amniocentesis. *Prenatal Diagnosis, 4,* 249–256.

Keirse, M. J. N. C., Kanhai, H. H. H., & Gravenhorts, B. J. (1985, December 7). Safety of chorionic villus sampling. *The Lancet,* p. 1312.

Ledbetter, D. H., Martin, A. O., Verlinsky, Y., Pergament, E., Jackson, L., Yang-Feng, T., Schonberg, St., Gilbert, F., Zachary, J. M., Barr, M., Copeland, K. L., DiMaio, M. S., Fine, B., Rosinsky, B., Schuette, J., de la Cruz, F. F., Desnick, R. J., Elias, S., Golbus, M. S., Goldberg, J. D., Lubs, H. A., Mahoney, M. J., Rhoads, G. G., Simpson, J. L., & Schlesselman, S. E. (1990). Cytogenetic results of chorionic villus sampling: High success rate and diagnostic accuracy in the United States collaborative study. *American Journal of Obstetrics and Gynecology, 162,* 495–501.

Lippman, A., Perry, T. B., Mandel, S., & Cartier, L. (1985). Chorionic villi sampling: Women's attitudes. *American Journal of Medical Genetics, 22,* 395–401.

Mahlstedt, P. P., MacDuff, S., & Bernstein, J. (1987). Emotional factors and the in vitro fertilization and embryo transfer process. *Journal of In Vitro Fertilization and Embryo Transfer, 4,* 232–236.

Marteau, T. M., Johnston, M., Shaw, R. W., Michie, S., Kidd, J., & New, M. (1989). The impact of prenatal screening and diagnostic testing upon the cognitions, emotions and behaviour of pregnant women. *Journal of Psychosomatic Research, 33,* 7–16.

Mikkelsen, M., Fischer, G., Hansen, J., Pilgaard, B., & Nielsen, J. (1983). The impact of legal termination of pregnancy and of prenatal diagnosis on the birth prevalence of Down syndrome in Denmark. *Annals of Human Genetics, 47,* 123–131.

Milne, B. J. (1987). Couples' experiences with in vitro fertilization. *Journal of Obstetric and Gynecological Neonatal Nursing, 17,* 347–352.

Perry, T. B., Vekemans, M. J. J., Lippman, A., Hamilton, E. F., & Fournier, P. J. R. (1985). Chorionic villi sampling: Clinical experience, immediate complication and patient attitudes. *American Journal of Obstetrics and Gynecology, 151,* 161–166.

Phipps, S., & Zinn, A. B. (1986). Psychological responses to amniocentesis: I. Mood state and adaptation to pregnancy. *American Journal of Medical Genetics, 25,* 131–142.

Reading, A. E., Chang, L. C., & Kerin, J. F. (1989). Attitudes and anxiety levels in women conceiving through in vitro fertilization and gamete intrafallopian transfer. *Fertility and*

Sterility, 52, 95–99.

Reading, A. E., & Kerin, J. F. (1989). Psychological aspects of providing infertility services. *The Journal of Reproductive Medicine, 34,* 861–871.

Rhoads, G. G., Jackson, L. G., Schlesselman, S. E., de la Cruz, F. F., Desnick, R. J., Golbus, M. S., Ledbetter, D. H., Lubs, H. A., Mahoney, M. J., Pergament, E., Simpson, J. L., Carpenter, R. J., Elias, S., Ginsberg, N. A., Goldberg, J. D., Hobbins, J. C., Lynch, L., Shiono, P. H., Wapner, R. J., & Zachary, J. M. (1989). The safety and efficacy of chorionic villus sampling for early prenatal diagnosis of cytogenetic abnormalities. *The New England Journal of Medicine, 320,* 609–617.

Robinson, G. E., Garner, D. M., Olmsted, M. P., Shime, J., Hutton, E. M., & Crawford, B. M. (1988). Anxiety reduction after chorionic villus sampling and genetic amniocentesis. *American Journal of Obstetrics and Gynecology, 159,* 953–956.

Rothman, B. K. (1986). *The tentative pregnancy.* New York: Penguin.

Sjögren, B., & Uddenberg, N. (1988). Decision making during the prenatal diagnostic procedure; A questionnaire and interview study of 211 women participating in prenatal diagnosis. *Prenatal Diagnosis, 8,* 263–273.

Sokal, D. C., Byrd, J. R., Chen, A. T. L., Goldberg, M. F., & Oakley, G. P. (1980). Prenatal chromosomal diagnosis: Racial and geographic variation for older women in Georgia. *Journal of the American Medical Association, 244,* 1355–1357.

Spencer, J. W., & Cox, D. N. (1987). Emotional responses of pregnant women to chorionic villi sampling or amniocentesis. *American Journal of Obstetrics and Gynecology, 157,* 1155–1160.

Spencer, J. W., & Cox, D. N. (1988). A comparison of chorionic villi sampling and amniocentesis: Acceptability of procedure and maternal attachment to pregnancy. *Obstetrics and Gynecology, 72,* 714–718.

Stanton, A. L., & Dunkel-Schetter, C. A. (Eds.). (in press). *Psychological adjustment to infertility.* New York: Plenum.

Stewart, S., & Glazer, G. (1986). Expectations and coping of women undergoing in vitro fertilization. *Maternal-Child Nursing Journal, 15,* 103–113.

Tedgård, U., Ljung, R., McNeil, T., Tedgård, E., & Schwartz, M. (1989). How do carriers of hemophilia experience prenatal diagnosis (PND)? *Acta Paediatr Scand, 78,* 692–700.

Tversky, A., & Kahneman, D. (1973). Availability: A heuristic for judging frequency and probability. *Cognitive Psychology, 5,* 207–232.

Wyatt, P. R. (1985, December 7). Chorionic biopsy and increased anxiety. *The Lancet,* pp. 1312–1313.

Zoeten, M. J. de, Tymstra, T., & Alberda, A. T. (1987). The waiting-list for IVF. The motivations and expectations of women waiting for IVF treatment. *Human Reproduction, 2,* 623–626.

Communicating About the New Reproductive Technologies: Cultural, Interpersonal, and Linguistic Determinants of Understanding

Rayna Rapp
New School of Social Research

In 1958 Jerome LeJeune (or a female researcher in his lab, in an alternate telling of origin tales) peered through the microscope at samples of smooth connective tissue taken from three patients with Down's syndrome, and identified the 47th chromosome whose presence spells the existence of that condition. In the late 1960s, several teams of doctors reported identifying the same extra chromosome in amniotic fluid extracted from pregnant women's uteruses, opening up the possibilities of prenatal diagnosis for Down's, and other inherited disabilities.

The practice of amniocentesis for prenatal diagnosis of inherited disabilities developed as the ability to identify, stain, and study chromosomes increased. At the same time, the DNA revolution transformed the fields of cytogenetics and cell biology, and by the late 1980s, over 200 inherited conditions, most of them extremely rare autosomal recessive diseases, could be diagnosed prenatally. Research frontiers in human genetics and molecular biology became inextricably tied to the routinization of amniocentesis. The rapid proliferation of information in human genetics has implications not only for health workers in the field of reproductive medicine, but for pregnant women and their families as well. But how were those technical and ever-shifting implications to be explained to the lay public? The profession of genetic counseling developed to translate the discourse of human genetics into usable and more popular language.

This chapter explores the social impact and cultural interpretations of prenatal diagnosis in the context of genetic counseling. It is based on 2 years' fieldwork in New York City following a team of genetic counselors through their hospital-based rounds, interviewing 35 genetic counselors about their work, observing a cytogenetics laboratory, and interviewing pregnant women and their families. A discussion of genetic counselors, and the development of genetic counseling as a new health profession introduces the analysis. An interpretation of genetic counseling sessions, using a language-based perspective, presents the core of my argument. This perspective allows me to understand genetic counseling as a discourse in which multicultural clients and science-based health professionals communicate and miscommunicate. Although the language of science claims to be universal, it must, in fact, confront the local idioms with which diverse groups and individuals respond to its powerful messages. Such salient social fault lines as class, ethnicity, race, and gender deeply influence clients' communication choices, however they do not determine them. Thus a counseling session is also a context in which meanings are actively, and interactively produced.

The third section concerns variability in the meanings of disabilities, and the ambiguities of "choice." Finally, I conclude with a discussion of the power of genetic communication: Counseling discourse has the power to create and highlight some problems, while masking and silencing others. Throughout the analysis, I implicitly describe the discourse of genetic counseling as caught in a contradiction: Developed to provide pregnant women and their families with more choices, it also inadvertently and unself-consciously replicates and extends the social hierarchies that limit choices, and within which it is embedded.

THE GENETIC COUNSELOR

In 1969, program developers at Sarah Lawrence College in Bronxville, New York planned a new masters'-level science degree, and in 1971, the first formally trained genetic counselor was born. "Genetic Counseling" is a label coined in 1947; it initially stood for a position of ethical neutrality and personal choice in the century-old eugenics debate about society's responsibility to encourage or discourage reproduction in certain individuals and families (Kevles, 1985; Reed, 1974). Prior to the invention of the modern genetic counselor at Sarah Lawrence, research pediatricians, geneticists, immune biologists — that is, medical doctors and researchers, the majority of whom were men — would counsel families with genetically disabled members about recurrence risks and disease management. Once amniocentesis was developing as a clinical service, the need for an "interface" also developed — someone to convey the risks and benefits of the test, to translate scientific possibilities into personal calculations for potential patients. That "gatekeeper" between science and social work, between epidemiology and empathy, became a woman.

Women students seemed especially suited to a field that was designed to counsel pregnant women. And "counseling" was a field in which "female qualities" seemed particularly appropriate. As the program at Sarah Lawrence was mounted through the School of Continuing Education, the first wave of genetic counselors tended to be well-educated homemakers living near the college, often wives of doctors, lawyers, and businessmen. Many had raised their children, and were ready to go back to school. They brought with them enormous resourcefulness, and a specific set of upper middle-class family values. The program promised an amalgam of hard science and counseling skills, and held out the possibility of part-time work. For the first wave of genetic counselors, advances in genetic science provided an exciting way to leave home and enter the world of public work.

Genetic counseling quickly became a profession-in-formation (Rollnick, 1984). Although Sarah Lawrence remains the largest and perhaps the most respected program in the country, there are now approximately nine others (depending on what "counts" as a program) located in seven states, the District of Columbia, and Canada. The curriculum varies somewhat, however all provide training in human genetics, medical genetics, counseling skills, and supervised clinical internships. Some programs include a seminar on bioethics, or ethical issues in genetic counseling, with a strong orientation toward individual choice. But according to the counselors I have interviewed, there is rarely much discussion of the cultural constraints and resources within which different pregnant women and their families may be operating. Most programs require 2 years of study. Board certification for practitioners is under way, and genetic counselors are insured by the medical centers for which they work. The National Society of Genetic Counselors (NSGC) estimates that there are currently about 600 to 700 practicing genetic counselors, including not only those who have completed a 2-year MS program, and served supervised internships, but also those "grandfathered" (in this case, "grandmothered") into the field through prior experience in nursing, social work, and related routes.

Genetic counseling remains a "women's field." Less than 1% of the graduates of genetic counseling programs are men, and many of them are employed in administration. Current students and recent graduates of genetic counseling programs are less likely to have attended elite women's colleges, are more likely to have considered a premed track, and rejected it, and are somewhat more diverse in class, ethnic, and racial background than the first wave of Sarah Lawrence graduates. Although consciousness of minority issues in counseling is growing, the numbers of NSGC counselors from Black-American, Hispanic, or Asian-American backgrounds remains small—not more than 5%.[1]

---

[1] The first NSCG workshop on "counseling the culturally different" was conducted by a team of minority genetic counselors at the annual meetings in 1985. Members of that team estimated

As part of an ongoing study of the social impact and cultural meaning of prenatal diagnosis, I have observed five genetic counselors working for New York City's Department of Health during their counseling sessions 1 to 2 days a week for over 2 years, sitting in on more than 200 intake interviews. As an observer, and sometimes, as a participant-translator, I have had extensive informal conversations with the five women who allowed me to observe their work. I have also interviewed 30 other genetic counselors who work in New York City, at least one from each medical center that offers amniocentesis. Although most of my sample would identify as White and middle-class, at least five spoke Spanish as their first language, and one was African-American.

In New York City, unlike many other parts of the country, a combination of State and City policies both fund and offer prenatal diagnosis to women regardless of their ability to pay for the test themselves. The City laboratory (through which my fieldwork has been conducted) collects amniotic fluid samples drawn from pregnant women who are approximately one-third Hispanic, one-third African-American, and one-third White. The City lab has contracts to perform cytogenetic analyses for 24 urban hospitals in all boroughs and neighborhoods, encompassing both municipal and voluntary facilities. Women seen by the City genetic counselors are roughly 50% private patients and 50% clinic patients (that is, poor and working class). The City genetic counselors are "circuit riders": In the period of my observations they rotated among six to eight hospitals, one of which saw private patients, four of which served an exclusively clinic population, and several of which served both. Genetic counselors thus must confront the polyglot diversity of their patients as they attempt to explain the test. In the process, they may help to shape experiences of knowledge and power in the reproductive lives of women, many of whose backgrounds are significantly different than their own.

As a new professional, the genetic counselor tends to be highly self-conscious of her ethical and scientific roots. The counselors I interviewed were very much aware of the anxiety, as well as the relief, that their services invoke. Most had thought deeply about why someone might reject, as well as accept, amniocentesis and possibly abortion. And many were curious and insightful about the problems of cross-cultural communication my interview schedule posed for them.

THE DISCOURSE OF GENETIC COUNSELING

A genetic counseling session almost always precedes the use (or nonuse) of amniocentesis. Counselors meet with their pregnant patients (and any

---

that no more than 30 minority counselors are trained and practicing nationally. But both the definition of "minority" and of "practicing" are open to interpretation.

supporters the woman brings with her) in the hospital where the test is offered. In the course of an hour's visit, counselors convey a great deal of medico-scientific information, ask and answer questions, and prepare women to take the test. The interaction is conversational: In a session, meanings are actively, and interactively, produced by patients and counselors together. But the discourse of genetic counseling is resolutely medico-scientific, revealing and creating some meanings, which mask or silence others. Medical language deploys a great authority that cannot always respond to the resources and questions particular women bring to this encounter. Miscommunication as well as communication, silence as well as conversation fill up a genetic counseling appointment.

Genetic counselors generally begin communication with pregnant patients with three goals in mind: to convey significant information about the risks of birth defects and the availability and nature of amniocentesis, to take a health and family history, and to communicate with the patient well enough so that her questions and concerns can be addressed. In order to accomplish these tasks, most genetic counselors begin by "setting up a dialogue." Many begin their intake session by posing some variant of the question, "Do you know why you are here talking to me?" From the beginning, interactions are context-sensitive to the responses and resources patients bring to the interaction. Middle-class, scientifically educated pregnant patients may respond, "We're planning to have amniocentesis," thus pushing the counseling script into high gear. Implicit in that answer is not only a knowledge of appropriate medical indications for the test, but also the existence of "the couple" as a decision-making unit. But a Dominican mother of three may answer, *"por culpa de mi edad"* (literally, "for the fault of my age"), thus presenting the counselor with several options. She can assume that the woman "knows," because "age" is the factor that sends her here. Or she can confront the *"culpa"* head-on, explaining that older women having babies present no shame, just medical risks. But wherever she begins her routine explanation, the counselor is likely to have to adjust her language to the language and assumptions of her pregnant patient (and sometimes the patient's mate).

In adjusting (or not adjusting) to the patients' language, genetic counselors are bound by the limits of their own communicative resources. Although many native languages are spoken by the pregnant women counselors see, most counseling sessions are conducted in English. But there are at least five counselors in New York hospitals who are native Spanish speakers, and another five who are comfortable counseling in Spanish. Many others have learned a bit of medical Spanish and work through translators, ranging from trusted assistants who understand their agenda (a secretary in the office, a clinic nurse) to catch-as-catch-can interpreters (the 10-year-old child brought along by the patient; a husband, brother, or male neighbor, who may be embarrassed to find himself discussing prior miscarriages and abortions). Availability of fluent translation is a significant problem: Depending on the hospital's catchment area, patients may be close to 100% Spanish speaking, 50% French/Creole speaking, or about 25% monolingual Spanish speaking, situations I observed at various New York City hospitals. "Native language" only approximates the variety of communicative differences that genetic counselors confront. "Hispanic" glosses a range of Spanish-speaking cultures, especially at the present time in New York City. Some genetic counselors distinguished "Hispanic" (which often meant Puerto Rican and Dominican — the "old" migrants) from new migrants who might be "middle-class" Colombians and Ecuadorians or the "field mice" (by which the speaker meant, "poor, rural, and humble") of Central America. Although exact cultural differences among Spanish-speaking groups may be unknown, most counselors recognize something of the diversity in educational levels, familiarity with medical terminology, and religious observation that different nationalities may represent.

Nominal or deep fluency in another tongue may aid, but it does not ensure, direct communication for science speakers. Language differences may signal communicative ambiguities far beyond the question of literal translation. Local metaphors of pregnancy, of birth, and of parenthood do not necessarily translate easily into the realm of medical discourse. Two native Spanish-speaking counselors pointed out the far-reaching impact of their conversations with pregnant patients:

> This knowledge is more than genetic. They learn about things that were completely hidden, where the eggs are, what sperm does, how children get to look like their parents. They have ideas, but this is female physiology, it is knowledge, not just information. For this, they come back.

> When I see confusion, I go to work, I tell them in language they will understand, language of the streets. They are comfortable here, it is a good place to visit, they come back to see me whenever they come to the hospital.

Of course, not everyone is equally open to the complex relation between native tongue, knowledge, and communicative power. Two counselors, one of whom conducts group sessions for patients in Spanish, expressed irritation that so few of their clients "bothered to learn English": "They're here 10, maybe 15 years. They learn enough English to pick up their welfare checks. Why don't they just learn the language? My grandparents did."

And if Spanish is a contested domain; French and Haitian Creole are virtual *terrae incognitae*. Only one genetic counselor feels comfortable counseling in French; none knows any Creole. The lack is significant: In at least one City hospital, Haitians make up about 50% of the current patients referred for counseling. In translating for counseling sessions, I discovered that there is no recognition of Down's syndrome or mongolism for recent immigrants coming from the Haitian countryside. No word exists in Creole for the condition. In principle, the incidence of Down's syndrome is invariant worldwide. But in a country with the worst infant mortality statistics in the Western hemisphere, babies may die from many causes, and this one may go unrecognized as a "syndrome." Nonrecognition of the label may also reflect other cultural and political experiences. Haitians living in New York City already have confronted alternative definitions of their children's vulnerabilities: As one Haitian evangelist father told me, while firmly rejecting amniocentesis on his wife's behalf, "What is this retarded? They always say that Haitian children are retarded in the public schools. But when we put them in the Haitian Academy (a community-based private school), they do just fine. I do not know what this retarded is." In his experience, "chromosomes" seem a weak and abstract explanation for the problems a Haitian child may face.

Language and cultural understandings are linked in other ways as well. Genre choice also constructs a field of understanding: The use of statistics and medical terminology both convey and delimit the quantity and quality of information that a counselor provides. The language of genetic counseling is resolutely statistical; it is an axiom of good counseling that a patient must be told her risks before she can decide to take or refuse the test. Yet statistics implies an abstract mathematical universe, which may not be shared by patients who have little formal schooling. The majority of genetic counselors confront this problem by simplifying the numbers and adding information, if it is requested:

(to someone perceived as unable to handle numbers:) At your age, the risk of having a baby with mongolism is about 1 in 100.

(to someone perceived as uneducated, but attentive:) Pregnant ladies your age have a 1 in 106 chance of having a baby with this condition. That means that of every 106 pregnant ladies your age, 105 will have no problems, and 1 will have a child with the problem.

(to someone perceived as scientifically sophisticated:) At 35, a woman's risk of bearing a liveborn child with Down's syndrome is 1 in 385; at 40, it increases to 1 in 106; at 45, it is 1 in 30.

Likewise, miscarriage rates must be shared: "This is a very safe test, but there's always *some* risk to any test in medicine. The risk of loosing the baby after amnio is very small, but it isn't zero."—versus: "Amnio adds 3 miscarriages per 1,000 to those having the test. Of 1,000 women your age 16 weeks pregnant who don't have amniocentesis, 32 will not have a liveborn child at the end of the pregnancy, through miscarriage or stillbirth. Of 1,000 women who have the test, 35 will lose the pregnancy."

But code switching and simplification of numbers only mark the professional side of the interaction. Such strategies may sit comfortably with information-seeking, medically compliant patients, especially those with some advanced education (read, middle-class), but they often gloss over the lived reality of less privileged women. Low-income African-American women, for example, often expressed a sense of statistics that varied radically from the sensibilities of middle-class couples. When a woman has given birth to four other children, comes from a family of eight, and all her sisters and neighbors have had similar histories, she has seen scores of babies born without recognizable birth defects. It requires a leap of faith in abstract reasoning to contrast these experiences with a number produced by a woman in a white coat proclaiming that the risk of having a baby with a birth defect is rising steadily with each pregnancy. Among middle-class professional families, where childbearing is likely to be delayed, the counselor is discussing a first, or at most a second pregnancy. Children are likely to be scarce throughout the network of the professional couple. To them, 1 in 300 sounds like a large and present risk, whereas for the low-income mother of four, the same number may appear very distant and small.

The vocabulary of biomedicine selects for concepts used to describe pregnancy and birth, abortion and disability, which may result in a tug-of-war of words. In a 45 minute intake interview, code switching occurs rapidly, as counselors feel out their clients: "Babies" vie with "fetuses" for space in "wombs," "tummies," or "uteruses"; "waters" or "liquid" or "fluids" may be "taken out with a needle," or "withdrawn through an insertion"; the "test" or "procedure" may involve "looking at the inherited material," or "examining chromosomes." And, in the worst-case scenario, women must decide to "terminate" or "abort" an "affected" or "sick" pregnancy in which "Down's syndrome" or "mongolism" has been diagnosed. In the war between medical and popular language, the more distant idiom may provide reassurance by suggesting to some pregnant women that their experiences are part of medical routine (Brewster, 1984). But for others, medical terminology may muffle anxiety-provoking choices until they are expressed through dramatic disruption:

> So I was sittin' and listenin', listenin' and sittin' and all the time gettin' more and more preoccupied. The counselor kept on talkin' but she never did say it, so finally I had to just say it, right while she was still talkin': "you can't take the baby out *then* (i.e., so late in pregnancy), can you now?" I finally asked. (Veronica Landry, 36, Trinidadian-born factory worker)

Much of the scientific information that counselors want to convey exists on technical and invisible terrains. Most counselors work with visual aids, especially with clinic patients, attempting to map what patients cannot see for themselves. These may include charts, graphs, and karyotypes (pictures of chromosomes arranged in pairs, to illustrate females and males, normal and abnormal genotypes). Many show pictures of children with Down's syndrome. And almost all discuss the sonogram accompanying amniocentesis, in which "you can see the baby moving around."

Developed to present the mysteries of the womb, the workings of heredity, and the universe of epidemiology graphically, such icons of professional knowledge are not, to be sure, self-evident. They require interpretation during which health professionals not only reveal some of their arcane wisdom but also shape the perceptions of the client:

> I saw the sonogram of the twins, and I was thrilled. But I really couldn't read it, I didn't know what it meant. They had to interpret it for you, to say, "here's a heart, these are arms." Afterwards, it made me queasy—they made the babies real for me by telling me what was there. If they hadn't interpreted, it would have just been grey blobs, and now, I'm more frightened to get the results of the amnio back. (Daphne McCarle, 41, U.S.-born professional)

> It was nothing, really, it looked like nothing. Then they showed it to me, and made it something. (Ileana Mendez, 37, Ecuadorian-born babysitter)

Virtually all counselors have a minimal "threshold" of information that they need to explain. For some, it includes the concept of chromosomes and genes; for others, it is the idea of heredity, especially, hereditary health problems. For most, it is the 2% to 3% risk of a birth defect involved in any pregnancy and the increased risk of chromosomal problems associated with childbearing later in life. Whatever her personal goal, no counselor is satisfied if she feels that a patient has failed to grasp her minimal scientific scenario. But medically significant lessons may mask the social experiences and meanings that disabling conditions hold, a point to which I return later. Scientific discourse silences as well as articulates.

In their training, counselors are taught to illustrate chromosomal problems by reference to a 47th chromosome that is clinically expressed in Down's syndrome, with accompanying mental retardation. Although this condition is recognized almost universally, the content of that recognition varies considerably. Many families share the counselor's concerns about the limitations on independence that mental retardation represents in our culture. But in families who have had direct experience with children with Down's, consciousness of disabilities is more finely honed: Down's children may be mildly, moderately, or profoundly retarded; may suffer from heart or esophagal problems, hearing loss, or increased risk for leukemia. "Mental retardation" provides an iconic description that blurs differences among Down's children, even as it categorizes them. And counselors do not offer routinely information on the social realities, rather than the medical diagnoses, that accompany this condition (or any other). Many counselors were open, in principle, to questions concerning support for families with genetically disabled members (especially if they worked in pediatric as well as prenatal services, they may have come into contact with such families quite often). However, they had little or no experience in discussing either the social stigmas or the infant stimulation programs that a newborn with Down's syndrome entails. Unless propelled by a patient's question, they did not transcend the medical frame of the discussion by offering a visit with a family whose child had the diagnosed condition about which the woman was concerned. Thus the counseling session is likely to reinforce a medical, rather than a social, definition of the problems of childhood disability.

Indeed, the assumptions of medicine weigh heavily throughout an intake interview. Genetic counselors elicit health histories, using a standard questionnaire. From a counselor's point of view, recent immigrants, especially from very poor countries, are likely to exhibit shallow knowledge of their own heredity. The cause of a father's death, the name of an uncle's form of mental retardation may be unknown, especially if births and deaths occurred after the immigrant left home. And although some health experiences can be recalled vividly — high fevers, exposure to X rays — others seem irrelevant, or badly named, from the migrant patients' point of view. Many Haitians, for example, routinely answer "no" to all questions concerning family histories of heart and kidney disease, diabetes, and venereal diseases. Their negative answers may well be ambiguous: Serious conditions may be unreported or unnamed, because they are virtually untreatable for all but the most privileged elite. A community health outreach worker from Jamaica now working in Brooklyn, for example, told me this part of her life story: "Sickle cell, do I counsel sickle cell, sure I do now. But then, I didn't know what it was. My brother, he died of it back then, we didn't know, no one told us. What's the difference? No transfusions back there, anyhow." But to the counselor, the "no" may result in one of a number of misinterpretations, for example, a lack of health problems in the family, or a lack of interest or intelligence on the part of the patient. These interpretations are overdetermined by the individual nature of a medical health history, minus its epidemiological and cultural context.

The codes, genres, and assumptions of biomedicine construct the limits of the conversations genetic counselors may have with their patients through claims of universality that silence other cultural resources and world views. The language of biomedicine also limits communication by locking counselors into a discourse that technical language must dominate, despite their sincere interests in reaching out to patients. Counselors are caught between the need to sound authoritative, and the desire to "glide on the patient's wavelength," as one counselor described the situation. Genetic counselors, as new professionals, must lay claim to a monopoly on the information that they offer. Such a claim must impress the rest of the medical hierarchy, in whose ball game they are new players. At the same time, genetic counselors are extremely interested in the public image of their field as a new field, and many are eager to further public education on their issues. Individually, many enjoy speaking at popular health forums, being interviewed by journalists, and serving as consultants to media projects in which they hope that scientific knowledge will be disseminated effectively. This tension between monopolizing an arcane body of information and popularizing it is inherent in a new profession: Members need to "sell their services" to both the medical establishment and the individual clients for whom they serve as translators (Brown, 1986). But this tension cannot be resolved easily in favor of popular language: Medical discourse is authoritative, it pervades the hospital setting, and it claims universality. The languages of patients are polyglot, and usually have no lexicon, or an unacceptable lexicon, for the expression of clinical and epidemiological facts.

This contradiction between speaking like doctors and talking with patients surfaces in nonverbal communication as well. Some counselors wear white coats "to appear like medical professionals," for example, whereas others forego that symbol of antiseptic separation, hoping to "make the patient right at home." One counselor described her dress code to me: "On clinic days, I like to dress comfortably, so they will feel at home, casual with me. I dress up like a professional when I see private patients; they expect more from their medical providers."

The inscriptions of professional status extend to briefcases, charts, and visual aids, isomorphic with those of both health-care professionals and their private clientele. But the poor carry inscriptions with them, too: Among non-English speakers, there are often electricity bills, check stubs, or personal letters, carried to communicate home addresses. And the ubiquitous Medicaid and clinic cards that define payment status and rights serve as passports into medical domains, marking the client status.

DISABILITY, VARIABILITY, AND "CHOICE"

In a genetic counseling intake interview, rich, many-layered, and powerful messages are being communicated. Officially, information about a new reproductive technology, its risks, limitations, and possible benefits is being conveyed. Unofficially, the power to define a pregnancy, fetus, disability, and maternal responsibility for fetal health are all under negotiation. Basic knowledge about human heredity, reproduction, and its control offers potentials for self-control and social control simultaneously, as several of the Spanish-speaking counselors tried to indicate. Ex-officio, women (and their families) are being given a set of choices about the kinds of babies they might, or might not, accept to bear:

> I was hoping I'd never have to make this choice, to become responsible for choosing the kind of baby I'd get, the kind of baby we'd accept. But everyone—my doctor, my parents, my friends—everyone urged me to come for genetic counseling and have amniocentesis. Now, I guess I'm having a modern baby. And they all told me I'd feel more in control. But in some ways, I feel less in control. Oh, it's still my baby, but only if it's good enough to be our baby, if you see what I mean. (Nancy Smithers, 36, U.S.-born lawyer)

Such choices are, of course, far more than individual, for they emerge from the embeddedness of specific pregnancies, contextualized by ethnic, class, racial, religious, and familial experiences. As my translation story earlier indicated, Creole-speaking Haitian immigrants from the countryside may not recognize Down's syndrome. In this case, being "offered the test" for a condition that holds no cultural meaning for them may make no sense. Recognition of a medical condition may be contextualized within other powerful discourses. For example, an Ecuadorian evangelical and a Colombian Catholic, both opposed to abortion but still wanting the test, made similar points to me: "Science can reveal God's miracles, let you know what He has in store." Their desire for the test might be interpreted as a bridging of religious and secular-scientific cultures, an expression of the necessities and possibilities of living in a multicultural world. And even for Black Americans raised in the shadow of medical discourse, its choices may seem inappropriate: One Black pregnant woman who was adamant about her antiabortion stance wanted the test in order to know whether she ought to move back to Georgia, where her mother would help her to raise a disabled child. Another, having recently given birth to a baby with Down's said to the genetic counselor, "My kid's got a heart problem. Let me deal with that first, then I'll figure out what this Down's business means." And low-income Puerto Rican parents I interviewed at an infant stimulation program said of their daughter with Down's syndrome, "She's growing really well, we were only concerned that she wouldn't grow, that she'd be really small. But now that she can walk, and she's growing, she seems like a normal child to us."

Mental retardation is the key focus when genetic counselors speak about Down's and offer amniocentesis, but it may not be the most significant factor in the consciousness and decisions of many of their clients. Among the Spanish speakers I interviewed, physical vulnerability, especially if it was highly visible, seemed a much more urgent problem for family life. The "choice" any pregnant woman makes to take or reject the test, and to keep or end any specific pregnancy, flows from the way the pregnancy is embedded in the totality of her life.

And if Down's syndrome represents the iconic case for genetic counseling, other potential diagnoses are more ambiguous and present complex problems for communication. The sex chromosome anomalies (XXY, or Klinefelter's syndrome, XYY, Triple X, and Turner's syndrome, or XO) all spell problems with growth and fertility, but none is "incompatible with life," as medicine would express it. There are controversial claims concerning mental retardation, learning disabilities, and, in the worst case, antisocial behavior associated with these conditions, but all are contested because there is no baseline population from which to make scientific comparisons. Only people who are diagnosed as having a clinical problem will ever have their chromosomes "read." And even when the ethical complexities of collecting baseline data on anomalous sex chromosomes are sorted out, epidemiological patterns cannot predict whether affected individuals will express many symptoms of the condition, and whether clinical expression will be severe or mild. So when one of these diagnoses emerges in a test tube of fetal cells, its meaning is open to interpretation.

One genetic counselor encountered two patients, each of whom chose to abort a fetus after learning that its status included XXY sex chromosomes (Klinefelter's syndrome). One professional couple told her, "If he can't grow up to have a shot at becoming the President, we don't want him." A low-income family said of the same condition, "A baby will have to face so many problems in this world, it isn't fair to add this one to the burdens he'll have." And a Puerto Rican single mother who chose to continue a pregnancy after getting a prenatal diagnosis of Klinefelter's said of her now 4-year-old son, "He's normal, he's growing up normal. As long as there's nothing wrong that shows, he isn't blind or deaf or crippled, he's normal as far as I'm concerned. And if anything happens later, I'll be there for him, as long as he's normal looking."

From a patient's point of view, most diagnoses are inherently ambiguous.[2] An extra chromosome spells out the diagnosis of Down's syndrome, but it does not distinguish mildly from severely retarded children, or indicate whether this particular fetus will need open heart surgery. A missing X-chromosome indicates a Turner's syndrome girl, but cannot speak to the meaning of fertility in the particular family into which she may be born. Homozygous status for the sickle cell gene cannot predict the severity of anemia a particular child will develop. All such diagnoses are

---

[2]Rothman (1986) argued forcefully that all prenatal diagnoses seem ambiguous to pregnant women.

interpreted in light of prior reproductive histories, community values, and aspirations that particular women and their families hold for the pregnancy being examined.

VALUES, DECISIONS, AND POWER IN
GENETIC COUNSELING

The ethical complexity of diagnoses is something all genetic counselors confront. Counselors are trained to be empathic as they convey statistics, and to practice Rogerian therapy—that is, a therapeutic style that is noninterventionist, aimed at helping the patient to make up her own mind. This counseling model assumes that the professional and the patient mutually participate in a decision-making process. Their task is short-term and well defined: Should the woman accept amniocentesis? If a positive diagnosis is made, should she end or continue the pregnancy? In distinction to a more directive model (which counselors associate with physicians), this protocol assumes that the patient can and must decide for herself. Yet counselors all know how hard it is to keep their own feelings out of a given situation:

We're supposed to ooze empathy, but stay aloof from decisions.

Oh, I know I'm supposed to be value-free. But when you see a woman on welfare having a third baby with one more man who's not gonna support her, and the fetus has sickle cell anemia, it's not hard to steer her toward an abortion. What does she need this added problem for, I'm thinking?

So I try to put it in neutral, to go where she goes, to support her whatever her decision. But I know she knows I've got an opinion, and it's hard not to answer when she asks me what I'd do in her shoes. "I'm not pregnant," I say, "remember that."

A social worker who trained me at Sloan-Kettering taught me something important: to clear my own agenda before I walk into the room, to let the patient set the agenda. It's the hardest lesson, and the most important one.

Despite this consciousness, counselors stand in a doubly binding position to their clients. On the one hand, they are always making decisions about what sort and how much information a pregnant woman needs and can use, and the form in which she can best absorb it. On the other, most of the information that the woman receives comes directly from the counselor, as she is unlikely to have a "folk model" of most of the diseases and risks associated with amniocentesis.[3] This is not true of any other aspect of pregnancy, or pregnancy loss, where the process of medicalization often is contradicted by ideas and images shared in communities of women. Here, communication about the health or illness of a potential child is shaped in a vocabulary that is exclusively medical, a grammar that is technological, and a syntax that has yet to be negotiated. As in so much of modern biomedicine, the genetic counselor really is the gatekeeper between science and social experience, regulating both the quantity and quality of the information on which decisions will be made.

At first glance, then, genetic counselors appear to control and shape communications because they hold near-exclusive access to the medical information on which its rules are predicated. But patients are not silent partners in these encounters, no matter how few sentences they utter. Ten percent of private patients and 50% of clinic patients break their appointments for genetic counseling, and somewhere between 20% and 50% of those counseled decide not to have amniocentesis.[4] Although their reasons are varied, they certainly include a disbelief or nonacceptance of the medical premises behind testing for fetal disabilities. This often takes the form of a clash of cultural assumptions, with pregnant women saying, "God will protect my baby," and counselors saying, "Most babies are born healthy, but 2% to 3% of all babies are born with birth defects."

---

[3]Folk models for children with Down's syndrome—highly stereotyped and badly out of date—surely exist for most people. And some African-Americans have opinions and images about the consequences of sickle-cell anemia. But virtually no one I have observed or interviewed knew about neural tube defects (e.g., spina bifida) for which the test is also being done, or about sex chromosome anomalies. And, with the exception of one African-American woman who claimed the authority of dreams to accurately predict the birth of her disabled (Down's syndrome) son, and one White middle-class woman who knew that her third pregnancy would produce a disabled child because "it didn't move right, it didn't really move at all," no one having the test, including women who subsequently received positive diagnoses of fetal disability, ever felt competent to predict the health status of the fetus she was carrying.

[4]These numbers are drawn from the counselors and medical centers in which I did direct observations, and they vary enormously from facility to facility. A small percentage of "no-shows" have miscarriages before they are scheduled to speak with the counselor, but most have opted out of the appointment. In some clinics, patients feel well served, and can communicate directly with a nurse or paramedic about their desire to see, or not see, the genetic counselor. In others, suspicion, anger, or resignation dominates the experience of medical care, and appointments are assigned coercively, and often broken in resistance. Those who choose not to have the test after counseling include women who discover that it cannot diagnose the problem they came to discuss, as well as those deemed "appropriate candidates" who do not want it. Their reasons may include religious and spiritual beliefs, conflict with other family or community members about the meaning of pregnancy, testing and having babies, fear of the test, especially needles (Hispanic women), and possible miscarriage (everyone).

Sometimes, an interaction will reveal an especially clear instance of the shifting meaning of motherhood — technocratic and traditional images uncomfortably located in the same sentence. As a low-income Chinese-American woman said after her husband finished signing her up for the test, and I queried her own desires:

> My mother, my grandmother, they all had babies in China, and nobody did this. They wouldn't do it now, if they were here. Now is modern times, everyone wants to know everything, to know as soon as possible, in advance, about everything. What kind of information is this? I don't know, but I will soon have it, faster than I can understand it.

Most counselors insist that "I'm not here to sell amnios," or "I don't feel like a success or failure according to whether or not she takes the test." Their interests lie in "informed consent," that particularly American legal-medical document that attests to an individual's acceptance of information properly produced. Such an individual contract model is highly appropriate to a litigious society without a national health plan, where the only remedy for lack of information or services, or harmful information or services, is the malpractice suit. When viewed in this larger context, the counselor is providing protection for the doctor and the medical center, ensuring their invulnerability despite the chaotic conditions of an "information revolution" in which the techniques and interpretations of genetic diagnoses are continuously under negotiation.

When viewed culturally, the process of obtaining informed consent might represent a less legalistic and more communitarian project. Decisions concerning amniocentesis are made with the sum total of the knowledge a pregnant woman (and often her shadow network of support) brings to her interaction with a new medical technology. Culturally informed consent (or its refusal) is not reducible to the exchange of information-for-signature negotiated at the intake interview, for it is based on all the assumptions, fears, and norms concerning healthy and sickly children with which any given woman undertakes a pregnancy. It includes the meaning of illness in family history; the shame and pride attached to the bearing (or nonbearing) of children; beliefs about fertility, abortion, femininity, and masculinity; as well as the social consequences and prejudices surrounding disability, including the "courtesy stigmas" borne by those close to disabled people (Goffman, 1963).

In this larger context, knowledge and power are not reducible to medical terminology, despite medicine's hegemonic claims. For surely this new technology has potentials that are at once emancipatory and socially controlling, depending on the context in which its use is shaped and practiced. Genetic counselors, no less than their polyglot patients, are heirs to a eugenic script in which our aspirations for the liberation of women and children necessarily confront the current conditions under which family life is enacted. If, and only if, the discourse on disability and reproductive rights is lifted out of medical context and negotiated as part of popular culture will it become possible to speak in another language.

We occasionally may catch glimpses of the effects of such displacements of medical culture in examining amniocentesis and disability among children as they are inscribed by mass media. To my question, "Where did you first learn about amniocentesis?" many women without advanced formal education answered, "Dallas," "St. Elsewhere," and the *National Enquirer.* An Ecuadorian domestic worker told me she'd learned about spina bifida (for which amniocentesis is offered) from "Jerry's Kids" (the Jerry Lewis telethon). Several clinic patients gave articulate, up-to-date descriptions of children with Down's syndrome after Phil Donahue devoted a recent show to them. Middle-class amniocentesis patients often arrived armed with new questions after genetics stories appeared in the "science section" of the *New York Times.* As teaching and learning about inherited disabilities, and even amniocentesis, increasingly permeates the world of mass culture, medico-scientific discourse will have to confront its own popularization, and challenges to it.

A more popular and widespread consciousness about both birth defects and technologies aimed at their screening may benefit both pregnant women and counselors. The first might then come to a decision from a more knowledgeable position, whereas the second would be relieved of some of the burdens of protecting the medical hierarchies within which they now practice, in favor of more mutually constituted conversations with their patients. Perhaps under those circumstances, we might discuss the shared responsibilities that surround education and decision making at the intersection of disability and reproductive rights.

ACKNOWLEDGMENTS

This chapter is drawn from an ongoing study, portions of which have been funded by the National Science Foundation, the National Endowment for the Humanities, and the Rockefeller Foundation's Program in Changing Gender Roles. I am deeply grateful to them all. I especially thank the hundreds of women who shared their amniocentesis stories with me, and the many health professionals whose commitment to better understanding their patients' experiences led them to cooperate in my research. All names have been changed to protect confidentiality. Helpful suggestions and criticisms were offered on earlier drafts of this essay by Robin Blatt, Robert Hahn, Alan Harwood, Marthe Gautier, Shirley Lindenbaum, and Judith Stacey, and an anonymous reviewer for *Medical Anthropology Quarterly.* I thank them all for their help in improving this work. Its weaknesses and conclusions remain my own. This chapter is reproduced by permission of the American Anthropological Association from *Medical Anthropology Quarterly* (Vol. 2, No. 2, June, 1988). Not for further reproduction. The chapter originally appeared as "Chromosomes and Communication: The Discourse of Genetic Counseling."

REFERENCES

Brewster, A. (1984). After office hours: A patient's reaction to amniocentesis. *Obstetrics and Gynecology, 64,* 443–444.

Brown, J. (1986). Professional language: Words that succeed. *Radical History Review, 34,* 33–52.

Goffman, E. (1963). *Stigma: Notes on the management of spoiled identity.* Engelwood Cliffs, NJ: Prentice-Hall.

Kevles, D. (1985). *In the name of eugenics.* New York: Knopf.

Reed, S. (1974). A short history of genetic counseling. *Social Biology, 21,* 332–339.

Rollnick, B. (1984). The National Society of Genetic Counselors: An historical perspective. *Birth Defects, 20,* 3–7.

Rothman, B. K. (1986). *The tentative pregnancy.* New York: Viking.

10

The New Reproductive Technologies: What Have We Learned?

Aila Collins
Karolinska Institute

Judith Rodin
Yale University

The past 10 years have witnessed the development of new reproductive technologies such as in vitro fertilization (IVF), embryo transfer, embryo freezing, prenatal screening, and artificial insemination, all of which have profound potential for affecting women's lives. In this chapter, we examine further some of the common and unifying themes of the preceding chapters and analyze the medical, ethical, and legal ramifications of the new reproductive technologies. As we have seen, these technologies are controversial because they touch upon issues of sexuality, genetics, parenting, and the family. They often probe the very limits of biology and demand decisions about complex matters of life and death, thus stirring up emotions and provoking debate about issues that in the past were determined biologically. In addition, they raise questions about the social control of science and technology and about the limits of state intervention in the lives of individuals.

The concept of reproductive choice is important in our society. Information and choice have been said to be the cornerstones of women's health care (Rothman, 1986). Some would argue that the freedom of choice may be the most important aspect of women's reproductive lives today. The degree of control women are able to exercise over their reproductive lives directly affects their educational and job opportunities, as well as level of income and physical and emotional well-being. Women as consumers of reproductive care have come to demand effective techniques to help them control their fertility. And new technology has provided them with a multitude of choices: Contraceptive methods enable women to plan their pregnancies; pregnant women can choose whether or not to continue their pregnancies; birthing women can choose alternative ways of managing their labor and deliveries; and couples who have been infertile for many years can circumvent their infertility and achieve pregnancies. The development of technologies such as in vitro fertilization, embryo transfer, and artificial insemination has truly revolutionized the field of reproductive medicine.

Do these new developments really ensure "reproductive freedom" for women? A critical analysis of the consequences of these techniques, as we have seen in the preceding chapters, reveals that there are potential drawbacks as well as benefits. Overall (1987) noted that new reproductive technologies have a paradoxical effect on the reproductive freedom of women: On the one hand, they provide more options and enhance the capacity to make choices; on the other hand, there are also many ways in which new technologies may serve to reduce choice. The new technologies carry an emotional cost, which is not immediately apparent and which has not been adequately assessed. As Whitbeck points out in chapter 5, technologies change human relationships, and the fact that they exist often has a powerful influence on the kind of decision making and negotiations that women have to carry out today.

In evaluating such techniques as ultrasound and fetal monitoring, Whitbeck raises the issue of how these technologies influence human relationships and the capacity to fulfill moral obligations. She argues that biological safety does not necessarily take precedence over questions of moral integrity, and emphasizes that technology never solves important problems of life and death. There is not merely a technical answer to these questions, and the social dimension must not be overlooked.

PRENATAL SCREENING

A study by Rothman (1986) serves to illustrate how amniocentesis can change the meaning of pregnancy and the relationship between the woman and her fetus. The possibility of finding an abnormality casts its shadow over the early months of the pregnancy, and the mother's developing relationship with her fetus is affected by the new technology. According to Rothman's terminology, many women are in a state of "tentative pregnancy"; in other words, under the condition imposed by the amniocentesis, a woman's commitment to her pregnancy can only be tentative until she knows the result of the test. A decision to continue or to terminate pregnancy is always very complex. Rothman remarked that aborting a wanted pregnancy because of a congenital abnormality can be more difficult than aborting for other reasons.

Another major problem with screening tests is that the information they yield is often ambiguous. The doctor cannot say with certainty whether the child will develop a disease or what will be the extent of a potential disability. It is up to the parents to make a final decision about whether to continue the pregnancy or whether to have an abortion, and often they must do so by making some probabilistic appraisal.

Another concern, which both Ruzek and Faden raise, is that of the safety of the tests. Many of the technologies, such as ultrasound and electronic fetal monitoring (EFM), were accepted as standards of care before they were assessed adequately. Visualization of the fetus by means of ultrasound has become routine prenatal care in most centers in the United States. However, much more scientific documentation is needed about possible negative long-term effects of using ultrasound and fetal monitoring. Diagnostic use of ultrasound has been of much benefit, making it possible to date the pregnancy more accurately and anticipating complications in delivery. Many experts also report beneficial effects in terms of increased bonding between parents and unborn children (Fletcher & Evans, 1983). However, others criticize the use of ultrasound. Petchesky (1987) argued that an overreliance on ultrasound reflects society's "obsession with the visual image" as being superior in giving objective and scientific evidence that the fetus is in good health. She pointed to the fact that ultrasound together with EFM are used to diagnose fetal distress and abnormal presentation of the fetus, which are indications for earlier delivery with cesarean section. Sometimes, though, the use of these technologies diagnoses abnormality where there is none and thus is one of the causes of the high number of cesarean sections being performed. Because of the fear of malpractice suits, physicians frequently feel that they should perform screening tests in order to be legally covered in cases where the child may be born with a congenital defect.

Another consequence of the availability of prenatal testing is that women feel the pressure to submit to screening. The fear of disability puts pressure on parents to produce only healthy children. Rapp raises the issue of too much emphasis being placed on identifying genetically impaired fetuses because of the tendency to devalue disability. To prevent having children with disabilities, the trend is for more and more sophisticated methods carried out earlier and earlier in pregnancy to ensure the health of the fetus. One of the newest techniques is chorionic villi biopsy, which is carried out in the 8th week of pregnancy. Other new techniques being developed include simple blood tests that can give information not only about chromosomal abnormalities, but also about potential carriers of disease that may develop later in life. At present, tests also are being developed for use on IVF embryos before they become implanted in a woman's uterus. If the embryos pass the "genetic inspection," they can be returned to the woman's uterus to develop. As prenatal tests are developed to detect diseases such as cancer, diabetes, Alzheimer's disease, and many other conditions that do not appear until later in life, parents will have to make increasingly difficult decisions. Soon society will have to face questions such as: Who can be held responsible for acting or not acting on a predisposition of a condition which may affect the child in adulthood?

It should be pointed out that the comfort and reassurance parents feel when their fetus does not have a detectable disability can be misleading, because so many of these are not congenital, but are acquired later in life. One consequence of prenatal testing is that parents may feel that they are responsible for their children's disabilities. Thus, the availability of sophisticated technology may increase parental guilt and feelings of personal failure. In this way, problems tend to become individualized and there is very little social support for parents with children who are born with disabilities (Hubbard, 1990). Henifin, Hubbard, and Norsigian (1989) suggested that laws must be enacted to prohibit discrimination on the basis of disability. Gallagher (1987) emphasized that we have to take steps to help build social supports and attitudes that make it possible for a woman to go through a pregnancy even when the amniocentesis shows that the baby may carry a defect. Only in a society that values people irrespective of their disabilities and provides support services for people who need them will prospective parents have a real choice concerning prenatal screening. Rapp points out in chapter 9 that religion, ethnicity, family history, cultural, and economic factors shape the responses to having a child with a genetic defect. She discusses the social and cultural meaning of disability and the cultural diversity in women's ability to control the conditions under which they are willing to mother children. Strategies for coping and perception of disabilities vary widely between different groups in society.

COMMODIFICATION OF LIFE

With the new reproductive technologies, the emphasis has shifted more and more to view the fetus as the focal point. Through prenatal diagnosis, the fetus has become a new type of patient, for whom therapies are being developed. Thus, a pregnant woman may feel compelled to accept diagnosis and treatment of her fetus despite the risks that are involved. How can she evaluate the information about the uncertainty of the outcome in order to make an informed decision? Faden and Clayton warn against possible mandatory screening in the future and the implications this would have for women in terms of commodification of life. The prenatal screening of fetuses serves the function of "quality control" and the demand for "the perfect baby." Rothman (1986) also remarked that by choosing prenatal testing, women are losing the choice of not controlling for quality, and accepting their children as they are.

Phrasing reproductive rights in the framework of choices makes it easier to regard babies as "consumer goods" (Overall, 1987). Parents are becoming consumers of special reproductive services designed to enhance the quality of their unborn children. Whitbeck in chapter 5 warns against the trend to regard everything as a potential resource. That the commodification process enters into all stages of women's reproductive lives is seen most clearly in the notion of surrogate motherhood. In a surrogacy contract, the contracting parties agree on the benefits each will receive: The surrogate mother will receive a fee and the agency and lawyers who facilitate the contract will receive their payment. Franklin (1990) remarked that reproduction is becoming an increasingly commercial activity at the "centre of a new market place" (p. 201) where surrogacy can command a fee and where eggs, sperm, and embryos can be exchanged as commodities.

The commodification of life is seen also in the recent trend of "wrongful life" and "wrongful births" suits, involving parents suing doctors for the birth of their children with congenital abnormalities. It is argued that the lives of these children are so difficult that they would have been better off not having been born, and the parents claim large sums of money as compensation for their suffering.

PARENTHOOD

Reproductive technologies powerfully address women's wish for a biological child. In many ways, technologies such as in vitro fertilization and embryo transfer, as well as oocyte donation and surrogacy, have deepened the anxieties about parenthood and genetic ties, because their relationship to parenthood is often ambivalent (Stanworth, 1987). In the past, we have been accustomed to distinguishing between biological and social parenthood. New technology adds another dimension: that of genetic parenthood. At the same time as IVF enables infertile couples to become genetic parents, artificial insemination with donor sperm and oocyte donation challenges the link between genetic parenthood and family.

Reproductive technologies reinforce the genetic link of the parent–child relationship. The underlying assumption is that the genetic link with a child is more important than social parenthood. The new reproductive technologies have the potential to significantly affect both the psychological state of the children who are born as a result of these technologies, as well as of the parents who use them. Surrogate motherhood offers couples a new way of family building. But what are the effects on the individuals involved in these transactions? The intentional separation of genetic, gestational, and social parenting may affect the well-being of the children born as a result of these arrangements.

Faden raises the issue of use of genetic technology in prenatal testing to determine the biological characteristics of the fetus. In the future, it may be simpler to choose the sex of the child. Being a parent may come to be seen as an act of "creating one's children" in a fuller sense than at present. Parents also may be held responsible by their children for choice of the wrong characteristics (Gallagher, 1989). This would certainly have implications for the parent–child relationship.

Reproductive technologies have made pregnancy and child bearing safer. However, they relate only to a limited part of parenthood, emphasizing the time before birth. Mothering involves responsibility not only for giving birth, but also for the physical, emotional, intellectual, and social development of children (Stanworth, 1987). Society offers little support to mothers during the first formative years of parenting, for example in terms of child care and maternity leave. Thus, we are left to wonder whether society does women a disservice by investing a disproportionate amount of its resources in reproduction, which is only one small period of parenthood.

BROADER ETHICAL ISSUES

Some legal commentators have suggested that a pregnant woman who is at risk for delivering a baby with disabilities and who refuses screening tests should be liable for "prenatal abuse." Shaw (cited by Gallagher, 1989) believed that it is unreasonable for a woman to carry a fetus to term knowing that it will suffer from a serious genetic disability. Shaw encouraged courts to take actions to ensure that fetuses are not "injured" by the "negligent acts" of others. According to some ethicists (Overall, 1987), the mother is seen as the greatest danger to the fetus, because it is she who exposes it to the reproductive hazards of the environment. This view tends to omit the social context of pregnancy and childbirth and societal responsibility for the health of pregnant women. Calls for court-ordered surgery or cesarean sections or legal punishment for negligent behavior during pregnancy are of great concern considering the lack of basic health care for many pregnant women.

Most of the debate about reproductive choice as it applies to the new reproductive technologies revolves around the right to make health-care decisions and to provide informed consent. However, as both Faden and Ruzek point out, the socioeconomic structure of American society today places many constraints on reproductive choice for women. Great socioeconomic inequalities deny many women access to prenatal care, as well as to perinatal and neonatal technologies. Women who have no access to basic prenatal care thus have no opportunity to exercise those aspects of reproductive choice that require the assistance of the health-care system. Ruzek stresses that there are many shortcomings in the present system, which is based on the fee-for-service principle. According to the Presidential Commission on Medical Ethics (cited in Buchanan, 1989), there are between 22 million and 25 million Americans who have neither private health-care insurance nor coverage under Medicare or Medicaid. Seen in this context, the fetal rights drive of legal actions against individual women raises many questions concerning health ethics. Targeting individual women for punitive policies and holding them responsible for poor fetal health or disability is unreasonable and serves to divert the attention from the need to change the health-care system (Gallagher, 1989).

As Ruzek points out, national policies vary widely in the extent to which they aim at reducing inequalities among women during pregnancy, childbirth, and the neonatal period. Some Western European countries, like the United Kingdom, the Netherlands, and the Scandinavian countries, have developed the most socialized health-care systems, and social policy is designed to reduce differences between socioeconomic groups. In the United States, the private sector still finances the largest portion of the health-care expenditure. Ruzek argues that health care is a core variable that influences what we consider to be important social and ethical issues. Both Faden and Ruzek emphasize the need to move toward a more integrated model of women's health that would cover all aspects of reproductive health with equal access for all women.

ETHICAL ISSUES ASSOCIATED WITH IVF

The development of expensive technologies, such as in vitro fertilization, raises the issue of how medical costs ought to be allocated. Currently in the United States, most third-party payers do not cover the cost of IVF. Five states have enacted legislation requiring the costs of IVF to be included in insurance plans (U.S. Congress Report, 1988). In Sweden, the cost of IVF treatment is covered by social health insurance, although the number of attempts is limited to three.

Many critics have expressed concerns about IVF as a therapy for infertility, considering the low success rates and the research needed to improve the technique. Most of the ethical and legal issues have been centered on the moral and legal status of the embryo. Women who undergo IVF treatment are subjected to hormonal stimulation, which results in "superovulation," enhancing the chances of getting more than one embryo for implantation and thus increasing the likelihood of a successful pregnancy. Because implanting more than three embryos increases the risk of multiple births, the extra fertilized eggs often are frozen for future attempts at implantation. It is the existence of these "spare" frozen embryos that raises many ethical questions. Can there be an ownership of embryos? Can they be sold or bought? Can embryos be the subject of experimentation? What is the status of the embryo when it develops? Who should have the custody of the embryos in the event of the couple's divorce?

Different countries are passing different rules and regulations concerning the use of embryos. The Swedish government has ruled that an embryo may be gestated only by the woman who produced the egg, thereby prohibiting embryo donation. Also, the frozen embryos may not be stored more than 3 years. In the United States, the use of embryos is so far not regulated. Different centers use different rules. For institutions that received federal funds, research on embryos was to be regulated by an ethics advisory board (Hubbard, 1990). The board, however, was dissolved; and there have been no federal funds allocated to basic research in this area since 1978. In the United Kingdom, the Warnock Committee recommended that the human embryo should be treated "with respect" and "should be afforded some protection in law" (Warnock, 1985, p. 63).

In order to make autonomous choices, those couples who seek IVF need accurate information about its efficacy. These couples are vulnerable in the sense that they have exhausted all other methods of conceiving a child of their own. They have a strong wish to do anything in their power to have a child. Therefore, particular care needs to be taken with these couples so that they can make informed decisions about the risks and benefits of IVF. IVF is an accepted treatment for infertility and has been regarded as a medical blessing by many women. Yet, it is very important to evaluate its impact on women and on society, as well as on scarce medical resources and its relation to other technologies, such as genetic engineering.

THE ROLE OF THE PHYSICIAN

Many of the authors emphasize that there is a need to widen the current debate to encompass the long-term social implications of technological reproductive interventions. These implications are very important, not only in terms of medical treatment. Ruzek, Dye, and Faden all point to the increasing medicalization of reproduction. Increasingly, women derive their understanding of pregnancy and childbirth in the language of medicine. It is the medical definition of women's reproductive capacity that has had the most important role in the formulation of legal definitions of reproductive processes, thereby conferring upon physicians and medicine a dispropor-tionate authority in this area. The states have permitted and encouraged physicians to act as moral gatekeepers.

Physicians are conferred significant authority in decisions about abor-tion, for example. Abortion, according to the formulation of *Roe v. Wade* (1973), is a decision between "the woman and her physician." Giving the doctor control over abortion means that "a woman's right to choose is always circumscribed by the physician's right not to perform" (Rothman, 1989, p. 117). As Clayton points out, this formulation of two-party decision making grants the physician and medicine unusual power over women's choices, the impact of which has not been understood fully. She questions whether medical doctors are more qualified than others to act as arbiters of moral and ethical issues. Faden addresses women's right to choose and points out that physicians' and patients' beliefs about the responsibility and authority appropriate to each are crucial factors for limiting or encouraging women's decision making.

As we move into the era of biotechnology and genetic engineering, these questions of policy making and ideology of health care are going to be an increasingly important area of political and legislative debate, the outcome of which will have tremendous importance for women's health care in the years to come.

REFERENCES

Buchanan, A. E., & Brock, D. W. (1989). *Deciding for others: The ethics of surrogate decision making*. Cambridge: Cambridge University Press.

Fletcher, J., & Evans, M. (1983). Maternal bonding in early fetal ultrasound examination. *New England Journal of Medicine, 308,* 282–293.

Franklin, S. (1990). Deconstructing desperateness: The social construction of infertility in popular representation of new reproductive technologies. In M. McNeill, J. Varcoe, & S. Yearley (Eds.), *The new reproductive technologies* (pp. 200–229). New York: St. Martins Press.

Gallagher, J. (1987). Eggs, embryos and fetuses: Anxiety and the law. In M. Stanworth (Ed.), *Reproductive technologies* (pp. 139–151). Minneapolis: University of Minnesota Press.

Gallagher, J. (1989). Fetus as patient. In S. Cohen & N. Taub (Eds.), *Reproductive laws of the 1990's* (pp. 185–236). Clifton, NJ: Humana Press.

Henifin, M. S., Hubbard, R., & Norsigian, J. (1989). Prenatal screening. In S. Cohen & N. Taub (Eds.), *Reproductive laws for the 1990's* (pp. 155–184). Clifton, NJ: Humana Press.

Hubbard, R. (1990). *The politics of women's biology*. New Brunswick, NJ: Rutgers University Press.

Overall, C. (1987). *Ethics and human reproduction*. Boston: Allen & Unwin.

Petchesky, R. (1987). Foetal images: The power of visual culture in the politics of reproduction. In M. Stanworth (Ed.), *Reproductive technologies* (pp. 57–80). Minneapolis: University of Minnesota Press.

Roe v. Wade, 410 U.S. 113 (1973).

Rothman, B. K. (1986). *The tentative pregnancy*. New York: Penguin.

Rothman, B. K. (1989). *Recreating motherhood*. New York: Norton.

Stanworth, M. (1987). Reproductive technologies and the deconstruction of motherhood. In M. Stanworth (Ed.), *Reproductive technologies* (pp. 10–35). Minneapolis: University of Minnesota Press.

U.S. Congress Report. (1988). *Infertility: Medical and social choices* (Office of Technology Assessment). Washington, DC: U.S. Government Printing Office.

Warnock, M. (1985). *A question of life*. Oxford, England: Blackwell.

Author Index

Subject Index